A Holiday in the Happy Valley with Pen and Pencil

by

T. R. Swinburne

Double 9
BOOKS

A Holiday in the Happy Valley
with Pen and Pencil
by T. R. Swinburne

ISBN: 978-93-62200-76-1

Published by

DOUBLE 9 BOOKS

2/13-B, Ansari Road
Daryaganj, New Delhi – 110002
info@double9books.com
www.double9books.com
Tel. 011-40042856

ABOUT THE AUTHOR

T. R. Swinburne, a celebrated author and artist, invites readers on a captivating journey through his masterpiece, "A Holiday in the Happy Valley with Pen and Pencil." With eloquent prose and exquisite illustrations, Swinburne vividly depicts the enchanting landscapes and vibrant culture of the Happy Valley, captivating readers with its charm and allure. Through his keen observations and lyrical narrative, Swinburne transports readers to a world of adventure and discovery, where every page unfolds a new facet of this picturesque locale. Whether traversing serene valleys or encountering the warmth of local hospitality, Swinburne's evocative storytelling paints a rich tapestry of experiences, immersing readers in the beauty and wonder of the Happy Valley. Seamlessly blending artistry with narrative, Swinburne's masterpiece stands as a testament to his talent and passion for exploration, inspiring readers to embark on their own journeys of discovery. "A Holiday in the Happy Valley with Pen and Pencil" is not merely a book but a window into a world of endless fascination, inviting readers to lose themselves in its pages and find solace in its beauty.

CONTENTS

PREFACE

I observe that it is customary to begin a book by an Introduction, Preface, or Foreword. In the good old days of the eighteenth century this generally took the form of a burst of grovelling adoration aimed at some most noble or otherwise highly important person. This fulsome fawning on the great was later changed into propitiation of the British public, and unknown authors revelled in excuses for publishing their earlier efforts.

But now that every one has written a book, or is about to do so, I feel that my apologies are rather due to the public for not having rushed into print before. I have really spared it because I had nothing in particular to write about, and I confess I am somewhat doubtful as to whether I am even now justified in invoking the kind offices of a publisher with a view to bringing forth this literary mouse in due form!

No admiring (if partial) relatives have hung upon my lips as I read them my journal, imploring me with tears in their eyes to waste not an instant, but give to a longing world this literary treasure. I have no illusions as regards my literary powers, and I do not imagine that I shall depose the gifted author of *Eöthen* from his pride of place.

I claim, however, the merit of truth. The journal was written day by day, and the sketches were all done on the spot; and if this account—bald and inadequate as I know it to be—of a very happy time spent in rambling among some of the finest scenery of this lovely earth, may induce any one to betake himself to Kashmir, he will achieve something worth living for, and I shall not have spilt ink in vain.

CHAPTER I
INTRODUCTION

A journey to Kashmir now—in these days of cheap and rapid locomotion—is in nowise serious. It takes time, I grant you, but to any one with a few months to spare—and there are many in that happy position— there can be few pleasanter ways of spending a summer holiday.

It would be as well to start from England not later than the middle of March, as the Red Sea and the Sind Desert begin to warm up uncomfortably in spring. Srinagar would then be reached fairly early in April, and the visitor should arrange, if possible, to remain in the country until the middle of October. We had to leave just as the gorgeous autumn colouring was beginning to blaze in the woods, and the first duck were wheeling over the Wular Lake.

The climate of Kashmir is fairly similar to that of many parts of Southern Europe. There is a good deal of snow in the valley in winter. Spring is charming, the brilliant days only varied by frequent thunderstorms—which, however, are almost invariable in keeping their pyrotechnics till about five in the afternoon. July and August are hot and steamy in the valley, and it is necessary to seek one of the cool "Margs" which form ideal camping-grounds on all the lofty mountain slopes which surround the valley.

Gulmarg is the most frequented and amusing resort in summer of the English colony and contingent from the broiling plains of the Punjab. Here the happy fugitive from the sweltering heat of the lower regions will find a climate as glorious as the scenery. He can enjoy the best of polo and golf, and, if he be not a misogynist, he will vary the 'daily round' with picnics and scrambles on foot or on horseback, in exploring the endless beauty of the place, coming home to his hut or tent as the sun sinks behind the great pines that screen the Rampur Road, to wind up the happy day with a cheery dinner and game of bridge. But if Gulmarg does not appeal to him, let him go with his camping outfit to Sonamarg or Pahlgam—he will find neither polo nor golf nor the gay little society of Gulmarg, but he will find equally charming scenery and, perhaps, a drier climate—for it must in fairness be admitted that Gulmarg is a rainy place. Likewise his pocket will benefit, as his expenses will surely be less, and he will still find neighbours dotted about in white tents under the pine trees.

Towards the middle of September the exodus from the high 'Margs' takes place—many returning sadly to Pindi and Sealkote—others merely to Srinagar, while those who yearn after Bara Singh and Bear, decamp quietly for their selected nullahs, to be in readiness for the opening of the autumn season.

Thus, from April to October, a more or less perfect climate may be obtained by watching the mercury in the thermometer, and rising or descending the mountain slopes in direct ratio with it.

It is quite unnecessary to take out a large and expensive wardrobe. Thin garments for the Red Sea and Indian Ocean, such as one wears in a fine English summer, and for Kashmir the same sort of things that one would take up to Scotland. For men—knickerbockers and flannel shirts—and for ladies, short tweed skirts and some flannel blouses. The native tailors in Srinagar are clever and cheap, and will copy an English shooting suit in fairly good material for about eleven rupees, or 14s. 8d.! One pair of strong shooting boots (plentifully studded with aluminium nails) is enough. For all mountain work, the invaluable but uncomfortable grass shoes must be worn, and both my wife and I invariably wore the native chaplies for ordinary marching. Foot-gear for golf, tennis, and general service at Srinagar and Gulmarg must be laid in, according to the traveller's fancy, in England.

Underwear to suit both hot and cold weather should be purchased at home—not on any account omitting cholera belts.

Shirts and collars should be taken freely, as it is well to remember that the native washerman—the well-abused "Dobie"—has a marvellous skill in producing a saw-like rim to the starched collar and cuff of the newest shirt; while the elegant and delicate lace and embroidery, with which the fair are wont to embellish their underwear, take strange and unforeseen patterns at the hands of the skilled workmen. It is surprising what an effect can be obtained by tying up the neck and sleeves of a garment, inserting a few smooth pebbles from the brook, and then banging the moist bundle on the bank!

The arrangement of clothing for the voyage is rather complicated, as it will probably be necessary to wear warm things while crossing Europe, and possibly even until Egypt is reached. Then an assortment of summer flannels, sufficient to last as far as India, must be available. We were unable to get any washing done from the date we left London, on the 22nd of February, until we reached Rawal Pindi, on the 21st March. Capacious canvas kit-bags are excellent things for cramming with grist for the dobie's mill.

In arranging for luggage, it should be borne in mind that large trunks and dress boxes are inadmissible. From Pindi to Srinagar everything must be transported by wheeled conveyance, and, in Kashmir itself, all luggage must be selected with a view to its adaptability to the backs of coolies or ponies. In Srinagar one can buy native trunks—or yakdans—which are cheap, strong, and portable; and the covered creels or "kiltas" serve admirably for the stowage of kitchen utensils, food, and oddments.

The following list may prove useful to any one who has not already been "east of Suez," and who may therefore not be too proud to profit by another's experience:—

1. "Compactum" camp-bed with case, and fitted with sockets to take mosquito netting.

2. Campaigning bedding-bag in Willesden canvas, with bedding complete.

3. Waterproof sheet.

4. Indiarubber bath.

If shooting in the higher mountains is anticipated, a Wolseley sleeping-bag should be taken.

5. Small stable-lantern.

6. Rug or plaid—light and warm.

7. Half-a-dozen towels.

8. Deck chair (with name painted on it).

We had also a couple of Roorkhee chairs, and found them most useful.

9. A couple of compressed cane cabin trunks.

9_a_. The "Ranelagh Pack" is a most useful form of "luggage."

10. Camp kit-bag.

11. Soiled-linen bag, with square mouth, large size. This is an excellent "general service" bag, and invaluable for holding boots, &c.

12. Large "brief-bag," most useful for stowing guide-books, flasks, binoculars, biscuits, and such like, that one wants when travelling, and never knows where to put. Our "yellow bag" carried even tea things, and was greatly beloved. Like the leather bottèl in its later stage, "it served to put hinges and odd things in"!

13. Luncheon basket, fitted according to the number of the party.

The above articles can all be bought at the Army and Navy Stores.

14. A light canvas box, fitted as a dressing-case.

Ours were made, according to our own wishes and possessions, by Williams, of 41 Bond Street. The innumerable glass bottles, so highly prized by the makers of dressing-cases, should be strictly limited in number. They are exceedingly heavy, and, as the dressing-case should be carried by its owner, the less it weighs the more he (or she) will esteem it.

15. A set of aluminium cooking-utensils is much to be recommended. They can easily be sold on leaving Kashmir for, at least, their cost price.

16. Pocket flask. This may be of aluminium also, although personally I dislike a metal flask.

17. Umbrella—strong, but cheap, as it is sure to be lost or stolen. There are few things your native loves more than a nice umbrella, unless it be

18. A knife fitted with corkscrew and screwdriver; therefore take two, and try to keep one carefully locked up.

19. Pair of good field-glasses.

I took a stalking telescope, but it was useless to my shikari, who always borrowed my wife's binoculars until she lost them—or he stole them!

20. Hats. It is obviously a matter of taste what hats a man should take. The glossy silk may repose with the frock-coat till its owner returns to find it hopelessly out of date, its brim being a thought too curly, or its top impossibly wide; but the "bowler" or Homburg hat will serve his turn according to his fancy, until, at Aden, he invests in a hideous, but shady "topee," for one-third of the price he would pay in London; and this will be his only wear, before sunset, until he again reaches a temperate climate. Ladies, who are rightly more particular as to the appearance of even so unlovely a thing as a sola topee, would do well, perhaps, to buy theirs before starting. Really becoming pith helmets seem very scarce in the East!

After sunset, or under awnings, any sort of cap may be worn.

21. Shirts and collars are obviously matters of taste. A good supply of white shirts and collars must be taken to cope with the destruction and loss which may be expected at the hands of the dobie. Flannel shirts can be made easily enough from English models in Srinagar.

22. Under-garments should be of Indian gauze for hot weather, with a supply of thicker articles for camping in the hills.

Cholera belts should on no account be omitted.

23. Socks, according to taste—very few knickerbocker stockings need be taken, as putties are cheap and usual in Srinagar.

24. Ties—the white ones of the cheap sort that can be thrown away after use, with a light heart. Handkerchiefs, and a few pairs of white gloves.

25. Sleeping-suits, both thick for camp work and light for hot weather, should be taken.

26. Dress suit and dinner-jacket.

27. Knickerbocker or knee-breeches, which can be copied in Kashmir by the native tailor.

Riding-breeches are not in the least necessary unless the traveller contemplates any special riding expedition. Ordinary shooting continuations do quite well for all the mounted work the tourist is likely to do. A pair of stohwasser gaiters may be taken, but even they are not necessary, neither is a saddle.

A lady, however, should take out a short riding-skirt, or habit, and a side-saddle.

28. A tweed suit of medium warmth for travelling, and a couple of flannel suits, will bring the wearer to Srinagar, where he can increase his stock at a ridiculously low price—about 22 rupees or £1, 9s. 4d. per suit.

29. Boots. Here, again, the wayfarer is at full liberty to please himself. A pair of strong shooting-boots, with plenty of spare laces and, say, a hundred aluminium nails, is a *sine quâ non*. A pair of rubbers, or what are known as "gouties" in Swiss winter circles, are not to be despised. Otherwise, boots, shoes, slippers, and pumps, according to taste.

30. A large "regulation" waterproof, a rain-coat or Burberry, and a warm greatcoat will all be required.

It is hard to give definite advice to a lady as to the details of her outfit. Let her conform in a general way to the instructions given above, always remembering that both Srinagar and Gulmarg are gay and festive places, where she will dine and dance, and have ample opportunity for displaying a well-chosen wardrobe.

Let her also take heed that she leaves the family diamonds at home. The gentle Kashmiri is an inveterate and skilful thief, and the less jewellery she can make up her mind to "do with," the more at ease will her mind be. But if she must needs copy the lady of whom we read, that

"Rich and rare were the gems she wore,"

then why not line the jewel-case—or rather the secret bag, which she will sew into some mysterious garment—with the diamonds of Gophir and the pearls of Rome?

If the intending visitor to Kashmir be a sportsman who has already had experience in big-game shooting, he will not need any advice from me (which, indeed, he would utterly disdain) as to the lethal weapons which should form his battery; but if the wayfarer be a humble performer who has never slain anything more formidable than a wary old stag, or more nerve-shattering than a meteoric cock pheasant rising clamorously from behind a turnip, he may not be too proud to learn that he will find an ordinary "fowling piece" the most useful weapon which he can take with him. If his gun is not choked, he should be provided with a dozen or more ball cartridge for bear.

If the pursuit of markhor and ibex is contemplated, a small-bore rifle will be required, but a heavy express is wanted to stop a bear. I had a "Mannlicher" and an ordinary shot-gun, with a few ball cartridges for the latter.

Duty has to be paid on taking firearms into India, and this may be refunded on leaving the country. This is not always done, however, as I found to my cost, my application for a refund being refused on the quibble that my guns were taken back to England by a friend, although I was able to prove their identity.

cartridges out, as it is exceedingly unlikely that the tyro will be able to shoot all the beasts allowed him by his game licence.[1] Smooth-bore cartridges of fair quality can be bought in Srinagar, and I certainly do not consider it worth the trouble and expense to convey them out from England.

[1] See Appendix 1.

To the amateur artist I would say: Be well supplied with brushes and paper—the latter sealed in tin for passage through the Red Sea and India. Colours, and indeed all materials can he got from Treacher & Co., Bombay, and also from the branch of the Army and Navy Stores there.

Paper is, however, difficult to get in good condition, being frequently spoilt by mildew.

It is almost impossible to get anything satisfactory in the way of painting materials in Kashmir itself; therefore I say: Be well supplied before leaving home.

Finally, a small stock of medicines should certainly be taken, not omitting a copious supply of quinine (best in powder form for this purpose), and also of strong peppermint or something of the sort, to give to the native servants and others who are always falling sick of a fever or complaining of an internal pain, which is generally quite cured by a dose of peppermint.

Neither Jane nor I love guide-books; we found however, in Kashmir, the little book written by Dr. Neve an invaluable companion;[2] while Murray's *Guide to India* afforded much useful information when wandering in that country.

[2] *The Tourist's Guide to Kashmir, Ladakh, Skardo, &c.*, edited by Arthur Neve, F.R.G.S.

The best book on Kashmir that I know is Sir Walter Lawrence's *Valley of Kashmir*.

Any one going out as we did, absolutely ignorant of the language, should certainly take an elementary phrase-book or something of the sort to study on the voyage. We forgot to do this, and had infinite trouble afterwards in getting what we wanted, and lost much time in acquiring the rudimentary knowledge of Hindustani which enabled us to worry along with our native servants, &c. No mere "globe-trotter" need attempt to learn any Kashmiri, as Hindustani is "understanded of the people" as a rule, and the tradesmen in Srinagar know quite as much English as is good for them.

CHAPTER II
THE VOYAGE OUT

It seems extraordinary to me that every day throughout the winter, crowds of people should throng the railway stations whence they can hurry south in search of warmth and sunshine, and yet London remains apparently as full as ever! We plunged into a seething mass of outward-bound humanity at Victoria Station on the 22nd of February, and, having wrestled our way into the Continental express, were whirled across the sad and sodden country to Dover amidst hundreds of our shivering fellow-countrymen.

Truly we are beyond measure conservative in our railway discomforts. With a bitter easterly wind searching out the chinks of door and window, we sat shivering in our unwarmed compartment—unwarmed, I say, in spite of the clumsy tin of quickly-cooled hot water procured by favour—and a gratuity—from a porter!

The Channel showed even more disagreeable than usual. A grey, cold sky, with swift-flying clouds from the east hung over a grey, cold sea, the waves showing their wicked white teeth under the lash of the strong wind. The patient lightship off the pier was swinging drearily as we throbbed past into the gust-swept open and set our bows for the unseen coast of France.

The tumult of passengers was speedily reduced to a limp and inert swarm of cold, wet, and sea-sick humanity.

The cold and miserable weather clung to us long. In Paris it snowed heavily, and I was constrained to betake myself in a cab—"chauffé," it is needless to remark—to seek out a kindly dentist, the bitter east wind having sought out and found a weak spot wherein to implant an abscess.

At Bâle it was freezing, but clear and bright, and a good breakfast and a breath of clean, fresh air was truly enjoyable after the overheated sleeping-car in which we had come from Paris.

It may seem unreasonable to grumble at the overheating of the "Sleeper" after abusing the under-heating of our British railways. Surely, though, there is a golden mean? I wish neither to be frozen nor boiled, and there can be no doubt but that the heating of most Continental trains is excellent, the power of application being left to the traveller.

The journey by the St. Gotthard was delightful, the day brilliant, and the frost keen, while we watched the fleeting panorama of icebound peaks and snow-powdered pines from the cushions of our comfortable carriage.

The glory of winter left us as we left the Swiss mountains and dropped down into the fertile flats of Northern Italy, and at Milan all was raw chilliness and mud.

Nothing can well be more depressing than wet and cheerless weather in a land obviously intended for sunshine.

We slept at Milan, and the next day set forth in heavy rain towards Venice. The miserable ranks of distorted and pollarded trees stood sadly in pools of yellow-stained water, or stuck out of heaps of half-melted and uncleanly snow.

No colour; no life anywhere, excepting an occasional peasant plodding along a muddy road, sheltering himself under the characteristic flat and bony umbrella of the country.

At Peschiera we had promise of better things. The weather cleared somewhat, revealing ranges of white-clad hills around Garda…. But, alas! at Verona it rained as hard as ever, and we made our way from the railway station at Venice, cowering in the coffin-like cabin of a damp and extremely draughty gondola, while cold flurries of an Alpine-born wind swept across the Grand Canal.

Sunshine is absolutely necessary to bring out the real beauty of Italy. This is particularly the case in Venice, where light and life are required to dispel the feeling of sadness so sure to creep over one amid the signs of long-past grandeur and decaying magnificence.

On a grey and wintry day one is chiefly impressed by the dank chilliness of the palaces on the Grand Canal, whose feet lie lapped in slimy water; the lovely tracery of whose windows shows ragged and broken, whose stately guest-chambers are in the sordid occupation of the dealer in false antiques, and whose motto might be "Ichabod," for their glory has departed.

It is five-and-twenty years since I was last in Venice, and I can truly say that it has not improved in that long time. The loss of the great Campanile of St. Mark is not compensated for by the gain of the penny steamer which frets and fusses its prosaic way along the Grand Canal, or blurts its noisome smoke in the very face of the Palace of the Doges.

Well! A steady downpour is dispiriting at any time, excepting when one is snugly at home with plenty to do, and it is particularly so to the unlucky traveller who has to live through half-a-dozen long hours intervening between arrival at and departure from Venice on a cold, dull, wintry afternoon.

The sombre gondola writhed its sinuous course and deposited us all forlorn in the near neighbourhood of the Piazza San Marco. Splashing our way across, and pushing through the crowd of greedy fat pigeons, we entered the world-famous church. I know my Ruskin, and I feel that I should be lost in wonder and admiration—I am not.

The gloom—rich golden gloom if you will—of the interior oppresses me; it is cavernous. A service is being held in one of the transepts, and the congregation seems noisier and less devout than I could have believed possible. My thoughts fly far to where, on its solitary hill, the noble pile of Chartres soars majestic, its heaven-piercing spires dominating the wide plain of La Beauce. In fancy I enter by the splendid north door and find myself in the pillared dimness softly lighted by the great window in the west. This seems to me to be the greatest achievement of the Christian architect, noble alike in conception and in execution.

There is no means of procuring a cold more certain than lingering too long in a cold and vault-like church or picture gallery, so we adjourned to the Palazzo Daniele, now a mere hotel, where we browsed on the literature—chiefly cosmopolitan newspapers—until it was time to start for Trieste.

The journey is not an attractive one, as we seemed to be perpetually worried by Custom-house authorities and inquisitive ticket-collectors! If possible, the wary traveller should so time his sojourn at Venice as to allow him to go to Trieste by steamer. The Hôtel de la Ville at Trieste is not quite excellent, but 'twill serve, and we were remarkably glad to reach it, somewhere about midnight, having left Milan soon after seven in the morning!

Trieste itself is rather an engaging town; at least so it seemed to us when we awakened to a fresh, bright morning, a blue-and-white sky overhead, and a copious allowance of yellow mud under foot!

There were various final purchases to be made. Our deck chairs were with the heavy luggage, which the passenger by Austrian Lloyd only gets at Port Saïd, as it is sent from London by sea; so a deck chair had to be got, also a stock of light literature wherewith to beguile the long sea hours.

A visit to our ship—the *Marie Valerie*—showed her to be a comfortable-looking vessel of some 4500 tons. She was busily engaged in taking in a large cargo, principally for Japan, and she showed no signs of an early departure. Her nominal hour for starting was 4 P.M., but the captain told us that he should not sail until next morning. So we descended to examine our cabin, and found it to be large and airy, but totally deficient in the matter of drawers or lockers.

Well! we shall have to keep everything in cabin trunks, and "live in our boxes" for the next three weeks.

There was cabin accommodation for twenty passengers, but at dinner we mustered but nine. This is, of course, the season when all right-minded folks are coming home from India, and we never expected to find a crowd; still, nine individuals scattered abroad over the wide decks make but a poor show.

The first meal on board a big steamer is always interesting. Every one is quietly "taking stock" of his, or her, neighbours, and forming estimates of their social value, which are generally entirely upset by after experience.

Of our fellow-passengers there were only five whose presence affected us in any way. A young Austrian, Herr Otto Frantz, with his wife, going out as first secretary of legation to Tokio; Major Twining, R.E., and his wife; and Miss Lungley, a cosmopolitan lady, who makes Kashmir her headquarters and Rome her *annexe*.

We became acquainted with each other sooner than might have been expected, by reason of an exploit of the stewardess—a gibbering idiot. The night was cold, so several of the ladies, following an evil custom, sent forth from their cabins those vile inventions called hot bottles. Only two came back..., and then the fun began. The stewardess, who speaks no known tongue, played "hunt the slipper" for the missing bottles through all the cabins, whence she was shot out by the enraged inhabitants until she was reduced to absolute imbecility, and the harassed stewards to gesticular despair.

The missing articles were, I believe, finally discovered and routed out of an unoccupied bed, where they had been laid and forgotten by the addle-pated lady, and peace reigned.

We sailed from Trieste early on the morning of the 28th of February, and steamed leisurely on our way. The Austrian Lloyd's "unaccelerated" steamers are not too active in their movements, being wont to travel at purely "economical speed," and so we were given an excellent view of some of the Ionian Islands, steaming through the Ithaca channel, with the snow-tipped peak of Cephalonia close on our starboard hand.

Then, leaving the far white hills of the Albanian coast to fade into the blue mists, we sped

"Over the sea past Crete,"

until the tall lighthouse of Port Saïd rose on the horizon, followed by the spars of much shipping, and the roofs of the houses dotted apparently over the waters of the Mediterranean. At length the low mudbanks which represent the two continents of Africa and Asia spread their dull monotony on either hand, and the good ship sat quietly down for a happy day's coaling.

Port Saïd has grown out of all knowledge since I first made its acquaintance in 1877. It was then a cluster of evil-looking shanties, the abode of the scum of the Levant, who waxed fat by the profits of the gambling hells and the sale of pornographic photographs. It has now donned the outwardly respectable look of middle age; it has laid itself out in streets; the gambling dens have disappeared, and the robbers have betaken themselves to the sale of the worst class of Japanese and Indian "curios," ostrich feathers from East Africa, and tobacco in all its forms.

Port Saïd has undoubtedly improved, but still it is not a nice place, and we were unfeignedly glad to repair on board the *Marie Valerie* as soon as we noted the cessation of the black coaly cloud, through the murkiness of which a chattering stream of gnome-like figures passed their burthens of "Cardiff" into the bowels of the ship.

Port Saïd was cold, and Suez was cold, and we started down the Red Sea followed by a strong north wind, which kept us clad in greatcoats for a day or two, and, as we got down into wider waters, obliged us to keep our ports closed.

An object-lesson on the subject of closed ports was given in our cabin, where the fair chatelaine was reclining in her berth reading, fanned by the genial air which floated in at the open port,—a truculent Red Sea billow, meeting a slight roll of the ship, entered the cabin in an unbroken fall on the lady's head. A damp tigress flew out through the door, wildly demanding the steward, a set of dry bedding, and the instant execution of the captain, the officer of the watch, and the man at the wheel!

How dull we should be without these little incidents!

A hoopoe took deck, or rather rigging, passage for a while, and evoked the greatest interest. Stalking glasses and binoculars were levelled at the unconcerned fowl, who sat by the "cathead" with perfect composure, and preened himself after his long flight.

The striking of "four bells" just under his beak unnerved him somewhat, and he departed in a great fuss and pother.

Our roomy decks afford many quiet corners in which to read or doze, and now that the weather is rapidly warming up we spend many hours in these peaceful pastimes, varied by an occasional constitutional—none of your fisherman's walks, "three steps and overboard"—but a good, clear tramp, unimpeded by the innumerable deck-chairs, protruding feet, and ubiquitous children which cover all free space on board a P. & O.

Then comes dinner, followed by a rubber of bridge, and so to bed.

On Saturday the 11th we passed the group of islands commonly known as the Twelve Apostles.

First, a tiny rock, rising lonely from the blue—brilliantly blue—waves; then a yellow crag of sandstone, looking like a haystack; and then a whole group of wild and fantastic islands, evidently of volcanic origin, and varying in rough peaks and abrupt cliffs of the strangest colours—brick-red, purple-black, grey, and yellow—utterly bare and desolate:

> "Nor tree, nor shrub, nor plant, nor flower,
> Nor aught of vegetative power,
> The weary eye may ken,"

save only the white lighthouse, which, perched on its arid hill, serves to emphasise the desolation of earth and sky.

The Red Sea is remarkably well supplied with lighthouses; and, considering the narrowness of the channel in parts, the strong and variable currents, and the innumerable islands and shoals, the supply does no more than equal the demand.

I cannot imagine a more grievous death in life than the existence of a lighthouse-keeper in the Red Sea!

Sunday, 12th.—We passed through the Gate of Tears this morning—the dismal, flat, and unprofitable island of Perim being scanned by me from the bathroom port, while exchanging an atmosphere of sticky salt air for an unrefreshing dip in sticky salt water.

The hoopoe is again with us; in fact I do not think he really left the ship, but simply sought a secluded perch, secure from prying observation. He reappeared upon the port stay, and proceeded to preen himself and observe the ship's course. He is evidently bound for Aden, casting glances of quiet unconcern on Perim and the coast of Araby the blest.

Towards sunset we passed the fantastic peaks of little Aden, and, drawing up to Steamer Point, cast anchor under the "Barren Rocks of Aden."

Monday, 13th.—We had a shocking time last night. All ports closed for coaling left us gasping, whilst a fiendish din arose from the bowels of the ship, whence cargo was being extracted. The stifling air, reeking with damp, developed in the early morning a steady rain, which dripped mournfully on the grimy decks. Rain in Aden! We are told on the best authority that this is most unusual.

Aden, to the passing stranger, shows few attractions. We went on shore when the rain showed signs of ceasing, and after buying a few odds and ends, such as a pith hat and some cigarettes, we betook ourselves to the principal hotel, where an excessively bad breakfast was served to us, after which we were not sorry to shake the mud of Aden off our feet, so we chartered a shore boat amid a fearful clamour for extra pay and backshish, and set forth to rejoin our ship, now swept and garnished, and showing little trace of the coal she had swallowed.

Monday, 20th.—We reached Karachi yesterday morning after a quiet, calm, and utterly uneventful passage across the Indian Ocean.

It was never hot—merely calm, grey, and even showery, our only excitements being an occasional school of porpoises or the sight of a passing tramp steamer.

Some time before leaving England I had written to my old friend General Woon, commanding the troops at Abbotabad, asking him to provide me with a servant capable of dry-nursing a pair of Babes in the Wood throughout their sojourn in a strange land. The General promised to supply us with such an one, who, he said, would rob us to a certain extent himself, but would take good care that nobody else did so!

Immediately, then, upon our arrival in Karachi roads, a dark and swarthy person, with a black beard and gleaming white teeth, appeared on board, and reported himself as Sabz Ali, our servant and our master!

His knowledge of English "as she is spoke" was scanty and of strange quality, but his masterful methods of dealing with the boatmen and Custom-house subordinates inspired us with awe and a blind confidence that he could—and would—pull us through.

There was no difficulty at the Custom-house until it transpired that I wanted to take three firearms into the country. This appeared to be a most unusual and reprehensible desire, and my statement that one weapon was a rifle which I was taking charge of for a friend did not improve the situation. It being Sunday, the principal authorities were sunning themselves in their back parlours, and the thing in charge (called a Baboo, I understand) became exceedingly fussy, and desired that the guns should be unpacked and exhibited lest they should be of service pattern. This was simple, as far as my battery was concerned, and I promptly laid bare the beauties of my Mannlicher and ancient 12-bore; but, alas! Mrs. Smithson's rifle was soldered like a sardine into a strong tin case, and no cold-chisel or screwdriver was forthcoming.

Messengers were sent forth to seek the needful instruments, while I proceeded to cut another Gordian knot.... An acquaintance of mine, hearing that I was coming to India, suggested that I should take charge of a parcel for a friend of hers, who wanted to send it to her fiancé in Bombay. As all the heavy baggage was sent from London to join us at Port Saïd, I had not seen the "parcel," and, finding no case or box addressed to any one but myself, I had to select one that seemed most likely to be right, and forward that.

At last the needful appliances were got and the rifle unpacked; but, although it proved to be (as I had said) a large-bore Express, the Baboo refused, like a very Pharaoh, to let it go, and I, after a two-hour vexatious delay, paid the duty on my own guns, and, leaving a note for the chief Customs official, explaining the case and begging him to send the rifle on forthwith, packed myself—hot, hungry, and angry—into a "gharri," and set forth to the Devon Place Hotel, whither the rest of the party had preceded me.

I have gone into this little episode somewhat at length in order to impress upon the voyager to India the necessity for limiting the number of firearms or getting a friend to father the extra ones through the Customs—a perfectly simple matter had one foreseen the difficulty. Also the danger of taking parcels for friends—of which more anon![1]

> [1] A big deal case which we unpacked at Srinagar proved to contain a "life-sized" work-table. The package holding our camp beds and bedding, having a humbler aspect, had been sent to Bombay and cost as a world of worry and expense to recover!

The Devon Place Hotel may be the best in Karachi, but it is pretty bad.... I am told that all Indian hotels are bad—still, the breakfast was a considerable improvement on the *Marie Valerie*, and we sallied forth as giants refreshed to have a look at Karachi and do a little shopping. It being Sunday, the banks were closed, but a kindly shopman cashed me a cheque for twenty pounds in the most confiding manner, and enabled us to get the few odds and ends we wanted before going up country—among them a couple of "resais" or quilted cotton wraps and a sola topee for Jane.

Karachi did not strike us as being a particularly interesting town, but that may be to a great extent because we did not see the best part of it. On landing at Kiamari we had only driven along a hot and glaring mole, bordered by swamps and slimy-looking flats for some two miles. Then, on reaching the city proper, a dusty road, bordered by somewhat suburban-looking houses, brought us to the Devon Place Hotel, near the Frere station. After breakfast we merely drove into the bazaars to shop before betaking ourselves to the station, in good time for the 6.30 train.

Passengers—at least first-class passengers—were not numerous, and Major Twining and I had no difficulty in securing two compartments—one for our wives and one for ourselves.

An Indian first-class carriage is roomy, but bare, being arranged with a view to heat rather than cold Two long seats run "fore and aft" on either side, and upon them your servant makes your bed at night. Two upper berths can be let down in case of a crowd. At the end of each compartment is a small toilet-room.

It was unexpectedly chilly at night, and Twining and I were glad to roll ourselves up in as many rugs and "resais" as we could persuade the ladies to leave to us.

CHAPTER III
KARACHI TO ABBOTABAD

This morning we awoke to find ourselves rattling and shaking our way through the Sind Desert—an interminable waste of sand, barren and thirsty-looking, covered with a patchy scrub of yellowish and grey-purple bushes.

I can well imagine how hatefully hot it can be here, but to-day it has been merely pleasantly warm.

Jane and I were deeply interested in the novel scenes we passed through, which, while new and strange to us, were yet made familiar by what we had read and heard. The quiet-eyed cattle, with their queer humps, were just what we expected to see in the dusty landscape. The chattering crowds in the wayside stations, their bright-coloured garments flaunting in the white sunlight—the fruit-sellers, the water-carriers, were all as though they had stepped out of the pages of *Kim*—that most excellent of Indian stories.

And so all day we rattled and shook through the Sind Desert in the hot sunlight till the dust lay thick upon us, and our eyes grew tired of watching the flying landscape.

In the afternoon we reached Samasata junction, where the Twinings parted company with us, being bound for Faridkot.

Sorry were we to lose such charming companions, especially as now indeed we become as Babes in the Wood, knowing nothing of the land, its customs, or its language!

Henceforward, Sabz Ali shall be our sheet-anchor, and I think he will not fail us. His English is truly remarkable, so much so that I regret to say I have more than once supposed him to be talking Hindustani when he was discoursing in my own mother-tongue. But he certainly is extraordinarily sharp in taking up what I and the "Mem-sahib" say.

He presented to me to-day a remarkable letter, of which the following is an exact copy. I presume it is a sort of statement as to his general duties:—

"To the MAGER SAHIB.

"Sir,—I beg to say that General 'Oon Sahib send me to you. He order me that the arrangement of Mager Sahib do.

"To give pice to porter kuli this is my work. This is usefull to you.

"You give him many pice.

"Your work is order and to do it my work. You give me Rupee at once. Then I will write it on my book, from which you will see it is right or wrong. Now I am going to Cashmir with you and Cashmiree are thief.

"If you will give me one man other it will usefull to you. I ask one cloth. All Sahib give cloth to Servant on going to Cashmir.

"If will give cloth then all men say that this Sahib is good. I am fear from General 'Oon Sahib. It is order to give cloth.

"I can do all work of cook and bearer. I wish that you will happy on me, also your lady, and say to General 'Oon Sahib that this man is good and honest man.

"I have servant to many Sahib.

"I have more certificate.

"You are rich man and king. I am poor man. I will take two annas allowance per day in Cashmir, you will do who you wish.

"I wish that you and lady will happy on me. This is begging you will.—I remain, Sir, your most obedient Servant,

"SABAZ ALI, *Bearer.*"

Wednesday, March 22.—We slept again in the train on Monday night, and arrived in Lahore about 6 o'clock yesterday morning.

We had been advised to tub and dress in the waiting-rooms at the station, as we had a break of some six hours before going on to Pindi; but, upon investigation, Jane found her waiting-room already fully occupied by an uninviting company of Chi-chis (Eurasians), and several men—their husbands and brothers presumably—were sleeping the sleep of the just in mine, so we left all our luggage stacked on the platform under the eye of Sabz Ali, and hurried off to Nedou's Hotel. Ye gods! What a cold drive it was, and how bitterly we regretted that we had not brought our wraps from their bundle.

I was fearfully afraid that Jane would get a chill—an evil always to be specially guarded against in a tropical climate, but a very hot tub and a good breakfast averted all calamity, and we set forth in a funny little trap to inspect Lahore.

This is the first large and thoroughly Indian city that we have seen—Karachi being merely a thriving modern seaport and garrison town—and we set to work to see what we could in the limited time at our disposal. We whisked along a road—bumpy withal in parts, and somewhat dusty, but broad. On either hand rose substantial stone mansions, half hidden by trees and flowering shrubs. Many of these fine-looking buildings were shops. I was impressed by their importance, for they were quite what would be described by an auctioneer or agent as "most desirable family mansions, approached by a carriage drive … standing within their own beautifully wooded and secluded grounds in an excellent residential neighbourhood," &c. &c.

Anon we whirled round a corner, and plunged into the seething life of the native city. The road was crammed with an apparently impenetrable crowd of men and beasts, the latter—water-buffaloes, humpy cattle, and donkeys—strolling about and getting in everybody's way with perfect nonchalance, while men in strange raiment of gaudy hue pursued their lawful occupations with much clamour. The variety of smells—all bad—was quite remarkable.

We could only go at a walk, as the streets were very narrow and the inhabitants thereof—particularly the cows—seemed very deaf and difficult to arouse to a sense of the need for making room, though our good driver yelled himself hoarse and employed language which I feel sure was highly flavoured. Our progress was a succession of marvellous escapes for human toes and bovine shoulders, but our "helmsman steered us through," and we emerged from the kaleidoscopic labyrinth into the open space before the Fort of Lahore, whose pinkish brick walls and ponderous bastions rose above us.

The last thing I would desire would be to usurp in any way the functions of grave Mr. Murray or well-informed Herr Baedeker, but there are certain points to which I will draw attention, and which it seems to me very necessary to keep in mind.

To the ordinary traveller in the Punjab and Northern India no buildings are more attractive, no ruins more interesting, than those of the Mogul dynasty, and the rule of the Mogul princes marks the high-water limit of Indian magnificence. It was but for a short time, too, that the highest level of grandeur was maintained.

For generations the Moguls had poured in intermittent hordes into Northern India, but it was only in 1556 that Akbar, by defeating the Pathans at Panipat, laid India at his feet. Following up his success he overthrew the Rajputs, and extended his dominion from Afghanistan to Benares. Having conquered the country as a great warrior, he proceeded to rule it as a noble statesman, being "one of the few sovereigns entitled to the appellation both of Great and Good, and the only one of Mohammedan race whose mind appears to have arisen so far above all the illiberal prejudices of that fanatical religion in which he was educated, as to be capable of forming a plan worthy of a monarch who loved his people and was solicitous to render them happy."[1] This "plan" was to study the religion, laws, and institutions of his Hindu subjects in order that he might govern as far as possible in conformity with Hindu usage. The Emperor Akbar was the first of the Mogul monarchs who was a great architect. The city of Fattepur Sikri being raised by him as a stately dwelling-place until want of water and the unhealthiness of the locality caused him to move into Agra, leaving the whole city of Fattepur Sikri to the owls and jackals, and later to the admiration of the Sahib logue.

[1] Robertson's *India*, Appendix.

A palace in Lahore, the fort at Allahabad, and much lovely work in the city of Agra testify to the creative genius of that contemporary of our own Good Queen Bess, the first "Great" Mogul. Jehangir, his son and successor, has left few buildings of note, but his grandson, Shah Jehan, was undoubtedly the most splendid builder of the Mogul Mohammedan period. To him Delhi owes its stately palace and vast mosque—the Jama Masjid— and Agra would be famous for its wonderful palace of dark red stone and fretted marble, even without that masterpiece of Mohammedan inspiration, the world-famed Taj Mahal. The brief period of supreme magnificence came to an end with the last of the "Great" Moguls—Aurungzeb, died in 1707— having only blazed in fullest glory for some century and a half, but leaving behind it some of the noblest works of man.

It seemed somehow very curious, as we drove up through the stately entrance of the Hathi Paon, or Elephant Gate of the fort, to be saluted with a "present arms" by British Tommies clad in unobtrusive khaki, and to reflect that we are the inheritors of the fallen grandeur of the Mogul Emperors; that we in our turn, on many a hard-fought field, asserted our power to conquer; and that since then we have (I trust) so far followed the sound principles of Akbar as to keep by justice and wise rule the broad lands with their teeming millions in a state of peace and security unknown before in India.

Opposite the entrance rise the walls of the Palace of Akbar, curiously decorated with brilliant blue mosaics of animals and arabesques.

We visited the armoury—a remarkably fine collection of weapons—not the least interesting being those taken from the Sikhs and French in the earlier part of the last century. Opposite the armoury, and across a small beautifully-paved court, were the private apartments of Shah Jehan. They reminded me very much of the Alhambra, only, instead of the honeycomb vaulted ceilings, and arches decorated in stucco by the Moors, the Eastern architect inlaid his ceilings with an extraordinary incrustation of glass, usually silvered on the back, but also frequently coloured, and giving a strange effect of mother-o'-pearl inlay, bordering on tawdriness when examined in detail.

It is possible that this coloured glass actually had its intended effect of inlaid jewels, and that the gem-encrusted walls, so enthusiastically described by Tavernier and others, as almost matching the peacock throne itself, may have been but imitation.

Many of the pilasters were, however, very beautiful—of white marble inlaid with flower patterns of coloured stones—while the arched window openings were filled in with creamy tracery of fair white marble.

Leaving the fort after an all too short visit, we crossed to the great mosque built by Aurungzeb. Ascending—from a garden bright with flowers and blossoming trees—a flight of broad steps, we found ourselves at the end of a rectangular enclosure, at each corner of which stood a red column not altogether unlike a factory chimney. In the centre was a circular basin, very wide, and full of clear water, while in front, three white marble domes rose like great pearls gleaming against the cloudless blue. The mosque itself is built of red—dark red—sandstone, decorated with floral designs in white marble.

We climbed one of the minarets, and had a view of the city at our feet, and the green and fertile plains stretching dim into the shimmering haze beyond the Ravee River.

Then back to the hotel through the teeming alleys and down to the station—the road, that we had found so bitterly cold in the early morning, now a blaze of sunlight, where the dust stirred up by the shuffling feet of the wayfarers quivered in the heat, and the shadows of men and beasts lay short and black beneath them.

We were not sorry to seek coolness in the bare railway carriage, and let the fresh wind fan us as we sat by the open window and watched the flat, monotonous landscape sliding past.

The journey from Lahore to Rawal Pindi is not a very long one—only about 170 miles, or less than the distance from London to York; but an

Indian train being more leisurely in its movement than the Great Northern Express, gave us ample time to contemplate the frequent little villages—all very much alike—all provided with a noisy population, among which dogs and children were extremely prevalent; the level plains, broken here and there by clumps of unfamiliar trees, and inhabited by scattered herds of water buffaloes, cattle, and under-sized sheep, all busily engaged in picking up a precarious livelihood, chiefly roast straw, as far as one could see!

We had grown so accustomed to the monotony of the plains, that when we suddenly became aware of a faint blue line of mountains paling to snow, where they melted into the sky, the Himalayas came upon us almost with a shock of surprise.

As we drew nearer, the rampart of mountains that guards India on the north, took form and substance, until at Jhelum we fairly left the plain and began to ascend the lower foothills.

Between Jhelum and Rawal Pindi the line runs through a country that can best be described by that much abused word "weird." Originally a succession of clayey plateaux, the erosion of water has worn and honeycombed a tortuous maze of abrupt clefts and ravines, leaving in many cases mere shafts and pinnacles, whose fantastic tops stand level with the surrounding country. The sun set while we were still winding through a labyrinth of peaks and pits, and the effect of the contrasting red gold lights and purple shadows in this strange confused landscape was a thing to be remembered.

We rolled and bumped into Pindi at 8 P.M., having travelled nearly 1000 miles during our two days and nights in the train.

Our friends the Smithsons were on the platform waiting to receive us and welcome us as strangers and pilgrims in an unknown land. They have only remained here to meet us, and they proceed to Kashmir to-morrow, sleeping in a carriage in the quiet backwater of a siding, to save themselves the worry of a desperately early start to-morrow morning.

The direct route into Kashmir by Murree is impassable, the snow being still deep owing to a very late spring following a severe winter. This will oblige us to go round by Abbotabad, so I wired to my friend General Woon to warn him that we propose to invade his peaceful home.

Sunday, March 26.—We stayed a couple of days at Pindi, in order to make arrangements for transporting ourselves and our luggage into Kashmir. The journey can be made *viâ* Murree in about a couple of days by mail tonga, but it is a joyless and horribly wearing mode of travel. The tonga, a two-wheeled cart covered by an arched canvas hood and drawn by two half-broken horses, holds a couple of passengers comfortably, who sit behind and stare at the flying white ribbon of road for long, long hours, while the driver urges his wild career. The horses are changed every ten miles or so, and horrible and blood-curdling tales are extant of the villainy and wrong-headedness of some of these tonga ponies, how they jib for sheer pleasure, and leap over the low parapet that guards them from the precipice merely to vex the helpless traveller. When we suggested that to sit facing the past might be conducive to a sort of sea-sickness and certainly to headache, and that a total absence of view was to be deprecated, it was impressed upon us that if the horses darted over the "khud," we could slip out suddenly and easily, leaving the driver and the ponies to be dashed to pieces by themselves! This appeared sound, but, upon inquiry I could not hear that any accident had ever happened to any traveller going into Kashmir by tonga.

Besides the tonga, there are other modes of going into Kashmir. For instance, the sluggish bullock-cart—safe, deliberate, and affording ample leisure for admiring the scenery; the light native cart, or ekka, consisting of a somewhat small body screened by a wide white hood, and capable of holding far more luggage than would at first sight seem possible, and drawn by a scraggy-looking but much enduring little horse tied up by a wild and complicated system of harness (chiefly consisting of bits of old rope) between a pair of odd V-shaped shafts.

Finally, there is the landau—a civilised and luxurious method of conveyance which greatly appealed to us. We decided upon chartering a landau for ourselves and servant, and two ekkas to carry the heavy baggage.

Mr. de Mars, the landlord of the hotel, was most obliging in helping us to arrange for our journey, promising to provide us with carriage and ekkas for a sum which did not seem to me to be at all exorbitant.

I soon found, however, that the worthy Sabz Ali did not at all approve of the arrangement. It was extremely hard to find out by means of his scant English what he proposed to do; but I decided that here was an excellent opportunity of finding out what he was good for, so we determined to give him his head, and let him make his own arrangements.

A smile broke over his swarthy face for a moment, and he disappeared, coming back shortly afterwards just as the already ordered ekkas made their appearance.

These he promptly dismissed—much to the vexation of Mr. de Mars; but I explained to him that I intended to see if my man was really to be depended upon as an organiser, and that I should allow him to work upon his own lines.

We had arranged to sleep in a carriage drawn into a siding at the station, to avoid a very early start next morning. So after dinner we strolled down towards our bedroom to find our henchman on the platform, full of zeal and energy. I found out (with difficulty) that he proposed to go on to Hassan Abdal with the luggage that night by goods train; that we should find him there next morning, and that all would be right. So he departed, and we rolled ourselves up in our "resais," and wondered how it would all turn out.

On Friday morning we rattled out of Rawal Pindi about seven, and slowly wound through a rather stony and uninteresting country, until we arrived at the end of our railway journey about ten o'clock, and scrambled out at the little roadside station.

Our excellent factotum, Sabz Ali, awaited us with a capacious landau, and informed us that the heavy baggage had gone on in the ekkas. So we set forth at once on our 42-mile drive to Abbotabad without "reposing for a time in the rich valley of Hussun Abdaul, which had always been a favourite resting-place of the Emperors in their annual migrations to Cashmere" (*Lalla Rookh*).

The landau, though roomy and comfortable, was, like Una's lion, a "most unhasty beast," and we rolled quite slowly and deliberately over a distinctly uninteresting plain for about twenty miles, until we came to Haripur, a pretty village enclosed in a perfect mass of fruit trees in full bloom.

Here we changed horses, and lunched at the dâk bungalow—a first and favourable experience of that useful institution. The dâk bungalow generally consists of a simple wooden building containing a dining-room and several bedrooms opening on to a verandah, which usually runs round three sides of the house. The furniture is strong and simple, consisting of tables, bedsteads, and some long chairs. A khansamah or cook provides food and liquor at a fixed and reasonable rate.

Travellers are only permitted to remain for twenty-four hours if the rooms are wanted, each person paying one rupee (1s. 4d.) for a night, or half that amount for a mere day halt.

The khansamah would appear to be the only functionary in residence until the hour of departure draws near, when a whole party of underlings—chowkidars, bheesties, and sweepers—appear from nowhere in particular; and the lordly traveller, having presented them with about twopence apiece, rolls off along the dusty white road, leaving the khansamah and his myrmidons salaaming on the verandah.

We made the mistake of over-tipping at first in India, not realising that a couple of annas out here go as far as a shilling at home; but it is a mistake which should be rectified as soon as possible, for you get no credit for lavishness, but are merely regarded as a first-class idiot. No sane man would ever expend two annas where one would do!

On leaving Haripur the road began to ascend a little, and at the village of Sultanpur we entered a valley, through which a shrunken stream ran, and which we crossed more than once.

Then a long ascent of about eleven miles brought us near our destination.

It had been threatening rain all the afternoon, and now the weather made its threat good, and the rain fell in earnest. It grew dark, too; and, finally, not having had any reply to my telegram to General Woon, we did not know whether we were expected or not.

Sabz Ali, however, had no doubts on the matter. We were approaching his own particular country, and whether "Gen'l 'Oon Sahib" was there to entertain us or not, *he* was; and so it was "alright."

Our poor horses were done to a turn, a heavy landau with five people in it, as well as a fair amount of luggage, being no trifle to drag up so long and steep a hill. So we had to walk up the last rise to the General's house in the dark and rain, mildly cheered, however, by finding the two ekkas just arrived with the baggage.

A most hearty greeting from my old friend and his charming wife awaited us, and after a hasty toilet and an excellent dinner we felt at peace with all the world.

Both yesterday (Saturday) and to-day it has been cold and disagreeable. The past winter, I am told, has been a very severe one, and the melancholy brown skeletons of all the eucalyptus trees in the place show the dismal results of the frost.

This forenoon the day darkened, and a very severe thunderstorm broke. So dark was it at lunch that candles had to be lighted in haste, and even now (4 P.M.) I can barely see to write.

Thursday, March 30.—Monday was showery, and Tuesday decidedly wet; but, in spite of the hospitable blandishments of our kind hosts, we were most anxious to get on, as, having arranged with the Smithsons to go into the Astor district to shoot, it was most important to reach Srinagar before the first of April—the day upon which the shooting passes were to be issued to sportsmen in rotation of application. Knowing that only ten passes were to be given for Astor, and that several men were ahead of me, I felt that we were running it somewhat fine to leave only three days for the journey.

General Woon, who knew Kashmir well, did his very best to dissuade us from attempting the passes into Astor, reading to us gloomy extracts from his journal, and pointing out that it was no fit country for a lady in early spring.

He did much to shake our enthusiasm, but still I felt we must do our best to "keep tryst" with the Smithsons. So, on Tuesday, we sent on the heavy luggage in two ekkas which Sabz Ali had procured, the two others being only hired from Hassan Abdal to Abbotabad.

Sabz Ali had pointed out that, although he himself was a wonderful man, and could do almost, if not quite, everything, a second servant would be greatly to our (and his) advantage. So, acting on my permission, he engaged one Ayata—a gentle person of a sheep-like disposition, who did everything he was told, and nothing that he was told not to, during our sojourn in Kashmir.

CHAPTER IV
ABBOTABAD TO SRINAGAR

Dismal tidings came in of floods and storms on the Hassan Abdal road. The river had swollen, and both men and beasts had been swept away while trying to cross. Undeterred, however, by such news, even when backed by warnings and persuasions from our friends, we set forth in the rain yesterday morning. The prospect was not cheerful—a grey veil of cloud lay over all the surrounding hills, here and there deepening into dark and angry thunder-clouds. The road was desperately heavy, but the General had most kindly sent on a pair of mules ahead, and, with another pair in the shafts, our own nags took a holiday as far as Manserah.

The weather grew worse. It rained very heavily and thundered with great vigour, and as we straggled up the deeply-muddied slope to the dâk bungalow at Manserah we felt somewhat low; but we did not in the least realise what was before us!

Our road had lain through fairly level plains, with low cuttings here and there, where the saturated soil was already beginning to give way and fall upon the road in untidy heaps; but this did not foreshadow what might occur later.

At Manserah we met Hill and Hunt, two young gunners, *en route* for Astor. They left in a tonga soon after we arrived, and we did not expect to see their speedier outfit again.

Being pressed for time, we only had a cup of cocoa, and then hastened on our dismal career.

The road grew steeper, winding over some low hills, but we could not see very much, as the whirling cloud masses blotted out all the view. By-and-by it bent towards a pine-clad hill, and began to ascend steeply. By this time we were very wet, as we had to walk up the hills to ease the horses. The scene was extraordinary, as the great thunder-clouds boiled up and over us—tawny yellow, and even orange in the lights, and dull and solid lead colour in the depths. The distance was invisible, but gleams now and again revealed, through the drifts of rain, wide stretches of cultivated land lying below us, and a ragged forest of pines piercing the mist above.

Dripping, we walked by our wet horses up to the top of the pass, hoping for a swift and easy descent on the farther side to Ghari Habibullah, where we intended to sleep, as we had given up all idea of being able to get on to Domel.

Presently the horses were pulled up sharply as a ton or two of rock and earth came crashing upon the road in front of us.

More fallen masses encumbering the way farther on made us feel rather anxious, until, on rounding a corner, we found the whole road barred by a huge mass of rock and soil.

It was blowing hard, the stormy wind striking chill and bleak through the bending pines; it was raining in torrents; it was 5 P.M., and we were still some six miles from the haven where we would be; so, after a short and utterly ineffectual attempt to get the carriage past the obstacle, Jane and I set off to walk down the hill and seek help.

It was exciting, as we had to dodge the rock-falls and run past the shaky-looking places! At a turn of the road we came upon the gunners' tonga, embedded in a mud-slide. The occupants had had an escape from total wreck, as one of the ponies had swerved over the khud, but the other saved the situation by lying down in the mud! Hunt had gone off into the landscape to try for a village and help, while Hill remained to wrestle with the tonga, which, however, remained obstinately immovable. We could do nothing to mend matters, so we fled on, meeting Hunt, with a few natives and a shovel, on his way back to the scene of action.

After an hour and a half of very anxious work, we emerged at dusk from the wood, hoping our troubles were over. We could dimly see, and hear, through the mist a stream below us; but, alas! no bridge was visible. I commandeered a man from the first hut we came to, and tried by signs to make him understand that he was to carry the lady across the river; but, luckily, just as we reached the bank of what was a very nasty-looking stream in full spate, the liberated tonga overtook us, and Jane was bundled into it, while we three men waded. The stream was strong and up to our knees, and level with the tonga floor, and the horses getting frightened began to jib. Hill seized one by the head, and Jane was safely drawn to shore and sent on her way under guidance of the driver, while we tramped on in the dark until a second torrent barred our way. Here, in the gloom, we made out the tonga empty, and stuck fast against the far bank. It was all right though, for Jane had crawled out at the front and wandered on in search of the dâk bungalow, leaving the driver squatting helplessly beside the water.

It was so dark that she missed the bungalow, which stands a little above the road, and struggled on till she came to a small cluster of native huts. One of the inhabitants, on being boldly accosted, was good enough to point out the way, and so the re-united party—tired, wet, and with no prospect of dry clothing—took possession of the cheerless-looking dâk bungalow. Things now began to improve. To our joy we found our ekkas with their contents drawn up in the yard. And while a fire was being encouraged into a blaze, and the lean fowl was being captured and slain on the back premises, we obtained dry garments—of sorts—from the baggage.

Madame's dinner costume consisted of a blue flannel garment—nocturnal by design—delicately covered by a quilted dressing-gown, and the rest of us were *en suite*, a great lack of detail as to collars and foot-wear being apparent! Nevertheless, the fire blazed royally, and we ate up all the old hen and called for more, and prepared to make a night of it until, about ten o'clock, our bearer Sabz Ali appeared, with a train of coolies carrying our bedding and the other contents of the derelict carriage.

This morning the two young gunners departed on foot, leaving their tonga, as the road to Domel is reported to be quite impassable. They intend to walk by a short cut over the hills, and get on as best they may, the race for Astor being a keen one.

We decided to remain here, the weather being still gloomy and unsettled, and the road being impossible for a lady.

At noon the landau was brought in, minus a step and very dirty, but otherwise "unwounded from the dreadful close."

Ghari Habibullah is not at all a cheerful spot, as it appears, the centre of a grey haze, with dense mist low down on the surrounding mountains. Sabz Ali, too, complains of fever, which is not surprising after the wetting and exposure of yesterday; and when a native gets "fever" he curls up and is fit for nothing, and won't try.

The dâk bungalow stands on a little plateau overlooking the road and a swift river, whose tawny waves were loaded with mud washed from the hills by recent storms. On a slope opposite, the queer, flat-roofed native village perched, and above it swirled a misty pall which hid all but the bases of the hills. To this village we strolled, but it was not interesting; the inhabitants did not seem wildly friendly, and the mud and dirt and dogs were discouraging. So we roamed along the Domel road till we came to a high cliff of conglomerate, which had recently been shedding boulders over the track to an alarming extent; so, deciding that it would be merely silly to risk getting our heads cracked, we turned back, and, re-crossing the river, clambered up a steep path above the right bank. Here we soon found great rents and rifts where falling rocks had come bounding down the steeps from above, so once more we turned tail, and, giving up the idea of any more country walks in that region, betook ourselves to the gloomy and chilly bungalow. The only really delightful things we saw during our doleful excursion were a lovely clump of big, rose-coloured primula, drooping from the clefts of a steep rock, and a pair of large and handsome kingfishers,[1] pursuing their graceful avocations by a roadside pool—their white breasts, ruddy flanks, and gleaming blue backs giving a welcome note of colour to the sedate and misty grey of the landscape.

[1] *N. Smyrnensis* (?).

Tuesday, April 4.—Thirty-six hours of Ghari Habibullah give ample time for the loneliest recluse to pant for the bustle of a livelier world. We were so bored on Thursday that we determined to push on, *coûte que coûte,* on Friday morning, although a note sent back by one of the gunners from Domel, by a coolie, informed us that the road about a mile short of that place was completely blocked by a fallen mass of some hundreds of tons.

Our henchman having somewhat recovered of his fever, thanks to a generous exhibition of quinine, we gave the order to pack and start, hoping to achieve the twelve miles which separated us from Domel, even though the last bit had to be done on foot. About two miles from Ghari Habibullah we came to the Kashmir custom-house, presided over by a polite gentleman, whose brilliant purple beard was a joy to look upon.

Most of the elderly natives dye their beards with, I think, henna, producing a fine orange effect, but purple...!

Bottom. What beard were I best to play it in?

Quince. Why, what you will.

Bottom. I will discharge it in either your straw-coloured beard, your orange-tawny beard, your purple-in-grain beard, or your French-crown-colour beard, your perfect yellow

Midsummer Night's Dream,
Act I. Sc. 2.

"What *coloured beard* comes next by the window?"

"A black man's, I think."

"I think a *red*: for that is most in fashion."

RAM ALLY.

Truly, until I beheld that tax-gatherer of the Orient, I had no idea that the "purple-in-grain" beard existed outside a poet's fancy!

The road took us along the left bank of the river, whose soil-stained waters churned their way through a wild and rocky gorge. On our left the mountain rose bare and steep, fringed with a few straggling bushes, and here and there a clinging patch of rose-coloured primula. Part of the conglomerate cliff had come down and obliterated the road, but a party of coolies was busily at work, and, after about an hour's delay, we triumphantly bumped our way past.

The road now led steadily upward, leaving an ever-increasing slope (or khud) between it and the river, until it attained a height of over a thousand feet, when, turning to the left, it swung over the watershed, and began to descend into the valley of the Kishenganga. Through the haze we could make out Domel, our goal, lying far below, and then the old Sikh fort of Musafferabad.

The road was so encumbered with rock-falls that we walked the greater part of it, until we came to the new bridge over the Kishenganga, whose dark red waters rush into the Jhelum about a mile below.

Here was Musafferabad, the whole place a confused jumble of wheeled traffic caught up by the big landslip in front. Passing, amid the chatter and clamour of men and beasts, through the medley of bullock-carts and ekkas that crowded every available space, we hauled the carriage through the bed of a watercourse whose bridge was broken. Up over the prostrate trunk of a fallen tree we regained the road, to find ourselves in front of the big landslip of which we had been warned. It consisted of some thousands of tons of dark red mud and loose boulders, and it blocked the road for fully a couple of hundred yards.

A large and energetic swarm of coolies was busily engaged in "tidying up." This was apparently to be achieved by means of shovels, each little shovel worked by two men—one to shovel, and the other to assist in raising it when full by means of a little rope round the head. This labour had to be lubricated by much conversation.

It seemed upon the whole unlikely that a path could be made for a considerable time, so we lunched peacefully in the carriage, a pair of extremely friendly crows assisting at the feast, and then, leaving our landau to follow as best it might, we walked into Domel, crossing the Jhelum by a fine bridge.

The dâk bungalow, prettily placed in a clump of trees, seemed the abode of luxury to us after the discomfort of Ghari Habibullah, and we fondly hoped that, being now upon the main road which runs from Rawal Pindi to Srinagar, our troubles were over.

Saturday was the 1st of April, the day upon which I should have applied for my pass for Astor. Wiring to Srinagar to explain that I was in Kashmir territory (which I subsequently found was enough to entitle me to a pass), and also to Smithson to say that we were making the best of our way to join him, we "took the road" after breakfast.

The carriage and the two ekkas had come in early, having been unloaded and then carried bodily over the "slide."

A broad and smooth road, whose gentle gradient of ascent was merely sufficient to keep us level with the river bank, opened up an alluring prospect of ease and comfort. We lay back on our comfortable cushions and watched the clouds as they swept over the mountains, hiding all but occasional glimpses of snow-streaked slopes and steep and barren ridges.

The valley of the Jhelum between Domel and Ghari is not beautiful—merely wide and desolate, with steep hills rising from the river, their lower slopes sparsely clad with leafless scrub, their shoulders merging into the dull mist which hangs around their invisible summits.

Alas! it soon became apparent that our troubles were not over. The cliffs above us became steeper, and the familiar boulder reappeared upon the road. Small landslips gave us a good deal of trouble, although we had no serious difficulty before reaching Ghari. Here we were told that a complete "solution of continuity" in the road at Mile 46 would prevent our reaching Chakhoti, so we reluctantly decided to remain where we were for the night. Although a cold and dull spring afternoon is not exciting at Ghari, where distractions are decidedly scanty, we found interest in the discovery of the Smithsons' heavy luggage, which had been sent on from Rawal Pindi ages ago. Here it lay in the peaceful backwater of a native caravansary, piled high on a bullock-cart, whose placid team lay near pensively chewing the "cud of sweet and bitter fancy," and apparently quite innocent of any intention of moving for a week or two!

We extracted the charioteers from a neighbouring hut, and gave them to understand, by means of Sabz Ali, that hanging was the least annoyance they would suffer if they didn't get under way "ek dam" at once. They promptly promised that their oxen—like Pegasus—should fly on the wings of the wind, and, having seen us safely round a corner, departed peacefully to eat another lotus.

The luggage arrived in Srinagar towards the end of the month.

Sunday morning saw us again battling with a perfect coruscation of landslips; so "jumpy" was it in many places that we sat with the carriage doors ajar, in hopes that a timely dart out might enable us to evade a falling rock. At Mile 46 we were held up for an hour until a ramp was made over a bad slide, and the carriage and ekkas were unloaded and got across. The landau looked for all the world like a great dead beetle surrounded by ants, as, man-handled by a swarm of coolies, it was hauled, step by step, over the improvised track. A landau is not at all a suitable or convenient carriage for this sort of work, and had we guessed what was before us we should most certainly have employed the handier tonga.

The road to-day, cut as it was out of the steep flank of the mountain, was magnificent, but, in its present condition, nerve-shattering. Fallen boulders and innumerable mud-slides constantly forced us to get out and walk, while the sturdy little horses tugged the carriage through places where the near wheels were frequently within a few inches of the broken edge of the road, while far below Jhelum roared hungrily as he foamed by the foot of a sheer precipice.

Reaching Chakhoti about four o'clock, we decided to remain there for the night, as it was growing late and the weather looked gloomy and threatening. Although we had only achieved a short stage of twenty-one miles, there was no suitable place for a night's halt until Uri, distant some thirteen miles and all uphill.

About half a mile above Chakhoti there is a rope bridge over the Jhelum, and after tea we set forth to inspect it.

The river is here about 150 yards wide and extremely swift, and I confess the means of crossing it, although practised with perfect confidence by the natives, did not appeal to me.

From two great uprights, formed from solid tree-trunks, three strong ropes were stretched—the upper two parallel, and the third, about four feet lower, was equidistant from each.

These three ropes were kept in their relative positions by wooden stretchers—something like great merrythoughts, lashed at intervals of a few yards—

"And up and down the people go,"

stepping delicately upon the lower rope, and holding on to the upper ones with their hands. The uncomfortable part seemed to the unpractised European to be where the graceful sweep of the long ropes brought the traveller to within a painfully close distance of the hurrying, hungry water, before he began to slither circumspectly up the farther slope!

We stood for some little time watching the natives going to and fro, passing one another with perfect ease by means of a dexterous squirm, and carrying loads on their backs, or live fowls under their arms, with the utmost unconcern.

We left Chakhoti early this morning—Tuesday—with the intention of getting right through to Baramula. The road was of course extremely bad, and the long ascent to Uri very hard upon our willing little nags. Of course they have had a remarkably easy time of it lately, as we have been limited to very short stages, and they are in excellent hard condition, so that we felt it no great hardship to ask them to do forty-two miles: albeit to drag a heavy landau containing five people and a good deal of luggage for that distance, with a rise of over 2000 feet, is a heavy demand upon a single pair of horses!

The scenery was very fine as we toiled up the gorge, in which Uri stands on a plateau over the river and guards the pass into Kashmir valley.

The ruins of an ancient fort rose on the near edge of the little plain. The Jhelum tore through a rocky gorge far below, and a dark semi-circle of mountains stood steeply up, their cloud-hidden summits giving fleeting glimpses of snow and precipice and pine-clad corries as the sun now and again shot through the clinging vapours.

The dâk bungalow of Uri, white and clean, was most attractive, and I should imagine the place to be charming in summer, but as yet the short crisp turf is still brown from recent snow, and although hot in the sun, which now began to shine steadily, it was extremely cold in the shade, while lunch (or should I say "tiffin"?) was being got ready. I strolled over to the post-office to find—as usual—another urgent wire from Smithson several days old, beseeching me to secure my pass for Astor at once. Directly after lunch we set forward, and as the road on leaving Uri takes a long bend of some miles to the right to a point where the Haji Pir River is crossed, and then sweeps back along its right hank to a spot almost opposite the dâk bungalow, we thought that a short cut down to the water, which from our height seemed quite insignificant, and thence up to the road on the other side, would be a desirable stroll. As we walked down the steep path into the nullah a brace of red-legged partridges (chikor) rose in a great fuss, and sailed gaily across the river, whose roaring gained ominously in volume as we drew near. It soon became plain to us that everything is on a very big scale in this country, and that the clearness of the atmosphere helps to delude the unwary stranger. The little stream that seemed to require but an occasional stepping-stone to enable us to pass over dry-shod, proved in the first place to be much farther off than we had supposed, and when, after a hot scramble, we found ourselves on the bank, the stepping-stones were no more, but only here and there we saw the shoulders of huge rocks which doggedly threw aside the flying foam of a fair-sized river. It was obviously impossible to cross except by deep wading, but, being unwilling to own defeat, I yelled to a brown native on the far bank, and made signs that he should come and do beast of burthen. He, however, stolidly shook his head, pointed to the water, and then to his chest, and finally we sadly and wrathfully toiled back to the road we had so lightly left, and expended all our energies on attracting the notice of the carriage, which, having crossed the bridge, was crawling along the opposite face of the nullah, and when, after a hot three miles, we once more embedded ourselves amongst the cushions with a sigh of relief, we swore off short cuts for the future.

We had been warned at Uri that there was a "bad place" at Mile 73, and sure enough, on rounding a bend, we came upon the familiar mass of semi-liquid red earth and a pile of boulders heaped across the road, the khud side of which had entirely given way. The usual crowd of coolies was busily engaged in trying to clear the obstruction by means of toothpicks and teaspoons.

We quitted the carriage with a celerity engendered of much practice, and, having crossed the obstacle on foot, sat down to await the coming of our conveyance.

It seemed perfectly marvellous that the heavy vehicle could be safely got over a jagged avalanche of earth and rock piled some eight or ten feet above the roadway, and having an almost sheer drop to the river entirely unguarded for some hundred yards, where the retaining parapet and even some of the road itself had gone.

Amid much apparent confusion and tremendous chattering, a sort of rough ramp was engineered up the slip, and presently the horseless landau appeared borne in triumph by a mob of coolies superintended by our priceless Sabz Ali.

For a minute we held our breath as one of the near wheels lipped the edge of the chasm, but the thing was judged to an inch, and in due time the sturdy chestnuts, the two ekkas, and all the luggage were assembled on the right side of what proved to be the last of the really bad slips.

The road engineer, who arrived in great state on a motor cycle while we were executing the portage, told us that there were no more difficulties, but an officer who was going out, and whose tonga was checked also at the big slip, informed us that about a mile farther were two great boulders on the road, lying so that although a short vehicle such as a tonga or motor cycle could wriggle round, yet a long four-wheeled landau could not possibly execute the serpentine curve required.

We therefore requisitioned a few coolies with crowbars, and set forward to attack the boulders. Sure enough there were two beauties, placed so that we could not possibly get by, until a large slice was chipped from the inner side of each.

This done, our most excellent and skilful driver piloted his ponies through the narrow strait, and we felt that, at last, our troubles were over, and that we could breathe freely and admire at leisure the snowy peaks of the Kaj-nag beyond the Jhelum, and the rough wooded heights that frowned upon our right.

I confess the relief was great, as we had endured six days of incessant strain on our nerves, never knowing when a turn of the road might bring us to an impassable break, or when the conglomerate cliffs beetling above might shed a boulder or two upon us!

Passing the somewhat uninviting little village of Rampur, we crossed a torrent pouring out of a dark pine-clad gorge, and halted for tea by the curious ruined temple of Bhanyar. The building consists of a rectangular wall, cloistered on two sides of the interior and surrounding a small temple approached by a dilapidated flight of stone steps. I regret to be obliged to own that I know but a mere smattering of architecture. I do not feel competent therefore to discuss this, the first Kashmiri temple I have seen, upon its architectural merits. I only know that it struck me as being extremely small, and principally interesting from its magnificent background of shaggy forest and snow-capped mountain.

Tea on a short smooth sward, starred with yellow colchicum, while the carriage, travel-stained and with one step lacking, stood on the road hard by, and the horses nibbled invigorating lumps of "gram" and molasses. Then the etna was returned to the "allo bagh" (yellow bag) and the tea things to the tiffin basket, and away we went along the now smooth and level road with only fifteen easy miles between us and Baramula.

The vegetation had gradually grown much richer. The sparse and storm-buffeted pines and the rough scrub merged into a tangled mass of undergrowth and forest, where silver firs and deodars rose conspicuous. The little streams that rushed down the hillsides were fringed with maidenhair fern, lighted up here and there with a bunch of pink primula or a tiny cluster of dog violets.

Jhelum had ceased from roaring, pursuing his placid path unwitting of the rush and fury that would befall him lower down, and by-and-by we emerged from the dark and forest-covered gorge into a wide basin where the river, now smooth and oily, reflected tall poplars and the red shoots of young dogwood.

A Holiday in the Happy Valley with Pen and Pencil | 43

Through a village, round a sweep to the left, over a tract said to be much frequented by serpents, and then in the deepening and chilly dusk we made out Baramula, lying engirdled by a belt of poplars about a mile away.

Glad were we, and probably gladder still our weary horses, to draw up before the uninviting-looking dâk bungalow, knowing that only thirty-five miles of level and open road lay now between us and Srinagar.

The dâk bungalow of Baramula is, upon the whole, the worst we have yet sampled. No fire seemed able to impart any cheerfulness to the gloomy den we were shown into, and the dinner finally produced by the khansamah-kitmaghar-chowkidar (for a single tawny-bearded ruffian represented all these functionaries when the morning tip fell due) was not of an exhilarating nature. Strolling out to have a look at the town of Baramula, I shivered to see a heap of snow piled up against the wall. It snowed here, heavily, three days ago, I am told.

We have not been, so far, altogether lucky in the weather. Bitter cold in Europe, cold at Port Saïd and Suez, chilly in the Red Sea, and wet at Aden! Distinctly chilly in India, excepting during the day; we seem to have hit off the most backward spring known here for many years. The Murree route, which was closed to us by snow, should have been clear a month earlier, and spring here seems not yet to have begun.

April 5.—We crept shivering to our beds last night, to be awakened at 6 A.M. by an earthquake!

I had just realised what the untoward commotion meant when I heard Jane from under her "resai" ask, "What *is* the matter—is it an earthquake?" Almost before I could reply, she was up and away, in a fearful hurry and very little else, towards the open country.

I followed, but finding hoar-frost on the ground and a nipping eagerness in the air, I went back for a "resai." The feeling was that of going into one's cabin in a breeze of wind, and the door was flapping about. Seizing the wrap in some haste, as I was afraid of the door jamming, I rejoined Jane in the open, to watch the poplars swaying like drunken men and the solid earth bulging unpleasantly. The shock lasted for three minutes, and when it seemed quite over we retired to our beds to try to get warm again.

The morning at breakfast-time was perfectly beautiful. Baramula lay serenely mirrored in the silver waters of the Jhelum, its picturesque brown wooden houses clustering on both banks, and joining hands by means of a long brown wooden bridge. No signs of any unusual disturbance could be seen among the chattering crews of the snaky little boats and deep-laden "doungas" that lined the banks or furrowed the waters of the shining river.

We left Baramula in high spirits to accomplish the five-and-thirty miles which still stretched between us and Srinagar. The scenery was quite different from anything we had yet known, for now we were in the broad flat valley of Kashmir, which stretches for some eighty miles from beyond Islamabad, on the N.E., to Baramula, planted at the neck where the Jhelum River, after spreading itself abroad through the fertile plain, concentrates to pour its many waters through the mountain barrier until it joins the Indus far away in Sind.

A broad and level road stretched straight and white between a double row of stark poplars, reminding one of the poplar-guarded ways of Picardy; also (as in France) not only were the miles marked, but also the thirty-two subdivisions thereof. On the right hand the ground sloped slowly up in a succession of wooded heights, the foothills of the Pir Panjal, whose snow-crowned peaks enclose the Kashmir valley on the south. Opposite, through a maze of leafless trees, one caught occasional gleams of water where the winding reaches of the river flowed gently from the turquoise haze where lay the Wular Lake, and beyond—clear and pale in the clear, crisp air—shone a glorious range of snow mountains, stretching away past where we knew Srinagar must lie, to be lost in the distant haze where sky and mountain merged in the north-east.

By the roadside we passed many small lakes, or "jheels," full of duck, but as there was never any cover by the sides I could not see how the duck were to be approached.

We lunched at the fascinating little bungalow at Patan (pronounced "Puttun"), about half-way between Baramula and Srinagar. The Rest House stands back from an apparently extremely populous and thriving village, the inhabitants whereof were all engaged in conversation of a highly animated kind! In the compound stood a fine group of chenar trees (*Platanus orientalis*) whose noble trunks and graceful branches showed in striking contrast to the slender stems of the poplars. The guide-book informed us that an ancient temple lay in ruins near by, but we trusted to a later visit and determined to push on. By-and-by a fort-crowned hill rose above the tree-tops. This we took to be Hari Parbat, the ancient citadel of Srinagar, and presently, through the poplars and the willows queer wooden huts or châlets began to appear, and the increasing number of men and beasts upon the road showed the proximity of the city.

Ekkas, white-hooded, with jingling bells hung round the scraggy necks of their lean ponies; brown men clad in sort of night-shirts composed of mud-coloured rags; brown dogs, humpy cattle, and children innumerable, swarmed upon the causeway in ever-increasing density until we drew up at the custom-house, and the usual jabber took place among Sabz Ali, the driver, and the officials.

All appeared satisfactory, however, and we were presented with bits of brown paper scrawled over with hieroglyphics which we took to be passes, and drove on, leaving the native town apparently on our left and making a détour through level fields and between rows of poplars, until we swung round and crossed the river by a fine bridge. Here we first got some idea of the city of Srinagar, which lay spread around us, bisected by the broad, but apparently far from sluggish river, which seems here to be about the width of the Thames at Westminster at high water.

Tier upon tier, the rickety wooden houses crowded either bank, the prevailing brown being oddly lighted up by the roofs, which were frequently covered with deep green turf. Here and there the steep and peculiar dome of a Hindu temple flashed like polished silver in the keen sunlight, while around and beyond all rose the ring of the everlasting hills, their peaks clear, yet soft, against a background of cloudless blue.

Close below us stood a remarkably picturesque pile of buildings, of a mixed style of architecture, yet harmonising well enough as a whole with its surroundings. Over it flew a great "banner with a strange device," and we assumed (and rightly) that we looked upon the palace of His Highness Sir Pratab Singh, Maharajah of Jammu and Kashmir.

Crossing the river, we dived into a bit of the native town, and were much struck by the want of colour as compared with an Indian street. Everything seemed steeped in the same neutral brown—houses, boats, people, and dogs! Emerging from the native street, with its open shop-fronts and teeming life, we drove for some little way along a straight level road, flanked, as usual, on either side by poplars of great size which ran through a brown, flat field, showing traces of recent snow, and finally finished our two-hundred-mile drive in front of the one and only hotel in all Kashmir.

Our two little chestnuts, which had brought us right through from Chakhoti to Srinagar—a distance of about seventy-eight miles—in two days, were as lively and fit as possible, and playfully nibbled at each other's noses as they were walked off to their well-earned rest.

The ekka horses, too, had brought our heavy luggage all the way from Abbotabad over a shocking road in the most admirable manner, and we had every reason to congratulate ourselves on having entrusted the arrangement of the whole business—the "bandobast" in native parlance—to our henchman Sabz Ali, who had thus proved himself an energetic and trustworthy organiser, and saving financier to the extent of some twenty rupees.

I may emphasise here the importance of keeping one's heavy baggage in sight, herding on the ekkas in front, if possible, and keeping a wary eye and a firm hand on the drivers at all halts. The Smithsons, who had sent on their gear from Rawal Pindi some days before we got there, did not receive it in Srinagar until the 22nd of April. It took about five weeks to do the journey, and the rifle which I was obliged to leave in Karachi on the 19th of March finally turned up in Srinagar, after an infuriating and vain expenditure of telegrams, on the 1st of May!

Of course, part of the delay was due, and all was attributed, to the unusually bad state of the roads. The heavy storms and floods which, by wrecking the road, had delayed us so much, naturally checked the heavy transport still more; and severe congestion of bullock-carts resulted at all the halting-places along the route. Still, the main cause of delay lies in the fact that the monopoly of transport has been granted by the Maharajah to one Danjibhoy, who charges what he pleases, and takes such time over his arrangements as suits his Oriental mind.

The motto over the Transport Office door might well be "*Ohne Hast — mit Rast!*"

The other (much-cherished) monopoly in this favoured land is that enjoyed by Mr. Nedou, the owner of THE HOTEL in Kashmir.

We were advised when at Lahore to approach Mr. Nedou (who winters in his branch there) with many salaams and much "kow-towing," in order to make a certainty of being received into his select circle in Kashmir. The great man was quite kind, and promised that he would do his best for us; and he was as good as his word, as we were immediately welcomed and permitted to add two to the four persons already inhabiting the hostelry. I confess that, even after a dâk bungalow of the most inferior quality—such as that at Ghari Habibullah or Baramula—Mr. Nedou's hotel fails to impress one with an undue sense of luxury. In fact, it presented an even desolate and forlorn appearance with its gloomy and chilly passages and cheerless bed-vaults.

CHAPTER V
FIRST IMPRESSIONS OF SRINAGAR

We learnt that the earthquake of this morning was far more than the ordinary affair that we had taken it to be. The hotel showed signs of a struggle for existence. Large cracks in the plaster, spanned by strips of paper gummed across to show if they widened, and little heaps of crumbled mortar on the floors, betrayed that the grip of mother earth had been no feeble one.

Telegrams from Lahore inquired if the rumour was true that Srinagar had been much damaged, and reported an awful destruction and loss of life at Dharmsala. I think if we had fully known what an earthquake really meant, we should not have so calmly gone back to bed again!

The advent of Mrs. Smithson upon the scene relieved a certain anxiety which we had felt as to immediate plans. The idea of rushing into Astor had been given up, we found—not so much on account of our tardy arrival, permits being still obtainable, but on account of the impossibility—at any rate for ladies—of forcing the high passes which the late season has kept safely sealed.

Walter, having pawed the ground in feverish impatience for some days, had gone off into a region said to be full of bara singh; so we decided to possess our souls in patience for a little time, and remain quietly in Srinagar. Accordingly, instead of unpacking our "detonating musquetoons," we exhumed our evening clothes, and began life in Srinagar with a cheerful dinner at the Residency.

Friday, April 7th.—We are evidently somewhat premature here as far as climate goes. The weather since our arrival has become cold and grey, and we have seemed on the verge of another snowfall. However, the clerk of the weather has refrained from such an insult, contenting himself with sending a breeze down upon us fresh from the "Roof of the World," and laden with the chilly moisture of the snows. We have consumed great quantities of wood, vainly endeavouring to warm up the den which Mr. Nedou has let to us as a sitting-room. Fires are not the fashion in the public rooms—probably because the only "public" besides ourselves consist of one or two enterprising sportsmen, who doubtless are acclimatising themselves to camp life amid the snows, and have implored the proprietor to save his fuel and keep the outer doors open.

Yesterday, we went on a shopping excursion down the river, our "hansom" being a long narrow sort of canoe, propelled and dexterously steered by four or five paddlers, whose mode of *digging* along by means of their heart-shaped blades reminded me not a little of the Kroo boys paddling a fish-canoe off Elmina on the Gold Coast.

We embarked close to the back of the hotel, at the Chenar Bagh, and went gaily enough down the strong current of what we took to be an affluent of the Jhelum. As a matter of fact, the European quarter forms an island, low and perfectly flat, the banks of which are heaped into a high dyke or "bund," washed on one side (the south) by the main river, and on the other by the Sunt-i-kul Canal, down which we have been paddling.

The river life was most fascinating—crowds of heavy doungas lay moored along the banks—their long, low bodies covered in by matting, and their extremities sloping up into long peaked platforms for the crew. These—many of them women and children—were all clothed in neutral-tinted gowns, the only bit of colour being an occasional note of red or white in the puggaree of the men or skull-cap of the children. The married women invariably wore whity-brown veils over the head. The wooden houses that lined the banks were all in the general low scheme of colour, but a peculiar charm was added by the roofs covered in thick, green turf.

Srinagar has been called the "Venice of the East," and, inasmuch as waterways form the main thoroughfares in both, there is a certain resemblance. Shikaras (the Kashmiri canoes) are first-cousins to gondolas—rather poor relations perhaps; both are dingy and clumsy in appearance, and both are managed with an extraordinary dexterity by their navigators.

Both cities are "smelly," though Venice, even at its worst, stands many degrees above the incredible filth of Srinagar.

Finally—both cities are within sight of snowy ranges; although it seems hardly fair to place in comparison the majestic range that overhangs Srinagar and the somewhat distant and sketchy view of the Alps as seen from Venice.

Here, I think, all resemblance ceases. The charm of Venice lies in its architecture, its art treasures, its historical memories, and its interesting people.

Srinagar has no architecture in particular, being but a picturesque chaos of tumble-down wooden shanties. It has no history worth speaking of, and its inhabitants are—and apparently have always been—a poor lot.

Shopping in Srinagar is not pure and unadulterated joy. Down the river, spanned by its seven bridges, amidst a network of foul-smelling alleys, you are dragged to the emporiums of the native merchants whose advertisements flare upon the river banks, and who, armed with cards, and possessed of a wonderful supply of the English language, swarm around the victim at every landing-place, and almost tear one another in pieces while striving to obtain your custom.

Samad Shall, in a conspicuous hoarding, announces that he can—and will—supply you with anything you may desire, including money—for he proclaims himself to be a banker.

Ganymede, in his own opinion, is the only wood-carver worth attention.

Suffering Moses is the prince of workers in lacquer, according to his own showing.

The nose of the boat grates up against the slimy step of the landing-place, and you plunge forthwith into Babel.

"Will you come to my shop?"

"No—you are going somewhere else."

"After?"

"Perhaps!"

"To-day, master?"

"No—no time to-day."

"To-morrow, then—I got very naice kyriasity [curiosity]—to-morrow, master—what time?"

"Oh! get out! and leave me alone."

"I send boat for you—ten o'clock to-morrow?"

"No."

"Twelve o'clock?" &c. &c.

After a short experience of Kashmiri pertinacity and business methods, you cease from politeness and curtly threaten the river.

Certainly the Kashmiri are exceedingly clever and excellent workers in many ways. Their modern embroideries (the old shawl manufacture is totally extinct) are beautiful and artistic. Their wood-carving, almost always executed in rich brown walnut, is excellent; and their *old* papier-mâché lacquer is very good. The tendency, however, is unfortunately to abandon their own admirable designs, and assimilate or copy Western ideas as conveyed in very doubtful taste by English visitors.

The embroidery has perhaps kept its individuality the best, although the trail of the serpent as revealed in "quaint" Liberty or South Kensington designs is sometimes only too apparent. Certain plants—Lotus, Iris, Chenar leaf, and so-called Dal Lake leaves, as well as various designs taken from the old Kashmir shawls, give scope to the nimble brains and fingers of the embroiderers, who, by-the-bye, are all male.

Their colours, almost invariably obtained from native dyes, are excellent, and they rarely make a mistake in taste.

The coarser work in wool on cushions, curtains, and thick white numdahs is most effective and cheap.

Curiously enough, the best of these numdahs (which make capital rugs or bath blankets) are made in Yarkand; and Stein, in his *Sand-Buried Cities of Kotan*, found in ancient documents, of the third century or so, "the earliest mention of the felt-rugs or 'numdahs' so familiar to Anglo-Indian use, which to this day form a special product of Kotan home industry, and of which large consignments are annually exported to Ladak and Kashmir."

The manufacture of carpets is receiving attention, and Messrs. Mitchell own a large carpet factory. Designs and colours are good, but the prices are not low enough to enable them to compete with the cheap Indian makes; nor, I make bold to say, is the quality such as to justify high prices. The shop of Mohamed Jan is well worth a visit, for three good reasons—first, because his Oriental carpets from Penjdeh and Khiva are of the best; second, because his house is one of the first specimens of a high-class native dwelling existing; and third, because he never worries his customers nor touts for orders—but, then, he is a Persian, and not a Kashmiri!

The famous shawls which fetched such prices in England in early Victorian days are no longer valued, having suffered an eclipse similar to that undergone by the pictures of certain early Victorian Royal Academicians, and the loss of the shawl trade was a severe blow to Kashmir. With the exception of occasional specimens of these shawls, which, however, can be bought cheaper at sales in London, there are no *old* embroideries to be got.

The wood-carving industry, too, is quite modern; but, although of great excellence and ingenuity in manipulation, it does not appeal to me, being too florid and copious in its application of design. A restless confusion of dragons from Leh, lotus from the Dal Lake, and the ever-present chenar leaf, hobnob together with British—very British—crests and monograms on the tops of tables and the seats of chairs—portions of the furniture that should be left severely plain.

British taste is usually bad, and to it, and not to Kashmiri initiative, must be ascribed the production of such exotic works as bellows embellished with chaste designs of lotus-buds, and afternoon tea-tables flaunting coats-of-arms (doubtless dating from the Conquest), beautifully carved in high relief just where the tray—the bottom of which is probably ornamented with a flowing design of raised flowers—should rest!

The lacquered papier-maché work—often extremely pretty when left to its own proper Cabul pattern or other native design—aims too often at attracting the eye of the mighty hunter by introducing an inappropriate markhor's head. The old lacquer-work is difficult to get, and, when obtained, is high in price; but comparison between the old and the new shows the gulf that lies between the loving and skilful labour of the artist and the stupid and generally "scamped" achievement of him who merely "knocks off" candlesticks and tobacco-boxes by the score, to sell to the English visitor— papier-maché being superseded by wood, and lacquer by paint.

The workers in silver, copper, and brass are many, but their productions are usually rough and inartistic. Genuine old beaten metal-work is almost unobtainable, although occasionally desirable specimens from Leh do find their way into the Srinagar shops.

Chinese porcelain is to be got, usually in the form of small bowls; but it is not of remarkably good quality, and the prices asked for it are higher than in London.

The jewellers' work is very far behind that of India. Amethysts of pale colour and yellow topaz are cheap. Fine turquoise do not come into Kashmir, but plenty of the rough stones (as well as imitations) are to be found, which, owing to a transitory fashion, are priced far above their intrinsic value. They come from Thibet.

A great deal of a somewhat soft and ugly-coloured jade is sent from Yarkand, also agates and carnelian; beads of these are strung into rather uncouth necklets, which may be bought for half the sum first asked.

Bargaining is an invariable necessity in all shopping in Kashmir, as everywhere else in the East, where the market value of an article is not what it costs to produce, but what can be squeezed for it out of the purse of the— usually—ignorant purchaser.

Three things are essential to the successful prosecution of shopping in Srinagar:—

(1) Unlimited time.

(2) A command of emphatic language, sufficient to impress the native mind with the need for keeping to the point.

(3) A liver in such thorough working order as to insure an extraordinary supply of good temper.

Without all these attributes the acquisition of objects of "bigotry and vertue" in Srinagar is attended with pain and tribulation.

The descent of the river is accomplished with ease and rapidity, but *revocare gradum* involves much hard paddling, with many pants and grunts; and it was both cold and dark when we again lay alongside the bank of the Chenar Bagh, and scurried up the slippery bund to the hotel, with scarcely time to dress for dinner.

Sunday, 9th April.—Friday was a horrible day—rainy, dull, and cold; but a thrill of excitement was sent through us by the news that Walter has shot two fine bara singh! Charlotte (who is nothing if not a keen sportswoman) was filled with zeal and the spirit of emulation, so we resolved to dash off down the river to Bandipur, join Walter—who has now presumably joined the ranks of the unemployed, being only permitted by the Game Laws to kill two stags—and take our pick of the remaining "Royals," which, in our vivid imaginations, roamed in dense flocks through the nullahs beyond Bandipur!

All Friday and yesterday, therefore, were devoted to preparation. I had already, through the kindness of Major Wigram, secured a shikari, who immediately demonstrated his zeal and efficiency by purchasing a couple of bloodthirsty knives and a huge bottle of Rangoon oil at my expense. I pointed out that one "skian-dhu" seemed to me sufficient for "gralloching" purposes, but he said two were better for bears. My acquaintance with bears being hitherto confined to Regent's Park, I bowed to his superior knowledge and forethought.

A visit to Cockburn's agency resulted in the hire of the "boarded dounga" *Cruiser*, which the helpful Mr. Cockburn procured for us, in which to go down the river; also a couple of tents for ourselves with tent furniture, one for the servants, and a cooking tent.

The local bootmaker or "chaplie-wallah" appeared, as by magic, on the scene, and chaplies were ordered. These consist of a sort of leather sandal strapped over soft leather boots or moccasins. They are extremely comfortable for walking on ordinary ground, but perfectly useless for hill work, even when the soles are studded with nails. The hideous but necessary grass shoe is then your only wear. The grass shoe, which is made as required by the native, is an intricate contrivance of rice straw, kept in position by a straw twist which is hauled taut between the big and next toe, and the end expended round some of the side webbing. The cleft sock and woollen boot worn underneath keep the feet warm, but do not always prevent discomfort and even much pain if the cords are not properly adjusted. However, the remedy is simple. Tear off the shoe, using such language as may seem appropriate to the occasion, throw it at the shikari's head, and order another pair to be made "ek dam"! Jane and I each purchased a yakdan, a sort of roughly-made leather box or trunk, strong, and of suitable size for either pony or coolie transport. Our wardrobe was stowed in these and secured by padlocks, and the cooking gear, together with a certain amount of stores in the shape of grocery, bread, and a couple of bottles of whisky were safely housed in a pair of large covered creels or "kiltas."

Each of the party provided him or herself with a khudstick, consisting of a strong and tough shaft about five feet long, tapering slightly towards the base, where it is shod with a chisel-shaped iron end.

Our staff of retainers had now been brought up to five—the shikari, Ahmed Bot, having procured a satellite, known as the chota shikari, a youth of not unprepossessing appearance, but whose necessity in our scheme of existence I had not quite determined. Ahmed Bot, however, was of opinion that all sahibs who wanted sport required two shikaris, so I imagined that while I was to be engaged with one in pursuit of bara singh, the other would employ himself in "rounding up" a few tigers for the next day's sport in another direction. Ahmed Bot agreed with me in the main, but did not feel at all sure about the tigers—he proposed ibex.

The fifth wheel to our coach was a strikingly ugly person, like a hippopotamus, whose plainness was not diminished by a pair of enormous goggles; this was the harmless necessary sweeper, that pariah among domestics, whose usefulness is undreamed of out of India.

After dinner last night we left the hotel, truly thankful to shake the dust of its gloomy precincts from our feet, and sought our boats, which were moored in the Chenar Bagh. How snug and bright the "ship" seemed after the murky corridors of Nedou! And yet the *Cruiser* was not much to boast of, really, in the way of luxury.

Let me describe a typical boarded dounga. Upon a long, low, flat-bottomed hull, which tapered to a sharp point at bow and stern, was raised a light wooden superstructure with a flat roof, upon which the passengers could sit. The interior was divided off into some half-a-dozen compartments, a vestibule or outer cabin held boxes, &c., and through it one passed into the dining or parlour cabin, which opened again to two little bedrooms and a couple of bathrooms. There was no furniture to speak of, but we had hired from Cockburn all that we required for the trip.

The servants, as well as the crew of the dounga, were all stowed in a "tender" known as the cook boat—no one, except for navigating duties, having any business on board the "flagship."

Charlotte Smithson had a smaller ship than ours—a light wooden frame, which supported movable matting screens or curtains, taking the place of our wooden cabins. The matted dounga looked as though it might be chilly, particularly if a strong wind came to play among the rather draughty-looking mats which were all that our poor friend had between her and a cold world!

CHAPTER VI
OUR FIRST CAMP

The fleet, consisting of four sail (I use this word in its purely conventional sense, a dounga having no more sails than a battleship), got under way about 5 A.M., while it was yet but barely daylight, and so we were well clear of Srinagar when we emerged from our cosy cabins into a world of clean air and brilliant colour.

The broad smooth current of the Jhelum flowed steadily and calmly through a level plain, bearing us along at a comfortable four miles an hour, the crew doing little more than keep steerage-way with pole and paddle.

Beyond the green, tree-studded levels to the south, the range of the Pir Panjal spread wide its array of dazzling peaks, while on the right towered the mountains which enclose the Sind Valley, culminating in the square-headed mass of Haramok. In the clear air the snows seemed quite close, although we knew that the snow-line was really some three thousand feet above the level of the valley.

A day like this, as we sit on the little roof of our floating home watching the silent river unfold its shining curves, goes far to obliterate the memory of the fuss and worry inseparable from the exodus from Srinagar. After lunch we tied up for a while, and I took my gun on shore to try and pick up a few of the duck that dotted the waters of the little lakes or jheels which lay flashing amid the hillocks beyond the river banks. The shores of these being perfectly bare and open, it was obviously impossible to escape the keenly observant eyes of the duck, which appeared, unlike all other birds in Kashmir, to retain their customary wariness.

Crouching low amid the furrows of a newly-ploughed field, I sent the shikari with a knot of natives to the far side of the water, whence they advanced in open line, splashing and shouting.

Presently, with much fuss and indignant quacking, a cloud of duck rose, and, circling after their fashion, as though reluctant to quit their resting-place, gave me several chances of a long shot before, working high into the air, they departed with loud expostulation to some quieter haunt.

Later in the afternoon we tied up to the bank for the night near a large jheel, where we all landed, Charlotte to try a rifle which she had borrowed, and I, if possible, to slay a few more duck, while Jane sat peacefully on a bank and enjoyed the glorious sunset.

The bag having been swelled by the addition of another dozen "specimens"—obtained by the same manoeuvres as before—we strolled back to our ships in the luminous dusk, visions of roast "canard" floating seductively before our mental vision.

There proved to be several varieties of duck among the countless flocks which I saw, notably mallard, teal, pochard, and shoveller. Likewise there were many coots, while herons, disturbed in their meditations by the untoward racket, flapped heavily away with disgusted squawks.

Jane is getting along remarkably well with her Hindustani. I have just found her diary, and hasten to give an extract:—

"Woke up very early; much bitten by pice. Tom started off to try and shoot a burra sahib, as he hears and hopes they've not yet shed all their horns."

"He really looked very nice in his new Pushtoo suit, with putty on his legs and chaplains on his feet…. His chickory walked in front, carrying his bandobast."

"9 A.M.—Sat down to my solitary breakfast of poached ekkas and paysandu tonga, with excellent chuprassies (something like scones). After breakfast, tried on my new kilta, which I have had made quite short for walking. I generally prefer walking to being carried in a pagdandy."

"Then took another lesson in Hindustani from my murghi, though I really think I hardly require it! My attention a good deal distracted by the antics of a pair of bul-buls (not at all the same as our coo-coos) in the jungle overhead."

"7 P.M.—T. returned after what he called a blank blank day. He found some bheesties (one of them a chikor ram or wild ghât) chewing the khud on a precipitous dâk."

"They were rather far off, about a mile he thinks, but he couldn't get any nearer owing to a frightful ghari-wallah with deep piasses which lay between, so he put up his ornithoptic sight for 2000 yards and 'pumped lead' into the bheesties for half-an-hour."

"He says he *thinks* he hit one, but they all went away—as his chickory remarked—'ek dam,' and Tom agreed with him."

"He fell into a budmash on his way home and was half-drowned, but the chickory, assisted by a friendly chota-hazri, managed to pull him out ... quite an eventful day!"

"10 P.M.—The body of the ram chikor has just been brought in. It looks as if it had been dead for weeks, but the doolie, who found it, says that in this climate a few hours is sufficient to obliterate a body.... Anyhow the head and tail seem all right.... Tom says the proper thing to do is to measure something—he can't quite remember whether it is the horns or the tail, but the latter seems the more remarkable, so we measured that, and found it to be 3 feet 4 inches."

"By a little judicious pulling, the chickory, who knows all about measuring things, elongated it to 4 feet 3 inches."

"This, he says, is a '*Record*'—how nice!"

Wednesday, April 12.—The place where we tied up was not far from the point where the Jhelum expands into the Wular Lake—a broad expanse of water, some seven or eight miles wide in places, which holds the proud record of being the largest lake in all India.

The mountains rise steeply from its northern shores, and from their narrow glens, squalls swift and strong are said frequently to sweep over the open water, particularly in the afternoons. The bold sailormen of Kashmir are not conspicuous for nautical daring—in fact their flat-bottomed arks, top-heavy and unwieldy, destitute alike of anchor and rudder, are not fit to cope with either wind or wave; they therefore aim at punting hurriedly across the danger space as soon after dawn as may be—panting with exertion and terror, they hustle across the smooth and waveless water, invoking at every breath the protection of local saints.

Long before we had left our beds, and blissfully unconscious of our awful danger, we were striking out for Bandipur, which haven we safely reached about 8 A.M. on a still and glorious morning.

Then came the business of collecting coolies and ponies, and loading them up with the tents and lesser baggage under the direction of Sabz Ali and the shikari.

By nine o'clock we were off. Charlotte and Jane, mounted astride a brace of native ponies, led the way, and, in ragged array, the rest of the procession followed. A quarter of a mile from the landing-place, clustered at the foot of a steep little hill—a spur from the higher ranges—lies the village of Bandipur, dirty and picturesque, with, its rickety-looking wooden houses, and its crowded little bazaar. It is a place of some importance in Kashmir, being the starting-point for the Astor country and Gilgit—and here the sahib on shikar bent, obtains coolies and ponies to take him over the Tragbal Pass into Gurais. A post and telegraph office stands proudly in the middle of the little village, and behind it lies a range of "godowns" filled with stores for the use of a flying column should the British Raj require to send troops quickly along the Gilgit road.

Passing through into the open country, we found ourselves on a good road—good, that is to say, for riding or marching, as no roads in Kashmir are adapted for wheeled traffic excepting the main artery from Baramula to Srinagar, and the greater portion of the route from Srinagar to Gulmarg. This road we followed up a gradually narrowing valley, and over a brawling little river, until at Kralpura the Gilgit road begins the steep ascent to the Tragbal by a series of wide zigzags up the face of a mountain. The pass which we should have had to tackle, had we carried out our original intention of going into Astor for markhor and ibex, is nearly 12,000 feet above sea level, and is still securely and implacably closed to all but the hardiest sportsmen. A short cut, which we took up the hill face, led us through a rough scrub of berberis and wild daphne (the former just showing green and the latter in flower) until, somewhat scant of breath, we regained the road, and followed it to the left up a gorge. As the mountains closed in on either side, we began to look out for the camp, which we knew was not far up the nullah. Presently, turning off the Gilgit road, along a track to the left, we came upon Walter—bearded like the pard—a pard which had left off shaving for about a week. He was pensively sitting on a big sun-warmed boulder, beguiling the time while awaiting us by contemplating the antics of a large family of monkeys, which he pointed out to Jane, to her great joy.

Tender inquiries as to camp and consequent lunch revealed the sad fact that some miles of exceedingly rough path yet lay betwixt us and the haven where we would be.

So we pricked forward, along a sort of cattle track, across dirty snow-filled little gullies, and over rock-strewn slopes, until the white gleam of Walter's tent showed clear on its perch atop of a flat-roofed native hut.

Crossing the stream which tumbled down the valley, by a somewhat "wobbly" bridge, and picking our way through the mixen which forms the approach to every well-appointed hut, we arrived upon the roof which supported the tent. This we achieved without any undue trouble, the building, like most "gujar" homes, being constructed on the side of a hill sufficiently steep to obviate the necessity for any back wall—the rear of the roof springing directly from the hillside. A Gujar village, owing to this peculiarity of construction, always looks oddly like a deposit of great half-open oysters clinging to the face of the hill.

After a welcome lunch, the ladies both pronounced decidedly against remaining in or near the highly-scented precincts of the village. The argument that there was no flat ground excepting roofs to be seen was overruled; so Walter and I climbed a neighbouring ridge, and selected a site on the crest.

It was not, certainly, a very good site for a camp, as it was so narrow that the unwary might easily step over the edge on either side, and toboggan gracefully either back on top of the aforesaid roof, or forward into a very rocky-bedded stream which employed its superfluous energy in tossing some frayed and battered logs from boulder to boulder, and which would have rejoiced greatly in doing the same to a fallen nestling from the eyry above.

Neither was the ridge level, and our tents were pitched at such an angle that the slumberer whose grasp of the bed-head relaxed

"In the mist and shadow of sleep"

was brought to wakefulness by finding his toes gently sliding out into the nipping and eager air of night.

The holding-ground for the tent-pegs was not all that could be desired, and visions of our tents spreading their wings in the gale and vanishing into space haunted us.

No—it was not an ideal camping-ground, and Jane, whose rosy dreams of camping in Kashmir had pictured her little white canvas home set up in a flowery mead by the side of a purling brook, gazed upon the rugged slopes which rose around—the cold snow gleaming through the shaggy pine-trees—with a shiver and a distinct air of disapproval.

It grew more than chilly too, as the sun dipped early behind the ridge that rose jealous between us and the western light, and an icy breeze from the snow came stealing down the gorge and whispering among the taller tree-tops in the nullah at our feet.

We were about 1500 feet above the Wular Lake, and snow lay in thick patches within a few yards of our tents, and had obviously only melted quite recently from the site of the camp, leaving more clammy mud about the place than we really required.

As it is reasonable to suppose that the bilingual lady who composes the fashion columns of the *Daily Horror* is most anxious to know how the fair sex was accoutred at our dinner party that night, I hasten to inform her that Charlotte was gowned in an elegant confection of Puttoo of a simply indescribable nuance of *crême de boue*—the train, extremely décolletée at the lower end, cunningly revealing at every turn glimpses of an enchanting pair of frou-frou putties.

The neat bottines, à la Diane Chasseresse, took a charming touch of lightness from the aluminium nails which decorated the "uppers" with a quaint and original Dravidian cornice.

She carried a spring bouquet of wild onions en branche—ornaments (of course), diamonds.

Every one remarked that Jane was simply too lovely for words, as, with the sweet simplicity of an ingénue, en combinaison with the craft of a Machiavella (I beg to point out that I know my Italian genders), she draped her lissom form in the clinging folds of an enormous habit de peau de brebis— portions of ear and the tip of her nose tilted over the edge of the deep turned-up collar, which, on one side, supported the coquettish droop of the hairy "Tammy" that, dexterously pinned to the spikes of a diamond fender, gave a clou to the entire "sac d'artifice."

Walter, having already shot two bara singh and a serow, came under the "statute of limitations" of the Kashmir Game Laws, and had to sound the "cease firing" as regards these animals; but Charlotte and I, having "khubbar" of game, started at 7 A.M. in pursuit. She, attended by Walter and in tow of Asna (the best shikari in all Kashmir), followed up the nullah which lay to our right, while I deflected to the north. Having donned grass shoes, I started off up a very steep slope which rose directly behind the camp. Reaching snow within a few minutes of leaving my tent, I was glad to find it hard and the going good, the early sun not yet having had time to soften and destroy the crisp surface.

Up and up we toiled, I puffing like any grampus—partly by reason of not yet being in good condition, and partly on account of the height, which was probably nearly 9000 feet above sea level. As we rose to the shoulder of the hill the gradient became much easier, and I had leisure to admire the panorama that stretched around the snowy ridge, which fell away abruptly on either side through dense pine forests. The day was quite glorious…. The sun, blazing in a cloudless sky, cast sharp steel-blue shadows where rock or tree stood between the snow and his nobility. The white peaks that rose around in marvellous array seemed so near in the bright air that it seemed as though one could see the smallest creature moving on their distant slopes. But there was little life observable in this still and silent world—nothing but an occasional pair of crows flapping steadily over the woods, or a far vulture circling at a giddy height in the "blue dome of the air." Silence everywhere, except for the distant and perpetual voice of many waters murmuring in the unseen depths below.

To the south—showing clear above the serrated back of the ridge beyond the camp—stood the Pir Panjal; pale ivory in the pale horizon below the sun. At the foot of the valley up which we had come yesterday, and partly screened by the intruding buttresses of its enfolding hills, the Wular Lake lay a shimmering shield of molten silver.

In front, the sheeted mountains which guard Gurais and flank the icy portals of the Tragbal stood, a series of glistening slopes and cold-crowned precipices, while to the east Haramok reared his 17,000 feet into a threefold peak of snowy majesty.

It was a sight to thank God for, and to remember with joy all the days of one's life. Doubtless there are many views as wonderful in this lovely land, but this was the first, and therefore not to be effaced nor its memory dimmed by anything that may come after.

The shikari had not climbed the mountain's brow to waste time over scenery; so, having apparently gone as far as he wanted on the ridge, he plunged down among the silver firs to the right, and I, with my heart in my mouth, went after him. At first it seemed to the inexperienced that we were slithering down the most awful places, and that, should the snow give way, I should have to swiftly embrace the nearest tree to avoid being shot down, a human avalanche, farther than I cared to think. However, I soon found it was all right. A welcome halt for lunch brought the tiffin coolie to the front. A blanket spread upon the hard snow at the foot of a fir made an excellent seat, and a cold roast teal, an apple, and a small flask of whisky were soon exhumed from the basket. Water, or rather the want of it, was a difficulty, for I was uncommonly thirsty, and no sign of any water was to be seen. A judicious blending of the dry teal with bits of succulent apple overcame the drought, and the half-hour for refreshment passed all too quickly.

The men considered it now time to get up some "shikar," so they invented a bear. This was exciting! They had separated (there were four of them) in search of traces of bara singh, &c., and some one found the bear, or its den, or a lock of its wool—I really couldn't quite ascertain which—but fearful excitement was the immediate result.

A consultation took place in frenzied whispers. My rifle was peeled from its case, and we proceeded to scramble stealthily down a horribly steep face much broken by rocks. The shikari being in front with my rifle over his shoulder, I was favoured with frequent glimpses down its ugly black barrel as I, like Jill, "came tumbling after," and I rejoiced that all the cartridges were safely stowed in my own pocket. Well! we searched like conspirators for that bear, peeped round rocks and peered into holes, and anxiously eyed all possible and impossible places where a bear might be supposed to reside, but there was no bear; and at length we arrived on the bank of the torrent which rioted noisily down the bottom of the nullah.

I now began to realise that plunging about in snow, often over one's knees, and scrambling among the fallen tree-trunks and great rocks selected by the torrent to make its bed, was distinctly tiring work!

Presently we came to a bridge over the river. It consisted of a single log, and appeared extremely slender. The stream was not deep enough to drown a man, but, all the same, a slip, sending one into the foaming water among a particularly large and hard collection of boulders, seemed most undesirable, and I stepped across, like Agag, delicately, carefully balancing myself with a khudstick. The men came prancing over as if they were on a good high-road, the careless ease with which they made the passage bordering on impertinence! I reflected, however, that sheep, and such like beasts of humble brain, can stroll upon the brink of gruesome precipices without any fear of falling, and my self-respect returned.

After another half-hour of stiff scrambling I sat down to rest awhile, leaving the men to spy the neighbourhood. Of course they had to find something, so this time they found a "serow" —a somewhat scarce beast. I awaited the coming of the serow at various coigns of vantage where they said it was bound to pass, while the four men surrounded it from different directions. Finally, like the Levite, it passed by on the other side—at least I never saw it. The shikari afterwards informed me, in confidence, that it was, like the inexcusable baby in *Peter Simple*, "a very little one."

We now made the best of our way down the nullah, and when an apology for a path became apparent I rejoiced greatly, and followed it along its corkscrew course until the camp came suddenly into view as we topped a spur, which gave the path a final excuse for dragging me up a stiff two hundred feet, and then sending me down a knee-shaking descent, for no apparent reason but pure "cussedness."

Charlotte had got home just before me, having seen nothing to shoot at. She, too, seemed anxious for tea!

During the day Sabz Ali had been doing his level best to improve the position in our sleeping-tent. The camp-beds had stood at such an angle that it was almost impossible to avoid sliding gradually into the outer darkness, but S.A. had scraped out earth from the head, and filled up a terrace at the foot, in a way which gave us hope of sound sleep. Our things had been carefully stowed, too, and a sort of hole scooped for the bath. Luxury stared us in the face!

The sunset certainly was a little dull last night, but we were quite unprepared for the dreary aspect of Dame Nature to which we awoke this morning. It was raining very heavily, and a dense pall of mist hung low among the pines, giving an impression of melancholy durability.

There was obviously nothing to do but exist as cheerfully as might be until the weather improved. The wet had shrunk canvas and rope gear till the tent-guys were as taut as fiddle-strings; and as it did not seem to have occurred to any of the servants to attend to this, an immediate tour of the camp had to be undertaken, in "rubbers" and waterproofs, to slack off guys and inspect the drainage system, as we had no wish to have our earthen floor—already sufficiently cold and clammy—turned into an absolute swamp.

These things done, we scuttled and slid down to the mess tent, and breakfasted as best we might; and the best was surprisingly good, considering the difficulties the wretched servants must have had in cooking anything in their wet lair, where the miserable fire of damp sticks produced apparently little but acrid smoke.

We passed a dismal day, as, wrapped in our warmest clothes, we sat upon our beds watching the rain turn to snow, then to hail and sleet, and finally back to rain again; while the ever-changing wisps of grey mist gathered thick in the glens, or "put forth an arm and crept from pine to pine."

Towards evening the clouds broke a little, and the forest-clad steeps appeared through them, powdered thickly with new snow. Walter and I sallied forth from our sodden tents and held a council of war in the mud. It was decided to quit our somewhat unsatisfactory and precarious position early to-morrow, if fine, as the weather looked so nasty, and a squall of wind might have awkward consequences.

Friday, April 14.—A very fairly fine morning enabled us to strike camp yesterday, and get the baggage off in good time. The Smithsons decided to make for the jheels near the river, in order to give the duck a final worry round before the season closes on the 15th.

My shikari having reported a good bara singh in a small nullah off the Erin, I arranged to go in search of him. The march down to Bandipur was a short and easy one, and we got comfortably settled on board our boats early in the afternoon. About sunset the clouds gathered thick over the hills which we had left, and a thunderstorm broke, its preliminary squall throwing the crews of our fleet into a fearful fuss, and sending them on to the bank with extra ropes and holdfasts to make all secure. An elderly lady, with a dirty red cap and very untidy ringlets, superintended the business with much clamour. We take her to be the wife or grandmother (not sure which) of the skipper.

It was with an undoubted sense of solid comfort that we lay in our cosy beds under a wooden roof, whereon the fat rain-drops sputtered, while the thunder still crackled and banged in the distance!

We shifted before dawn to a small village a couple of miles to the east, and at 6.30 Jane and I set out to attack the bara singh, of which the shikari held out high hope. My wife, mounted on a rough pony, was able to accomplish with great comfort the two miles of flat country which we had to traverse before turning off sharp to the right along a track which led steeply upwards through the scrub that clothed the lower part of the nullah.

There is something unusually charming in the dawn here—the crisp, buoyant air, the silent hills, their lower slopes and corries still a purple mystery; on high, the silver peaks—looking ridiculously close—change swiftly from their cold pallor into rosy life at the first touch of the risen sun.

The first part of our day's work was easy enough. The sun was still hidden from us behind the mountain flange on our left; the snow patches on the sky-line ahead seemed comparatively near, and the diabolical swiftness of the shikari's stealthy walk was yet to be fully realised.

Up and up we went, first through a thick scrub or jungle of a highly prickly description, over a few small streams, then out upon a grassy ridge, up which we slowly panted. The gradient became sharper, and I began to feel a little anxious about Jane, as the short, brown grass was slippery with frost—a slip would be very easy, and the results unpleasant. However, with the able assistance of the shikari, she did very well, and, having crossed a shelving patch of snow by cutting steps with our khudstick, we found ourselves, after an hour and a half's stiff climbing, on the sky-line of the ridge that had seemed but an easy stroll from below. The heights and distances are most deceptive, partly on account of the crystal clearness of the air, and partly because of the magnitude of everything in proportion. The mountains are not only high themselves, but their spurs and foothills would rank as able-bodied mountains were they not dwarfed by peaks which average 15,000 feet in height above the sea. The pines which clothe their sides, the chenars and poplars in the valley, are all enormous when compared with their European cousins.

The view was most remarkable as we gained the crest of the ridge—a sea of white cloud came boiling up from the valley to the east, and, pouring over the saddle upon which we stood, gave only occasional glimpses of snow and pine and precipice above, or the glint of water in the rice-fields far below. Once, between the swirling cloud masses, the near hills lay clear in the sunshine for a few moments and revealed a party of five bara singh hinds, crossing the slope in front of us, and not more than 150 yards away. Alas! there was no stag.

This was not satisfactory weather for stalking. However I was hopeful, as I have noticed that in the fine forenoons a thick white belt of cloud often forms about the snow level—roughly, some 8000 feet above the sea, or 3000 above the Wular Lake—and hangs there for an hour or two, to disappear entirely by midday. And so it came about to-day; after a halt for tiffin, I set forward in brilliant sunshine, while Jane remained quietly perched on the hillside, as the shikari said the road was not good for a lady. The shikari was right, as, within ten minutes of starting, we had to drop from the crest of the ridge to circumvent a big rock which barred our way, to find ourselves confronted by a very unpleasant-looking slope of short brown grass, which fell away at an angle of about 50° to what seemed an endless depth. This grass, having only just become emancipated from its winter snow, had all its hair—so to speak—brushed straight down, and there was mighty little stuff to hold on to! Carefully digging little holes with our khudsticks, and not disdaining the help of my shikari, I got across, and thankfully scrambled back to the safety of the ridge.

Now we reached snow, and the going became easier, whereupon Ahmed Bot promptly set a pace which left me struggling far behind. As the sun grew stronger the surface-crust of the snow became soft, and at every few steps one went through to the knees, until both muscles and temper became sorely tried. For an hour or so we kept climbing up what was evidently one of the many steep and rugged ranges which, radiating from Haramok, on this side flank the Wular with their lofty bastions. Having apparently attained the height he deemed necessary, and got well above the part of the pine forest in which he expected to find game, Ahmed Bot turned to the left of the ridge, and we were immediately involved in the deep drifts which covered the pine-clad slope of the nullah. Over snow-covered trunks of prostrate trees, over hidden holes and broken rocks, we toiled and scrambled until, emerging breathless on a bare knoll—smooth and white as a great wedding-cake—we obtained a searching view into the neighbouring gullies. Still no sign or track of any "beast," so we worked back until, tired and hot, I regained the place where Madame lay basking beneath her sunshade. The shikari and his myrmidons departed to "look" another bit of country, while I, nothing loth, remained to await events in the neighbourhood of the refreshment department.

On the return of the men, who had of course seen nothing, we set off for home, climbing down the edge of the ridge where yellow colchicum starred the turf. It was steep—verging on the precipitous in places—and Jane frankly expressed her satisfaction when we accomplished the worst part and entered a dense jungle of scrubby bushes, all of which seemed to grow spines of sorts. A bear was said to have been seen here yesterday, so we kept our weather eyelids lifting, but were not favoured with a sight of him. We had almost gained the bottom of the hill, with but two short miles to dinner and a tub, when weird shrieks and whistles were exchanged between our people and an excited villager below. The shikari, his eyes gleaming with uncontrollable excitement, announced that the "big stag" was waiting for me at that very moment!—and therewith Ahmed Bot dashed off down the hill, leaving me to follow as best I might. Leaving my wife in charge of the tiffin coolie, I tumbled off after the shikari, whom I found gloating with the messenger over the inspiriting particulars of the monarch of the glen, which, I understood, crouched expectant some paltry 2000 feet above us, near the top of the nullah!

It was past six o'clock, and the light already showing signs of waning, so we lost no time in attacking the hill again. I was pretty well "done," and had to accept a tow from the shikari, and hand in hand we pressed up that accursed hill until, at seven o'clock, the sun set and it began to grow dusk. Lying down near the edge of the snow, to gain breath and let the shikari crawl round and "look" the face of the hill, I was soon moved to activity by the news that the stag was lying under a pine tree within a few hundred yards. A short "crawl" brought me within sight of the beast, who lay half-hidden by a rock. It was now so dark that even with my glasses I could only make sure that it was a "horn beast" and not a hind; there was no time to lose, so, putting up my sight for 150 yards, I let him have it, and was nearly as much surprised as gratified to see him roll out on the snow to the shot. My vexation and disgust may be imagined when I found the noble beast to be a miserable 8-pointer, which I would never have fired at if I could have seen its head properly. Heartily consigning the shikari, together with the mendacious villager and all his kind, to a hot place, I dolefully stumbled away downhill again in the gathering dark, and finally deposited my weary and dejected self on board the boat, after fourteen hours of the hardest walking I have ever done.

There is a confused tale prevalent that the bear, taking a mean advantage of my absence, has been down to the village and eaten a few ponies, or frightened them—I can't make out which.

CHAPTER VII
BACK TO SRINAGAR

Easter Day, *April* 23.—We left the Erin district early in the morning following the bara singh fiasco, and punted and poled up the river to join the Smithsons in a last attack upon the duck. We found the bold Colonel,

"Rough with slaughter and red with fight,"

enjoying himself hugely among the jheels, and we prepared to join in the fray; but our *chasse* was put an end to by the discovery that the 14th, and not the 15th, was the last legal day for shooting. So we packed away our guns and towed up to Srinagar, which we reached on Sunday afternoon.

Our brief experience of camping and "shikar" had proved to my wife that she was not cast in the heroic mould of a female Nimrod. Not being a shot herself—as Charlotte is—she saw that, as far as she was concerned, a shooting expedition with the Smithsons would entail a great deal of solitary rumination in camp, while the rest of the party pursued the red bear to his den, or chased the nimble markhor up and down the precipices. The joys of reading, knitting, and washing the family clothes might—probably would—pall after a time; and the physical exertion of "walking with the guns" in Kashmir is decidedly more of an undertaking than over a Perthshire grouse moor! Our original arrangement, before coming out to join the Smithsons, was that the time should be spent in camping, boating, "loafing," and shooting. Being perfectly ignorant of the conditions of life out here, we were unaware of the fact that it is practically impossible to combine serious shooting with any other form of amusement. In Scotland one may stalk one day, fish the next, and golf the third, but out here it is not so. The worshipper of Diana must be prepared to sacrifice everything else at her shrine; he must go far afield, and be prepared to live hard and work hard, and even then it may befall that his trophies of the chase are none too plentiful. That will depend a good deal on his shikari and his own knowledge, together with luck.

Walter had the good fortune to come upon two fine stags not far from his camp almost as soon as he got there. He was within fifty yards of them as they were moving slowly in deep snow, and he killed them both; the best of these was a remarkably fine 10-pointer, length of horn 41 inches and span 38-1/2 inches. His wife spent an equal time in the same neighbourhood and never saw anything.[1]

> [1] That lady subsequently killed a remarkably good
> 13-pointer bara singh and some bears in October.

When we talked over plans with Colonel and Mrs. Smithson at Pindi, the general idea had crystallised into a scheme for going into Astor to shoot, immediately upon our arrival in Kashmir, and, in order to reach Srinagar before April 1st—the date of issue of shooting passes—we had struggled hard to make our way into the country before it was really attractive to the ordinary visitor.

When we did reach Srinagar we found that our friends had abandoned all idea of an expedition to Astor, partly on account of expense, but principally on account of the backwardness of the season, which practically precluded ladies from crossing the Tragbal and Boorzil Passes for some time. The merits and demerits of the Tilail district and Baltistan came up for review, and then we almost decided to go to Leh until we reflected that the return journey over a bare and open country—arid and hot as an Egyptian desert—in the month of August might not be unmixed joy, and the Smithsons were assured that they would find no sport whatever *en route*, but would have to go several marches beyond Leh to obtain the chance of an Ovis Ammon or Thibetan antelope.

The Leh scheme thus having come to naught, and our friends being still wholly intent on "shikar" to the exclusion of all other pursuits, we decided to be independent, so we hired a nice-looking boarded dounga, whose fresh and clean appearance pleased us, for a term of three months. Nedou's Hotel offered so few attractions and so many drawbacks that we were prepared to do anything rather than return to it, and, as a matter of economy, we scored heavily, as, on working it out, we found that the boat, including the cook-boat, would cost 60 rupees per month. Our food and the wages of those servants whom we should not have required at the hotel came to approximately 80 rupees per month, making a total of 140 rupees, or £9, 6s. 8d.; whereas our hotel bill would have come to 12 rupees per day, without extras—or 360 rupees (£24) per month—a clear saving in money as well as in comfort.

Our new habitation—the house dounga *Moon*—was owned and partly worked by Satarah, an astute old rascal, whose "tawny beard," like Hudibras'—

"Was the equal grace
Both of his wisdom and his face;
In cut and dye so like a tyle
A sudden view it would beguile:
The upper part whereof was whey,
The nether orange mixt with grey."

His costume consisted of a curious sort of short nightgown worn over white and flappy trousers, below which were revealed a pair of big, flat naval feet. The first lieutenant, Sabhana—sleek and civil-spoken, but desperately afraid of work—was, we understand, son-in-law to the Admiral Satarah, having to wife the Lady Jiggry, eldest daughter of that worthy, who, with her younger sisters Nouri, Azizi, and "the Baba," completed the ship's company.

The *Moon* differed from an ordinary house-boat in being narrower, and possessing a long bow and stern which projected far enough from the body of the boat to enable men to pole or paddle with ease; a house-boat can only be towed. On embarking by means of a narrow gangway—a plank possessed of an uncontrollable desire to "tip-up" at unexpected and disconcerting moments—one entered first a small vestibule, or "ante-cabin," which held our big boxes and opened into the drawing-room—quite a roomy apartment, about fifteen feet by ten feet, fitted with a fireplace, a rough writing-table, and overmantel, surmounted by a photograph—something faded—of Mrs. Langtry! A small table and a couple of deck chairs graced the floor, while upon the walls a heterogeneous collection of pictures, including a coloured lithograph of a cottage and a brook, a fearful and wonderful portrayal of an otter, and a very fancy stag of unlimited points dazzled the eye. The ceiling was decorated with an elaborate and most effective design in wood—a fashion very common in Srinagar, consisting of a sort of patchwork panelling of small pieces of wood, cut to length and shape, and tacked on to a backing in geometrical designs. At a little distance the effect is rich and excellent, but close inspection shows up the tintacks and the glue, and a prying finger penetrates the solid-looking panel with perfect ease.

The drawing-room was separated from the dining "saloon" by a sliding door—which frequently refused to slide at all, or else perversely slid so suddenly as to endanger finger-tips and cause unseemly words to flow. This noble apartment of elegant dimensions (to borrow the undefiled English of the house-agent) could contain four feasters at a pinch. Sabz Ali having cooked the dinner, the cook-boat was laid alongside, and Sabz Ali, clambering in and out of the window, proceeded to serve the repast, a black paw, presumably belonging to Ayata, the kitchenmaid-man, appearing from time to time to retrieve the soiled plates or hand up the next course.

A funny little sideboard and cupboard contained a slender stock of knives, forks, and glasses, and part of a broken-down dinner set, while the fireplace easily held three dozen of soda-water.

Then came Jane's bedroom, fitted with a cupboard and shelves, which were a constant source of covetousness to me, who had none. A small bathroom completed our suite of apartments, and, after the bare boards of the *Cruiser*, the *Moon* seemed to overflow with luxury.

We have been taking life easily here for the last week. The Smithsons intend going into Tilail as soon as the Tragbal becomes feasible; we propose to remain in Srinagar for a while. The weather has not been very fine—cold winds and a good deal of rain, varied by thunderstorms, being our daily experience. The spring is, I am told, exceptionally backward, and, although the almond is in full and lovely flower, the poplars and chenars are barely showing a sign of life.

My wife having gone to lunch at the Residency this afternoon, I walked half-way up the Takht-i-Suleiman, whose sharp, rock-strewn pyramid rises a thousand feet above Srinagar.

The view of the Kashmir plain, through which the river winds like a silver snake; the solemn ring of mountains, enclosing the valley with a rampart of rock and snow; the innumerable roofs of the city, glittering like burnished scales in the keen sunlight, densely clustered round the fort-crowned height of Hari Parbat, went to make up such a picture as Turner would have kneeled to.

Of course it is simply futile to compare one magnificent view with another which differs entirely in kind. All that one can do is to lay by in the memory a mental picture-gallery of recollection; and as I sat in the shelter of a big rock, gazing out over the level plain stretching below, where the changing shadows as they swept by turned the amber masses of the trees to gold, I conjured up in my mind's eye other scenes whose beauties will remain with me while life shall last:—The purple and gold of a glorious sunset over Etna, the Greek theatre of Taormina in front of me, with the sea below—a shimmering opal that melted away in the haze beyond Syracuse; the awful rapids raging furiously below Niagara, a very ocean tortured and maddened to blind fury, pouring its irresistible torrents through the chasm above the whirlpool; and again, a cloudless October morning, with just the keen zest of early autumn in the air, as I lay high up on a hillside in Ardgour watching for deer—with the hills of Lochaber and Ballachulish reflected in all their glory of purple and russet in the waters of Loch Linnhe, windless and still!

Chills can be caught amidst the most glorious scenery—the little tufts of purple self-heal at my feet were shivering and shaking in a biting breeze that swept down from the snows to the north-east, and although I am an admirer of Kingsley, I do not hold with him in his wrong-headed admiration for a "nor'-easter"—so I quitted my perch in search of tea.

Easter Monday.—The Smithsons scuttled away in a great hurry to-day, their shikari, Asna (the best shikari in Kashmir), having heard that, owing to the lateness of the season, the bara singh have not even yet all shed their horns—so Charlotte is filled with high hope. The bears, too, are said to be waking from their winter's doze and poking around in warm and balmy corners.

Armed to the teeth and thirsting for blood, the hunter and the huntress cast loose their matted dounga and paddled away merrily down the Jhelum to Bandipur, thence to pursue the royal bara singh, and later, if possible, scale the snow-barred slopes of the Tragbal and penetrate the lonely Tilail Valley to assail the red bear and the multitudinous ibex.

Jane and I having decided that a purely shikar expedition into the more difficult parts of the country was not suited to our prosaic habits, remained to enjoy the effeminate pleasures of Srinagar till the weather should grow a few degrees warmer.

As we are bidden to a sort of state luncheon to-morrow, given by the Maharajah, it appeared to me to be but right and seemly to go and inscribe my name in the visitors' book of His Highness, and also to call upon his brother, the Rajah Sir Amar Singh. I went with the more alacrity as I thought it might prove interesting. Strolling across the big bridge above the Palace, I soon found myself in the purely native quarter, immersed in a seething crowd of men and beasts, from beneath whose passing feet a cloud of dust rose pungent. The water-sellers, the hawkers of vegetables and of sweets, the cattle, the loafers and the children got into the way and out of it in kaleidoscopic confusion. By the side of the street, money-changers, wrapped in silent consideration, bent over their trays of queer and outlandish coins. Bright cottons and silks flaunted pennons of gorgeous colours. Brass, glowing like gold, rose piled on low wide counters. In front stood the Palace, looking its best from this point, and showing huge beside the huddle of wooden and plaster huts which hem it in.

General Raja Sir Amar Singh lives in a sort of glorified English villa. Were it not for the flowering oleanders and hibiscus in front and the silvery gleam of temple domes beyond, one might suppose oneself near the banks of Father Thames. And were it not for the group of stalwart retainers at the door, the illusion need not be lost on entering the house.

The hall and staircase were decorated with a profusion of skins and horns, somewhat modern and brilliant rugs, and tall glasses full of flowers closely copied from Nature; while the drawing-room was of a type very frequently seen near London.

Like so many British reception-rooms, it shone replete with *objets d'art*, rather inclining to Oriental luxury than Japanese restraint.

My host, who came in almost immediately, was charming, speaking English with fluency, although he has never been in England.

He is essentially a strong man, and remarkably well posted in everything, both political and social, that occurs in the state, mixing far more freely than his brother with the English, towards whom his courtesy is proverbial.

His elder brother, the Maharajah of Jammu and Kashmir, is in many respects of a different type. Keeping more aloof from the English colony, he spends much of his time in devotion and the privacy of the inner Palace.

On leaving Sir Amar Singh, one of his henchmen conducted me across the iron bridge spanning a cut from the Jhelum, and into the warren-like precincts of the Palace; presently we emerged from an obscure passage, and found ourselves at the "front door," where, in the visitors' book, by means of the stumpy pencil attached thereto, I inscribed my name and condition.

April 27.—His Highness the Maharajah having invited us to a luncheon given by him in honour of Colonel Pears, the new Resident, we prepared to cross the famous Dal Lake to the Nishat Bagh, the scene of the present feast, which we fondly hoped might recall the glorious days of the Moguls when Jehangir dallied in the historic Shalimar with the fair Nourmahal.

> "Th' Imperial Selim held a feast
> In his magnificent Shalimar:—
> In whose saloons ...
> The valleys' loveliest all assembled."

Our shikara, a sort of canoe paddled by four active fellows, with the stern, where we sat on cushions, carefully screened from the sun by an awning, was brought alongside the dounga at about 11.30, as we had some seven or eight miles to accomplish before reaching the Nishat Bagh.

Leaving the main river just above the Club, we paddled down the Sunt-i-kul Canal, which runs between the European quarter and the Takht-i-Suleiman, the rough brown hill which, crowned with its temple, forms a constant background to Srinagar.

The canal was closely lined with house-boats and their satellite cook-boats, clinging to the poplar-shaded banks. The golf-links lay on our left, and on a low spur to the right stood the hospital, which the energy and philanthropy of the Neves has gained for the remarkably ungrateful Kashmiri. It is told that a man, being exceedingly ill, was cared for and nursed during many weeks in the Mission Hospital, his whole family likewise living on the kindly sahibs. When he was cured and shown the door, he burst into tears because he was not paid wages for all the time he had spent in hospital!

Just before entering the waterway of noble chenars, known as the Chenar Bagh (a camping-ground reserved for bachelors only), we ported our helm (or at least would have done so had there been any rudders in Kashmir), and pushed through the lock-gate, which gives entrance to the Dal Lake, against a brisk current.

This gate, cunningly arranged upon the non-return-valve principle, is normally kept open by the current from the Dal; but if the Jhelum, rising in flood, threatens to pour back into the lake and swamp the low ground and floating gardens, it closes automatically, and so remains sealed until the outward flow regains the mastery.

A sharp bout of paddling, puffing, and splashing shot us into the peaceful waters of the Dal Lake, over which every traveller has gushed and raved. It is difficult, indeed, not to do so, for it is truly a dream of beauty.

A placid sheet of still water, its surface only broken here and there by the silvery trails of rippled wake left by the darting shikaras or slow-moving market boats, lay before us, shining in the crystal-clear atmosphere. On the right rose the Takht, his thousand feet of rocky stature dwarfed into insignificance by holy Mahadeo and his peers, whose shattered peaks ring round the lake to the north, their dark cliffs and shaggy steeps mirrored in its peaceful surface.

On the lower slopes strong patches of yellow mustard and white masses of blossoming pear-trees rose behind the tender green fringe of the young willows.

As we swept on, the lake widened. On the left a network of water lanes threaded the maze of low-growing brushwood and whispering reeds, and round us extended the half-submerged patches of soil which form the celebrated "floating gardens" of the lake. From any point of view except the utilitarian, these gardens are a fraud. A combination of matted and decaying water-plants, mud, and young cabbages kept in place by rows and thickets of willow scrub, is curious, but not lovely; and our eyes turned away to where Hari Parbat raised his crown of crumbling forts above the native city, or to the mysterious ruins of Peri Mahal, clinging like a swallow's nest to the shelving slopes above Gupkar.

> "Still onward; and the clear canal
> Is rounded to as clear a lake;"

and we emerged from the willow-fringed water lanes, and saw across the wider shield of glistering water the white cube of the Nishat Bagh Pavilion—the Garden of Joy, made for Jehangir the Mogul—standing by the water's edge, and at its foot a great throng and clutter of boats, amidst whose snaky prows we pushed our way and landed, something stiff after sitting for two hours in a cramped shikara.

Other guests—some thirty in all—were arriving, either like us by boat, or by carriage *viâ* Gupkar, and we strolled in groups up the sloping gardens, which still show, in their wild and unrestrained beauty, the loving touch of the long-vanished hand of the Mogul.

Down seven wide grassy terraces a series of fountains splashed and twinkled in the sun. Broad chenars, just beginning to break into leaf, gave promise of ample shade against the day when the blaze should become overpowering. So far so good, but the grass that bordered the path was not the sweet green turf of an English lawn, and the way was edged by big earthen pots, into which were hastily stuck wisps of iris blooms and Persian lilac. The topmost terrace widened out, enclosing a large basin of clear water, in the middle of which played a fountain. On one side was raised a marquee, revealing welcome preparations for lunch. On the opposite side of the fountain a profusion of chairs, shaded by a great awning, stood expectantly facing a bandstand. Here we were welcomed by His Highness, a somewhat small man with exceedingly neat legs and an enormous white pugaree, in his customary gracious manner.

It was now half-past two, and we had breakfasted early, so that a move towards the luncheon tent was most welcome. Finding the fair lady whom I was detailed to personally conduct, and the ticketed place where I was to sit, I prepared to make a Gargantuan meal. Was it not almost on this very spot that

> "The board was spread with fruit and wine,
> With grapes of gold, like those that shine
> On Casbin's hills;—pomegranates full
> Of melting sweetness, and the pears
> And sunniest apples that Cabul
> In all its thousand gardens bears.
> Plantains, the golden and the green,

Malaya's nectar'd mangusteen;
Prunes of Bokara, and sweet nuts
  From the far groves of Samarcand,
And Basra dates, and apricots,
  Seed of the sun, from Iran's land;—
With rich conserve of Visna cherries,
Of orange flowers, and of those berries
That, wild and fresh, the young gazelles
Feed on in Erac's rocky dells..
Wines, too, of every clime and hue
Around their liquid lustre threw;
Amber Rosolli..
And Shiraz wine, that richly ran..
Melted within the goblets there!"

This reckless, but unsubstantial and very unwholesome meal, was not for us, and while waiting patiently for the first course to appear, I glanced down the long table to admire the decorations. They were delightful, consisting of glass flower-vases spaced regularly along the festive board, and filled to overflowing with tufts and clumps of flowers. Innumerable plates filled with fruit and sweetmeats graced the feast, and a magnificent array of knives and forks gave promise of good things to come.

Presently the expected dainties arrived, resembling but little the lately-described poetic feast; a strict attention to business enabled us to keep the wolf from the door, and a very cheerful party finally emerged from the big tent to stroll by the fountains that flashed under the chenars.

The Maharajah, of course, did not lunch with us, but held aloof, peeping occasionally into the cook-house to satisfy himself that the lions were being fed properly, and in accordance with their unclean customs.

Finally, he and his chief officers of state vanished into a secluded tent, where he probably took a little refreshment, having first carefully performed the ablutions necessary after the contamination of the unbeliever.

His Highness reappeared from nowhere in particular as his guests strolled across the terrace, and, after a little polite conversation, we took our leave and set forth for Srinagar.

It was a glorious afternoon, and we deeply regretted that time would not permit us to visit the neighbouring Shalimar Bagh, which lay hidden among the trees near by. The excursion must remain a "hope deferred" for the present, as we had again to thread the maze of half-submerged melon plots and miniature kitchen gardens which, even in the golden glow of a perfect evening, could not be made to fit in with our preconceived ideas of "floating gardens." Jane was frankly disappointed, as she admitted to having pictured in her mind's eye a series of peripatetic herbaceous borders in full flower, cruising about the lake at their own sweet will and tended by fair Kashmirian maidens.

By-the-bye, here let me expose, once for all, the fallacy of Moore's drivel about the lovely maids of fair "Cashmere." *There are none!* This appears a startling statement and a sweeping; but, as a matter of fact, the Eastern girl is not left, like her Western sister, to flirt and frivol into middle age in single "cussedness," but almost invariably becomes a respectable married lady at ten or twelve, and drapes her lovely, but not over clean, head in the mantle of old sacking, which it is *de rigueur* for matrons to adopt.

The good Tommy Moore did not know this, but, letting his warm Irish imagination run riot through a mixed bag of Eastern romancists and their works, he evolved, amid a *pôt pourri* of impossibilities, an impossible damsel as unlike anything to be found in these parts as the celebrated elephant evolved from his inner consciousness by the German professor!

> As I traversed the main, or rolled by train,
>   From my Western habitation,
> I frequently thought—perhaps more than I ought—
>   Upon many a quiet occasion
> Of the elegant forms and manifold charms
>   Of the beautiful female Asian.

> For the good Tommy Moore, in his pages of yore,
>   Sang as though he could never be weary
> Of fair Nourmahal—an adorable "gal"—
>   And of Paradise and the Peri,
> Until, I declare, I was wild to be where
>   I might gaze on the lovely Kashmiri.

> Through the hot plains of Ind I fled like the wind,
>   Unenchanted by mistress or ayah,
> The dusky Hindu, I soon saw, wouldn't do,
>   So I paused not, until in the sky——Ah!—
> Far upward arose the perpetual snows
>   And the peaks of the proud Himalaya.

> But in Kashmir, alas! I found not a lass
>   Who answered to Tommy's description—
> For the make of such maid I am sadly afraid

A Holiday in the Happy Valley with Pen and Pencil | 77

The fond parents have lost the prescription,
And I murmured; "No doubt, the old breed has died out,
At least such is my honest conviction."

In the horrible slums which form the foul homes
  Of the rag-covered dames of the city,
I saw wrinkled hags, all wrapped in old rags,
  Whose appearance excited but pity.
Beyond question the word which it would be absurd
  To apply to these ladies is "pretty."

In the high Gujar huts were but brats and old sluts,
  These last being the plainest of women;
Then I sought on the waters the sisters and daughters
  Of the Mangis—those "bold, able seamen"
(I have often been told that the Mangi is bold,
  And as brave as at least two or three men).

One lady I saw—I am told her papa
  In the market did forage and "gram" sell—
Decked all over with rings, necklets, bangles and things,
  She appeared a desirable damsel;
And I cried "Oh, Eureka! I've found what I seek:
  Tell me quick—Is she 'madam' or 'ma'mselle'?"

It was comical, but to this question I put—
  A remarkably innocent query—
I received but a sigh or evasive reply,
  Or a blush from the modest Kashmiri;
And I gathered at last that the lady was "fast,"
  And her name should be Phryne, not Heré.

Toddled up a small tot—her hair tied in a knot—
  Who remarked, "I can hardly consider
You've the ghost of a chance on this wild-goosie dance
  Unless you should hap on a 'widder!'
For our maidens at ten—ay, and less now and then—
  Are all booked to the wealthiest bidder."

"My dear man, it's no use to indulge in abuse
  Of our customs, so be not enraged, sir—
No woman a maid is—we're all married ladies.

Our charms very early are caged, sir—
I'm eleven myself," remarked the small elf,
  "And a year ago I was engaged, sir!"

Ah, well! The country is the loveliest I ever saw, and that goes far to make up for its disgusting population.

Here, indeed, it is that

"Every prospect pleases, and only man is vile."

We stopped to look at the ruins of an ancient mosque, built in the days of Akbar by the Shiahs. Its remains may be deeply interesting to the archaeologist, but to me a neighbouring ziarat, wooden, with its grassy roof one blaze of scarlet tulips, was far more attractive. Moving homeward, we floated under a lovely old bridge, whose three rose-toned arches date from the sixteenth century—the age of the Great Moguls. The extreme solidity of its piers contrasts strongly with the exceedingly sketchy (and sketchable) bridges manufactured by the Kashmiri.

In fairness, though, I must point out that, as the bridge in Kashmir usually spans a stream liable at almost any moment to overwhelming floods, it would appear to be a sound idea to build as flimsily as possible, with an eye to economical replacement.

The Kashmiri carries this plan to its logical conclusion when he fells a tree across a raging torrent, and calls it a bridge, to the unutterable discomfiture of the Western wayfarer.

CHAPTER VIII
THE LOLAB

May 1.—The pear and cherry blossom has been so lovely in and around Srinagar that we determined to go to the Lolab Valley and see the apple blossom in full flower.

We started in some trepidation, for the warm weather lately has melted much snow on the hills, and Jhelum is so full that we were told that our three-decker would be unable to pass under the city bridges—of which there are seven. We decided to see for ourselves, so set forth about eleven, and soon came to the first bridge, the Amira Kadal, which carries the main tonga road into Srinagar, tying up just above it, amid the clamour and jabber of an idle crowd.

The Admiral solemnly measured the clear space between the top of the arch and the water with a long pole, consulted noisily with the crowd, yelled his ideas to the crew, and decided to attempt the passage.

Hen-coops, chairs, half-a-dozen flower-pots containing sickly specimens of plants, and all other movables being cleared from the upper deck, we set sail, and shot the bridge very neatly, only having a few inches of daylight between the upper deck and the wooden beams upon which the roadway rests.

Ce nest que, le premier "pont" que coute.

The other bridges were all easier than the first, and we shot them gaily, spending the rest of the day in floating quietly down the river, and finally anchoring—or rather mooring, for anchors are, like boat-hooks, masts, sails, rudders, and rigging, alike unknown to the "jollye mariners" of the Jhelum—some two or three miles above the entrance to the dreaded Wular Lake.

This awful stretch of water, so feared by the Kashmiri that his eyes goggle when he even thinks of it, is an innocent enough looking lake, generally occupied in reflectively reproducing its surroundings upside down, but occasionally its calm surface is ruffled by a little breeze, and it is reported that wild and horrible squalls sweep down the nullahs of Haramok at times, and destroy the unwary. These squalls are said to be most frequent in the afternoons, and are probably the accompaniments of the thunderstorms.

It is only considered possible to cross the Wular between dawn and 10 or 11 A.M., and no persuasion will prevail upon a native boatman to risk his life on the lake after lunch.

Before turning in, I gave orders that a start should be made next morning at five o'clock, but a heavy squall of rain and thunder during the night had the effect of causing orders to be set at naught, and at breakfast-time there was no sign of "up anchor" nor even of "heaving short." An interview with the Admiral showed me that the Wular, in his opinion, was too dangerous to cross to-day—in fact he wouldn't dream of asking coolies to risk it. He was given to understand that we intended to cross, and that the sooner he started the safer it would be.

No coolies being forthcoming, I inhumanly gave orders to get under way—the available crew consisting of the wicked Satarah, the first lieutenant, and the Lady Jiggry. Sulkily and slowly we wended our way past the wide flats which border the Wular, all blazing golden with mustard in full pungent flower.

Before entering the lake the Admiral meekly requested to be allowed to try for coolies in a small village near by. He was allowed quarter of an hour for pressgang work, and sure enough he came back within a very reasonable time with a few spare hands, and then—paddling and poling for dear life— we glided swiftly through the tangled lily-pads and the green rosettes of the Singhara, and soon were *in medias res* and fairly committed to the deep.

The Wular lay like a burnished mirror, reflecting the buttresses of Haramok on our right, and the snowy ranges by the Tragbal ahead, its silvery surface lined here and there with the wavering tracks of other boats, or broken by bristling clumps of reeds and tall water-plants. Our transit was perfectly peaceful, and by lunch-time we were safely tied up to a bank, purple with irises, just below Bandipur.

A visit to the post-office and a stroll up the rocky hill behind it, where we sat for some time and watched a pair of jackals sneaking about, completed a peaceful afternoon.

May 3.—We were up with the lark, and, having moved along the coast a few miles to the west of Bandipur, left the ship before six of the clock in pursuit of bear. I had "khubbar" of one in the Malingam Nullah, and, after a brisk walk over the lower slopes, we entered the nullah and clambered up about 1500 feet to a quiet and retired spot under a shady thorn-bush, where we breakfasted.

We thereafter climbed a little higher, and then sat down while the shikaris departed to spy, their method of spying being, I believe, somewhat after this fashion:—Leaving the sahib with his belongings—notably the tiffin coolie—in a spot carefully selected for its seclusion, the miscreants depart hurriedly and rapidly up the nearest inaccessible crag; this is "business," and throws dust, so to say, in the eyes of the sahib, by means of an exhibition of activity and zeal. Passing out of sight over the sky-line, the hunters pause, wink at one another, and, choosing a shady and convenient corner, proceed to squat, light their pipes, and discuss matters—chiefly financial—until they deem it time to return, scrambling and breathless with excitement, to relate all that they have seen and done.

So, while the shikaris unceasingly spied for bear, for nine mortal hours Jane and I camped out on a remarkably hard and unyielding stone, varied by other seats equally tiresome.

Fortunately we had brought books with us, and we relieved the monotony by observing the habits of a pair of "kastooras," a hawk, and a brace of chikor at intervals, but it was truly a tedious chase.

At four o'clock the sons of Nimrod returned, declaring that the bear had been seen, but that as we had on chaplies and not grass shoes, it would be impossible for us to pursue him. I asked the shikari why the — — goose he had let me come out in chaplies instead of grass shoes if the country was so rough? His reply was to the effect that whatever it pleased me to wear pleased him!

May 4.—Armed *cap-à-pie* so to speak, with pith helmets and grass shoes, we again set forth at dawn of day to hunt the bear. Breakfast under the same tree, sitting on the same patch of rose-coloured flowers—a sort of fumitory (*Corydalus rutaefolia*)—followed by another nine-hour bivouac, brought us to 5 P.M. and the extreme limit of boredom, when lo! the shikaris burst upon us in a state of frenzied excitement to announce the bear! Off we went up a steep track for a quarter of an hour, until, at the foot of a rough snow slope, the shikari told the much disgusted Jane that she must wait there, the rest of the climb being too hard for her, and, in truth, it was pretty bad. Up a very steep gully filled with loose stones and rotten snow, scrambling, and often hauling ourselves up with our hands by means of roots and trailing branches, we slowly worked our way up a place I would never have even attempted in cold blood.

Twenty minutes' severe exertion brought us to a shelf, or rather slope, of rock on the right, sparsely covered with wiry brown grass from which the snow had but very recently gone, and crowned by a crest of stunted pines.

Up this we wriggled, I being mainly towed up by my shikari's cummerbund, and, lying under a pine, we peered over the top.

A steep gully divided us from a rough ridge, upon a grassy ledge of which, about 200 yards off, a big black beast was grubbing and rooting about.

The shikari, shaking with excitement, handed me the rifle, urging me to shoot. I did nothing of the sort, having no breath, and my hand being unsteady from a fast and stiff climb.

I regret to be obliged to admit that, not realising that it would be little short of miraculous to kill a bear stone-dead at 200 yards with a Mannlicher, and being also, naturally, somewhat carried away by the sight of a real bear within possible distance, I waited until I was perfectly steady, and fired. The brute fell over, but immediately picked himself up again and made off. I saw I had broken his fore-shoulder and fired again as he disappeared over the far side of the ledge, but missed, and I saw that bear no more.

We had the utmost difficulty in crossing the precipitous gully to a spot below the ledge upon which the beast had been feeding—the ledge itself we could not reach at all; and the lateness of the hour and the difficulty of the country in which we were, prevented us from trying to enter the next ravine and work up and back by the way the bear had gone. A neck-breaking crawl down a horrible grass slope brought us to better ground, and I sadly joined Jane to be well and deservedly scolded for firing a foolish shot. The lady was very much disgusted at having been defrauded of the sight of a bear "quite wild," as she expressed it—a certain short-tempered animal which had eaten up her best umbrella in the Zoo at Dusseldorf not having fulfilled the necessary condition of wildness.

Next day I sent out coolies to search for traces, promising lavish "backshish" in the event of success, but I got no trustworthy news, "and that was the end of that hunting."

May 6.—Jane took a respite from the chase, and I sallied forth alone at dawn up a nullah from Alsu to look for a bear which was said to frequent those parts. A brisk walk of some four miles over the flat, followed by a climb up a track—steep as usual—to the left of the main track to the Lolab, brought us to a grassy ridge, where I sat down patiently to await the bear's pleasure. I took my note-book with me, and whiled away some time in writing the following:—

Let me jot down a sketch of my present position and surroundings; it will serve to bring the scene back to me, perhaps, when I am again sitting in my own particular armchair watching the fat thrushes hopping about the lawn.

Well, I am perched in a little hollow under a big grey boulder, which serves to shelter me to a certain, but limited, extent from the brisk showers that come sweeping over from the Lolab Valley. The hollow is so small that it barely contains my tiffin basket, rifle, gun, and self—in fact, my grass-shod and puttied extremities dangle over the rim, whence a steep slope shelves down some 200 feet to a brawling burn, the hum of which, mingling with the fitful sighing of the pines as the breeze sweeps through their sounding boughs, is perpetually in my ears. Across the little torrent, and not more than a hundred yards away, rises a slope, covered with rough grass and scrub, similar to that in the face of which I am ensconced.

Here the bear was seen at 7 A.M. by a Gujar, who gave the fullest particulars to Ahmed Bot (my shikari) in a series of yells from a hill-top as we came up the valley. We arrived on the scene about seven, just in time to be too late, apparently. It is now 3 P.M., and the bear is supposed to be asleep, and I am possessing my soul in patience until it shall be Bruin's pleasure to awake and sally forth for his afternoon tea.

There is certainly no bear now, so I pass the time in sleeping, eating, smoking, writing, and observing the manners and customs of a family of monkeys who are disporting themselves in a deep glen to the left. Beyond this ravine rises a high spur, beautifully wooded, the principal trees being deodar, blue pine (*Excelsa*) and yew. This is sloped at the invariable and disgusting angle of 45 degrees. Beyond it rise further wooded slopes, with snow gleaming through the deep green, and above all is the changing sky, where the clear blue gives way to a billowy expanse of white rolling clouds or dark rain-laden masses, which pour into the upper clefts of the ravine, and blot out the serried ranks of the pines, until a thorough drenching seems inevitable—when lo! a glint of blue through the gloomy background, and soon again,

"With never a stain, the pavilion of Heaven is bare."

The immediate foreground, as I said before, slopes sharply from my very feet, where a clump of wild sage and jasmin (the leaves just breaking) grows over a charming little bunch of sweet violets. Lower down I can see the lilac flowers of a self-heal, and the bottom of the little gorge is clothed with a bush like a hazel, only with large, soft whitish flowers.

My solitude has just been enlivened by the appearance of a cheerful party of lovely birds. They are very busy among the "hazels," flying from bush to bush with restless activity, and wasting no time in idleness. They are about the size of large finches—slender in shape, with longish tails. They are divided into two perfectly distinct kinds, probably male and female. The former have the back, head, and wings black; the latter barred with scarlet, the breast and underparts also scarlet. The others—which I assume to be the females—replace the black with ashy olive, the wings being barred with yellow, the underparts yellowish. The very familiar note of the cuckoo, somewhere up in the jungle, reminds me of an English spring.

4 P.M.—I knew it! I knew that if the wind held down the nullah I should be dragged up that horrible ridge opposite. Hardly had I written the above when I was hunted from my lair, and rushed down 200 steep feet, and then up some 500 or 600 on the other side of the stream, through an abattis of clinging undergrowth that made a severe toil of what could never have been a pleasure. There can be no doubt but that a pith helmet—a really shady, broad one—is a most infernal machine under which to force one's way through brushwood.

Well, all things come to an end—wind first, temper next, and finally the journey.

My shikari is a fiend in human shape. He slinks along on the flat at what *looks* like a mild three-miles-an-hour constitutional, but unless you are a *real* four-mile man you will be left hopelessly astern; but when he gets upon his favourite "one in one" slope, then does he simply sail away, with the tiffin coolie carrying a fat basket and all your spare lumber in his wake, while you toil upward and ever upwards—gasping—until with your last available breath you murmur "Asti," and sink upon the nearest stone a limp, perspiring worm!

5.30 P.M.—That bear has taken a sleeping draught!

I am now perched on a lonely rock, my hard taskmaster having routed me out of a very comfortable place under a blue pine, whose discarded needles afforded me a really agreeable resting-place, and dragged me away down again through the pine forest and jungle; hurried me across a roaring torrent on a fallen tree trunk; personally conducted me hastily up a place like the roof of a house; and finally, explaining that the bear, when disturbed, must inevitably come close past me, has departed with his staff (the chota shikari, the tiffin coolie, and a baboon-faced native) to wake up the bear and send him along.

After the first flurry of feeling all alone in the world, with only a probable bear for society, and having loaded all my guns, clasped my visor on my head and my Bessemer hug-proof strait-waistcoat round my "tummy," I felt calm enough to await events with equanimity.

6.15 P.M.—A large and solemn monkey is sitting on the top of a thick and squat yew tree regarding me with unfeigned interest. The torrent is roaring away in the cleft below. Nothing else seems alive, and I am becoming bored— —What? A bear? No! The shikari, thank goodness!

"Well, shikari—Baloo dekho hai?" No, it is passing strange, but he has *not* seen a bear. "All right! Pick up the blunderbuss, and let us make tracks for the ship."

Wednesday, May 10.—Beguiled by legends of many bears, detailed to me with apparently heartfelt sincerity by Ahmed Bot, I have been pursuing these phantoms industriously.

On Monday we quitted our boat, and started upon a trip into the Lolab Valley. The views, as the path wound up the green and flower-spangled slope, were very beautiful, and, when we had ascended about 1500 feet and were about opposite to the supposed haunt of Saturday's bear, we determined to camp and enjoy the scenery, not omitting an evening expedition in search of our shy friend.

Jane joining me, we had a most charming ramble down a narrow track to the bed of the stream which rushes down from the snow-covered ridge guarding the Lolab. Here we crossed into a splendid belt of gaunt silver firs, the first I have seen here; whitish yellow marsh-marigolds and a most vivid "smalt" blue forget-me-not with large flowers were abundant, also an oxalis very like our own wood-sorrel.

Emerging from the pines, we crossed a grassy slope covered with tall primulas (P. *denticulata*) of varying shades of mauve and lilac, and sat down for a bit among the flowers while the shikaris looked for game. (I need hardly remark that the noble but elusive beast had appeared on the scene shortly after I left on Saturday; a Gujar told the shikari, and the shikari told me, so it must be true.) When we had gathered as many flowers as we could carry, we strolled back to the camp to watch the sunset transmute the snowy crest of Haramok to a golden rose.

Yesterday, Tuesday, I left the camp at dawn, and went all over the same ground, but with no better success, only seeing a couple of bara singh, hornless now, and therefore comparatively uninteresting from a "shikar" point of view. After a delightful but bearless ramble I returned to breakfast, and then we struck camp, and completed the ascent of the pass over into the Lolab. Arrived at the top, we turned off the path to the right, and, climbing a short way, came out upon the lower part of the Nagmarg, a pretty, open clearing among the pines where the grass, dotted thickly with yellow colchicum, was only showing here and there through the melting snow. Choosing a snug and dry place on some sun-warmed rocks at the foot of a tree, we prepared to lunch and laze, and soon spread abroad the contents of the tiffin basket.

There is something, nay much, of charm in the utter freedom and solitude of Kashmir camp life. There is no beaten track to be followed diligently by the tourist, German, American, or British, guide-book in hand and guide at elbow. No empty sardine-tins, nor untidy scraps of paper, mar the clean and lonely margs or village camping-grounds.

The happy wanderer, selecting a grassy dell or convenient shady tree with a clear spring or dancing rivulet near by, invokes the tiffin coolie, and if a duly watchful eye has been kept upon that incorrigible sluggard, in short space the contents of the basket deck the sward. What have we here? Yes, of course, cold chicken—

"For beef is rare within these oxless isles."

Bread! (how lucky we sent that coolie into Srinagar the other day). Butter, nicely stowed in its little white jar, cheese-cakes (one of the Sabz Ali's masterpieces), and a few unconsidered trifles in the form of "jam pups" and a stick of chocolate.

Whisky is there, if required, but really the cold spring water is "delicate to drink" without spirituous accompaniment.

Hunger appeased, the beauty of the surrounding scenery becomes intensified when seen through the balmy veil of smoke caused by the consumption of a mild cheroot, and peace and contentment reign while we feed the sprightly crows with chicken bones and bits of cheese rind.

Shall we ever forget—Jane and I—that simple feast on the Nagmarg?

The sloping snow melting into little rills which trickled through the fresh-springing flower-strewn grass; the extraordinary blue of the hillsides overlooking the Lolab Valley seen through the sloping boughs of the pines; the crows hopping audaciously around or croaking on a dried branch just above our heads; and above all, the glorious sense of freedom, of aloofness from all disturbing elements, of utter and irresponsible independence in a lovely land unspoiled by hand of man?

The afternoon sun smote us full in the face as we descended the bare and not too smooth path that led into the valley, and we were right glad to reach the shade of a grove of deodars that covered the lower slopes of the hill. The Lolab Valley, into which we had now penetrated, is a rich and picturesque expanse of level plain, some fifteen miles long by three or four broad, apparently completely surrounded by a densely-wooded curtain of mountains, rising to an elevation of some 3000 feet above the valley on the south and west, but ranging on the other sides up into the lofty summits which bar the route into Gurais and the Tilail. The mountain chain is not really continuous, the river Pohru, which drains the valley, finding outlet to the west e'er it bends sharply to the south and enters the Wular near Sopor.

Perhaps the most noticeable objects in the Lolab are the walnut trees; they are now just coming into full leaf, and their great trunks, hoary with age and softly velveted with dark green moss, form the noble columns of many a lovely camping-ground. We pitched our tents at Lalpura in a grove of giants, the majesty of which formed an exquisite contrast to the white foam of a cluster of apple trees in bloom.

It has been so hot to-day that we have stayed quietly in camp, reading, sketching, and enjoying the *dolce far niente* of an idle life.

Sunday, May 14.—On Thursday we left Lalpura and marched to Kulgam, a short distance of some eight or ten miles. Mr. Blunt, the forest officer,[1] had most kindly placed the forest bungalows of the Lolab at our disposal; but, as they all lie on the other side of the valley, we are obliged to camp every night. We have been working along the north side of the Lolab, as the shikari is full of bear "khubbar," and as long as the weather remains fair we really do not much care where we go! Skirting the foot of the wooded ridge on our right, and with the flat and populous levels of the valley on our left, we marched along a good path shaded in many places by the magnificent walnuts and snowy fruit-trees for which the Lolab is justly famed, until, crossing the Pohru by a rickety bridge, and toiling up a hot, bare slope, we reached Kulgam, nestling at the foot of the hills.

[1] Commonly called the "Jungly-sahib."

After tiffin and a short rest we set forth up the nullah behind the village to look for (need I say?) a bear. The gradient was stiff, as usual, and the path none too good. Feeling that our laborious climb deserved to be rewarded by, at any rate, the sight of game, and Ahmed Bot having sent a special message to the Lumbadhar at Kulgam directing him to keep the nullah quiet, we were justly incensed when, having toiled up some couple of thousand weary feet, we met a gay party of the *élite* of Kulgam prancing down the hill with blankets stuffed with wild leeks, or some such delicacy.

Ahmed Bot showed reckless courage. Having overwhelmed the enemy with a vituperative broadside, he fell upon them single-handed, tore from them their cherished blankets, and spilt the leeks to the four winds.

I expected nothing less than to be promptly hurled down the khud, with Jill after me, by the six enraged burghers of Kulgam. But no. They simply sat down together on a rock, and blubbered loud and long; we sat down opposite them on another rock and laughed, and laughed—tableau!

On Friday I went for a delightful walk through the pine and deodar forests, the ostensible objective being, of course, a bear. Putting aside all ideas of sport, I gave myself up to the simple joy of mere existence in such a land; noting a handsome iris with broad red lilac blooms, which I had not seen before; listening to the intermittent voice of the cuckoo, and pausing every here and there to gaze over the fair valley, backed by its encircling ranges of sunlit mountains.

The chota shikari is a youth of great activity, both mental and physical. He almost wept with excitement on observing the mark of a bear's paw on a dusty bit of path. He said it was a bear which had left that paw-mark, so I believed him. Late in the dusk of the afternoon he *saw* a bear sitting looking out of a cave. I could only make out a black hole, but he saw its ears move. I regarded the spot with a powerful telescope, but only saw more hole; still, I cannot doubt the chota shikari. The burra shikari saw it too, but was of opinion that it was too late to go and bag it. I think he was right, so we went back to camp without further adventure.

Yesterday we left Kulgam, and followed up a track to a small village which lies at the foot of the track leading over to Gurais and the Tilail country. Here we camped in a grove of walnuts, which stood by an icy spring. Jane and I went for a stroll, watched a couple of small woodpeckers hunting the trunk of a young fir within a few feet of us, but retreated hurriedly to camp on the approach of a heavy thunderstorm. This was but the prelude to a bad break in the weather; all to-day it has rained in torrents, and everything is sopping and soaked. The little stream which yesterday trickled by the camp is become a young river, and it is a perfect mystery how Sabz Ali manages to cook our food over a fire guarded from the full force of the rain by blankets propped up with sticks, and how, having cooked it, he can bring it, still hot, across the twenty yards of rain-swept space which intervenes between the cook-house and our tent.

Monday, May 15.—The deluge continued all night, and only at about ten o'clock this forenoon did the heavy curtain of rain break up into ragged swirls of cloud, which, torn by the serrated ridges of the gloomy pines, rolled dense and dark up the gorges, resonant now with the roar of full-fed torrents.

The men are all beginning to complain of fever, and have eaten up a great quantity of quinine. Considering the dismal conditions under which they have been living for the last couple of days, this is not surprising; so, with the first promise of an improvement in the weather, we struck camp, determined to make for the forest bungalow at Doras and obtain the shelter of a solid roof. Many showers, but no serious downpour, enlivened our march, and we arrived at the snug little wooden house just in time to escape a particularly fine specimen of a thunderstorm. The Doras bungalow seemed a very palace of luxury, with its dry, airy rooms and wide verandah, all of sweet-smelling deodar wood. The men, too, were thankful to have a good roof over their heads, and we heard no more of fever.

Wednesday, May 17.—Yesterday it rained without ceasing, until the valley in front of us took the appearance of a lake—A party of terns, white above and with black breasts, skirled and wrangled over the "casual" water. It was still very wet this morning, but as it cleared somewhat after breakfast, we made up our minds to quit the Lolab and get back to our boat.

Doras has sad memories for Jane, for here died the "chota murghi," a black chicken endowed with the most affectionate disposition. It was permitted to sit on the lady's knee, and scratch its yellow beak with its little yellow claw; but I never cared to let it remain long upon my shoulder—a perch it ardently affected. Well! it is dead, poor dear, and whether from shock (the pony which carried its basket having fallen down with it *en route* from "Walnut Camp"), or from a surfeit of caterpillars which were washed in myriads off the trees there, we cannot tell. Sabz Ali brought the little corpse along, holding it by one pathetic leg to show the horrified Jane, before giving it to the kites and crows. He has many "murghis" left; baskets full, as he says, for they are cheap in the Lolab, but we shall never love another so dearly.

We had a shocking time while climbing to the pass which leads over to Rampur, the road being deep in slimy mud, and so slippery that the unfortunate baggage ponies could hardly get along. Jane, who is in splendid condition now, toiled nobly up a track which would have been delightful had the weather been a little less hideous.

Reaching the ridge which divides the Lolab from the Pohru Valley, we turned to the left, along the edge, instead of descending forthwith, as we had hoped and expected to do. It was raw and cold, with flying wreaths of damp mist shutting out the view, and we were glad of a comforting tiffin, swallowed somewhat hurriedly, under a forlorn and stunted specimen of a blue pine. Then on along a rough and slippery catwalk that made us wonder if the baggage ponies would achieve a safe arrival at Rampur.

Crossing a steep, rock-strewn ridge, covered with crown imperial in full flower, we began a sharp descent through a wood of deodars; and now the thunder, which had been grumbling and rumbling in the distance, came upon us, and a deafening peal sent us scurrying down the hill at our best pace; the lightning-blasted trunks stretching skywards their blackened and tempest-torn limbs in ghastly witness of what had been and what might be again.

At last we cleared the wood, and, plunging across a perfect slough of deep mud, crawled on to the verandah of the Rampur forest-house, where we sat anxiously watching the hillside until we saw our faithful ponies safely sliding down the hill.

Thursday, May 18.—The changes of weather in this country are sudden and surprising. This morning we woke to a perfect day—the sun bathing the warm hillsides, the picturesque brown village, and the brilliant masses of snowy blossoming fruit-trees with a radiant smile. And, but for the tell-tale riot of the streams and the sponginess of the compound, there was nothing to betray the past misdeeds of the clerk of the weather.

At noon we set out to cover the short distance that lay between us and Kunis, where we had made tryst with Satarah. The country was like a series of English woodland glades—watered by many purling streams, and bright with masses of apple blossom; the turf around the trees all white and pink with petals torn from the branches by the recent storms. Clumps of fir clothed the hills with sombre green—a perfect background to a perfect picture.

The flowers all along our path to-day were much in evidence after the rain. Little prickly rose-bushes (*R. Webbiana*) were covered with pink blossoms just bursting into full glory; bushes of white may, yellow berberis, Daphne (*Oleoides?*), and many another flowering shrub grew in tangled profusion, while pimpernel (red and blue), a small androsace (*rotundifolia*), hawks-bit, stork's bill, wild geranium, a tiny mallow, eye-bright, forget-me-not, a little yellow oxalis, a speedwell, and many another, to me unknown, blossom starred the roadside. In the fields round Kunis the poppies flared, and the iris bordered the fields with a ribbon of royal purple.

We reached Kunis at two o'clock, and found the village half submerged, the water being up and over the low shores from the recent rain. Our boats were moored in a clump of willows, whose feet stood so deeply in the water that we had to embark on pony-back! After lunch came the usual difference of opinion with the Admiral, who seems to have great difficulty in grasping the fact that our will is law as to times and seasons for sailing. He always assumes the rôle of passive resister, and is always defeated with ignominy. He insisted that it was too late to think of reaching Bandipur, but we maintained that we could get at any rate part of the way; so he cast off from his willow-tree, and sulkily poked and poled out into the Wular, taking uncommon good care to hug the shore with fervour.

Here and there a group of willows standing far out into the lake, or a half-drowned village, drove us out into the open water, and once when, like a latter-day Vasco de Gama, the Admiral was striving to double the dreadful promontory of a water-logged fence, a puff of wind fell upon us, lashing the smooth water into ripples, whereupon the crew lost their wits with fright, and the lady mariners in the cook-boat set up a dismal howling; the ark, taking charge, crashed through the fence, her way carrying us to the very door of a frontier villa of an amphibious village. With amazing alacrity the crew tied us up to the door-post, and prepared to go into winter quarters.

This did not suit us at all, and

"The harmless storm being ended,"

we ruthlessly broke away from our haven of refuge, and safely arrived at Alsu.

Friday, May 19.—An ominous stillness and repose at 3 o'clock this morning sent me forth to see why the windlass was not being manned. A thing like a big grey bat flapping about, proved, on inspection, to be that rascal the Lord High Admiral Satarah. He said he could not start, as the hired coolies from Kunis had been so terrified by the horrors of yesterday that they had departed in the night, sacrificing their pay rather than run any more risks with such daredevils as the mem-sahib and me. This was vexatious and entirely unexpected, as I had never before known a coolie to bolt before pay-day. Sabz Ali and Satarah were promptly despatched on a pressgang foray, while I put to sea with the first-lieutenant to show that I meant business. A crew was found in a surprisingly short time, and a frenzied dart was made for the mouth of the Jhelum.

All day we poled round the shore of the lake, over flooded fields where the mustard had spread its cloth of gold a short week ago, over the very hedges we had scrambled through when duck-shooting in April, until in the evening we entered the river just below Sumbal.

The towing-path was almost, in many places quite, under water, and the whole country looked most forlorn and melancholy as the sun went down—a pale yellow ball in a pale yellow haze.

Sunday, May 21.—All yesterday we towed up the river against a current which ran swift and strong.

The passage of the bridge at Surahal gave us some trouble, as the flooded river brought our upper works within a narrow distance of the highest point of the span, but we finally scraped through with the loss of a portion of the railing which decorated our upper deck.

The strain of towing was severe, so, when a brisk squall and threatening thunder-shower overtook us at the mouth of the Sind River, we decided to tie up there for the night.

This morning we started at four o'clock, but only reached our berth at Srinagar at two, having spent no less than six hours in forcing the boats by pole and rope for the last three miles through the town! An incredible amount of panting, pushing, yelling, and hauling, with frantic invocations to "Jampaws" and other saints, was required to enable us to crawl inch by inch against the racing water which met us in the narrow canal below the Palace.

All's well that ends well, and here we are once more in Srinagar, after a trip which has been really delightful, albeit the weather latterly has not been by any means all that could have been desired, and we have slain no bears![2]

[2] Can it be that Bernier was right? "Il ne s'y trouve ni serpens, ni tigres, ni ours, ni lions, si ce n'est très rarement." — *Voyage de Kachemire.*

CHAPTER IX
SRINAGAR AGAIN

We have spent the last three weeks or so quietly in Srinagar, our boats forming links in the long chain that, during the "season," extends for miles along both banks of the river. A large contingent of amphibians dwells in the canal leading to the Dal gates, and the Chenar Bagh, sacred to the bachelor, shows not a spare inch along its shady length.

Not being either professional globe-trotters or Athenians, we have not felt obliged to be perpetually in high-strung pursuit of some new thing; and to the seeker after mild and modest enjoyment there is much to be said in favour of a sojourn at Srinagar.

Polo, gymkhanas, lawn-tennis, picnics, and golf are everyday occurrences, followed by a rendezvous at the club, where every one congregates for a smoke and chat, until the sun goes down behind the poplars, and the swift shikaras come darting over the stream like water-beetles to carry off the sahibs to their boats, to dress, dine, and reassemble for "bridge," or perhaps a dance at Nedou's Hotel, or at that most hospitable hub of Srinagar, the Residency.

Polo is, naturally, practically restricted to the man who brings up his ponies from the Punjab, but golf is for all, and the nine-hole course, although flat, is not stale, and need not be unprofitable, unless you are fallen upon—as I was—by two stalwart Sappers, sons of Canada and potent wielders of the cleek, who gave me enough to do to keep my rupees in my pocket and the honour of the mother country upheld!

On May 26th we took shikara and paddled across the Dal Lake to see something of the Mohammedan festival, consisting in a pilgrimage to the Mosque of Hasrat Bal, where a hair of the prophet's beard is the special object of adoration.

As we neared the goal the plot thickened. Hundreds of boats—from enormous doungas containing the noisy inhabitants of, I should suppose, a whole village, down to the tiniest shikara, whose passenger was perched with careful balance to retain a margin of safety to his two inches of freeboard—converged upon the crowded bank, above which rose the mosque.

How can I best attempt to describe the din, the crush, the light, the colour? Was it like Henley? Well, perhaps it might be considered as a mad, fantastic Henley. Replace the fair ladies and the startling "blazers" with veiled houris and their lords clad in all colours of the rainbow; for one immortal "Squash" put hundreds of "squashes," all playing upon weird instruments, or singing in "a singular minor key"; let the smell of outlandish cookery be wafted to you from the "family" boats and from the bivouacs on the shore; let a constant uproar fall upon your ears as when the Hall defeats Third Trinity by half a length; and, finally, for the flat banks of Father Thames and the trim lawns of Phyllis Court, you must substitute the Nasim Bagh crowned with its huge chenars, and Mahadco looking down upon you from his thirteen thousand feet of precipice and snow.

Half-an-hour of this kaleidoscopic whirl of gaiety satisfied us. The sun, in spite of an awning, was a little trying, so we sought the quiet and shade of the Nasim Bagh for lunch and repose.

Returning towards Srinagar about sundown, we stopped to visit the ancient Mosque of Hassanabad, which stands on a narrow inlet or creek of the Dal Lake, shaded by chenars and willows in all their fresh spring green. A little lawn of softest turf slopes up gently to the ruined mosque, of which a portion of an apse and vaulted dome alone stand sentinel over its fallen greatness. Around lie the tombs of princes, whose bones have mouldered for eight hundred years under the irises, which wave their green sabres crowned with royal purple in the whispering twilight.

Near by, the mud and timber walls of a ziarat stand, softly brown, supporting a deeply overhanging, grass-grown roof, blazing with scarlet tulips. Through its very centre, and as though supporting it, pierces the gnarled trunk of a walnut tree, reminding one of Ygdrasil, the Upholder of the Universe.

May 27.—What an improvement it would be if a house-dounga could be fitted with torpedo netting! Jane finds herself in the most embarrassing situations, while dressing in the morning, from the unwelcome pertinacity of the merchants who swarm up the river in the early hours from their lairs, and lay themselves alongside the helpless house-boats.

By 10 A.M. we have to repel boarders in all directions. Mr. Sami Joo is endeavouring to sell boots from the bow, while Guffar Ali is pressing embroidery on our acceptance from the stern. Ali Jan is in a boat full of carved-wood rubbish on the starboard side, while Samad Shah, Sabhana, and half-a-dozen other robbers line the river bank opposite our port windows and clamour for custom. A powerful garden-hose of considerable calibre might be useful, but for the present I have given Sabz Ali orders to rig out long poles, which will prevent the enemy from so easily getting to close quarters.

June 17.—It is quite curious that it should be so difficult to find time to keep up this journal. Mark Twain, in that best of burlesques, *The Innocents Abroad* affirms, if I remember rightly, that you could not condemn your worst enemy to greater suffering than to bind him down to keep an accurate diary for a year.

It is the inexorable necessity for writing day by day one's impressions that becomes so trying; and yet it must be done daily if it is to be done at all, for the only virtue I can attain to in writing is truth; and impressions from memory, like sketches from memory, are of no value from the hand of any but a master.

The time set apart for diary-writing is the hour which properly intervenes between chota hasri and the announcement of my bath; but, somehow, there never seems to be very much time. Either the early tea is late or bath is early, or a shikar expedition, with a grass slipper in pursuit of flies, takes up the precious moments, and so the business of the day gets all behindhand.

The fly question is becoming serious. Personally, I do not consider that fleas, mosquitoes, or any other recognised insect pests (excepting, perhaps, harvest bugs) are so utterly unendurable as the "little, busy, thirsty fly." It seems odd, too, as he neither stings nor bites, that he should be so objectionable; but his tickly method of walking over your nose or down your neck, and the exasperating pertinacity with which he refuses to take "no" for an answer when you flick him delicately with a handkerchief, but "cuts" and comes again, maddens you until you rise, bloody-minded in your wrath, and, seizing the nearest sledgehammer, fall upon the brute as he sits twiddling his legs in a sunny patch on the table, then lo—

"Unwounded from the dreadful close "—

he frisks cheerfully away, leaving you to gather up cursefully the fragments of the china bowl your wife bought yesterday in the bazaar!

How he manages to congregate in his legions in this ship is a mystery. Every window is guarded by "meat safe" blinds of wire gauze; the doors are, normally, kept shut; and yet, after one has swept round like an irate whirlwind with a grass slipper, and slain or desperately wounded every visible fly in the cabin, and at last sat down again to pant and paint, hoping for surcease from annoyance, not five minutes pass before one, two, nay, a round dozen of the miscreants are gaily licking the moisture off the cobalt (may they die in agony!), or trying to swim across the glass of water, or playing hop-scotch on the nape of my neck.

From what mysterious lair or hidden orifice they come I know not, but here they are in profusion until another massacre of the innocents is decreed.

It is a sound thing to go round one's sleeping-cabin at night before "turning in," and make a bag of all that can be found "dreaming the happy hours away" on the bulkheads and ceiling. It sends us to bed in the virtuous frame of mind of the Village Blacksmith—

"Something attempted, something done,
Has earned a night's repose"

There are other microbes besides flies in Kashmir which are exasperating—coolies, for instance.

I had engaged men through Chattar Singh (the State Transport factotum at Srinagar) to take us up the river, and decreed that we should start at 4 A.M. yesterday.

We had been to an *al fresco* gathering at the Residency the night before, and so were rather sleepy in the early morning, and I did not wake at four o'clock. At six we had not got far on our way, and at ten we were but level with Pandrettan, barely three miles from Srinagar as the crow (that model of rectilinear volition) flies.

I was busy painting all the forenoon, and failed to note the sluggish steps of our coolies, but in the afternoon it was borne in upon us that if we wanted to reach Avantipura that night, as we had arranged, a little acceleration was necessary.

Then the trouble began. The coolies were bone-lazy, the admiral and first-lieutenant were sulky, and the weather was stuffy and threatened thunder—the conditions were altogether detrimental to placidity of temper.

By sunset we had the shikari, the kitchen-maid, and the sweeper on the tow-rope, and even the great and good Sabz Ali was seen to bear a hand in poling. Much recrimination now ensued between Sabz Ali and the Admiral, and the whole crowd made the air resound with Kashmiri "language," every one, apparently, abusing everybody else, and making very nasty remarks about their lady ancestors.

At 10 P.M. I got four more coolies from a village, apparently chiefly inhabited by dogs, who deeply resented our proximity, and at 2 o'clock this morning we reached the haven where we would be—Avantipura.

This morning I discharged the Srinagar coolies and took a fresh lot, who pull better and talk less.

How differently things may be put and yet the truth retained. Yesterday we reclined at our ease in our cosy floating cottage, towed up the lovely river by a picturesque crew of bronze Kashmiris, the swish of the passing water only broken by their melodious voices. The brilliancy of the morning gave way in the afternoon to a soft haze which fell over the snowy ranges, mellowing their clear tones to a soft and pearly grey, while the reflections of the big chenars which graced the river bank deepened us the afternoon shadows lengthened and spread over the wide landscape. Towards evening we strolled along the river bank plucking the ripe mulberries, and idly watching the terns and kingfishers busily seeking their suppers over the glassy water; and at night we sat on deck while the moon rose higher in the quiet sky, and the dark river banks assumed a clearer ebony as she rose above the lofty fringe of trees, until the towing-path lay a track of pure silver reaching away to the dim belt of woodland which shrouded Avantipura.

That is a perfectly accurate description of the day, and so is this:—

It was very hot—and there is nothing hid from the heat of the sun on board a wooden house-dounga. The flies, too, were unusually malevolent, and I could scarcely paint, and my wife could hardly read by reason of their unwelcome attentions.

The coolies were a poor lot and a slack, and as the day grew stuffier and sultrier so did their efforts on the tow-path become "small by degrees and beautifully less."

That irrepressible bird—the old cock—refused to consider himself as under arrest in his hen-coop, and insisted upon crowing about fifteen times a minute with that fidgeting irregularity which seems peculiar to certain unpleasant sounds, and which retains the ear fixed in nervous tension for the next explosion of defiance or pride, or whatever evil impulse it is which causes a cock to crow.

Driven overboard by the cock, and a feeling that exercise would be beneficial, we landed in the afternoon, and plodded along the bank for some miles. The innumerable mulberry trees are loaded with ripe fruit, the ground below being literally black with fallen berries. We ate some, and pronounced them to be but mawkish things.

After dinner we sat on deck, as the lamp smelt too strongly to let us enjoy ourselves in the cabin, and the coolies on the bank and the people in our boat and those in the cook-boat engaged in a triangular duel of words, until the last few grains of my patience ran through the glass, and I spake with *my* tongue.

There is certainly some curious quality in the air of this country which affects the nerves: maybe it is the elevation at which one lives—certain it is that many people complain of unwonted irritability and susceptibility to petty annoyances. And, while travelling in Kashmir is easy and comfortable enough along beaten tracks, yet the petty worries connected with all matters of transport and supply are incessant, and become much more serious if one cannot speak or understand Hindustani.

It takes some little time for the Western mind to grasp the fact that the Kashmiri cannot and must not be treated on the "man and brothel" principle.

He is by nature a slave, and his brain is in many respects the undeveloped brain of a child; in certain ways, however, his outward childishness conceals the subtlety of the Heathen Chinee.

He has in no degree come to comprehend the dignity of labour any more than a Poplar pauper comprehends it, but fortunately his Guardians, while granting certain advantages in his tenure of land and payment of rent, have bound him, in return, to work for a fair payment, when required to do so by his Government, as exercised by the local Tehsildhar.

The demand made upon a village for coolies is not, therefore, an arbitrary and high-handed system of bullying, but simply a call upon the villages to fulfil their obligation towards the State by doing a fair day's work for a fair day's pay of from four to six annas.

I do not, of course, propose to entangle myself in the working of the Land Settlement, which is most fully and admirably explained in Lawrence's *Valley of Kashmir*.

The coolie, drawn from his native village reluctant, like a periwinkle from its shell, is never a good starter, and when he finds himself at the end of a tow-rope or bowed beneath half a hundredweight of the sahib's trinkets, with a three-thousand-feet pass to attain in front of him, he is extremely apt to burst into tears—idle tears—or be overcome by a fit of that fell disease—"the lurgies." Lest my reader should not be acquainted with this illness, at least under that name, here is the diagnosis of the lurgies as given by a very ordinary seaman to the ship's doctor.

"Well, sir, I eats well, and I sleeps well; but when I've got a job of work to do—Lor' bless you, sir! I breaks out all over of a tremble!"

CHAPTER X
THE LIDAR VALLEY

We were glad enough to leave Srinagar, as that place has been undoubtedly trying lately, being extremely hot and relaxing. The river, which had been up to the fourteen-foot level, as shown on the gate ports at the entrance to the Sunt-i-kul Canal, had fallen to 9-1/2 feet, and the mud, exposed both on its banks and in the fields and flats which had been flooded, must have given out unwholesome exhalations, of which the riverine population, the dwellers in house-boats and doungas, got the full benefit.

Jane has certainly been anything but well lately, and I confess to a certain feeling best described as "slack and livery."

We had not intended to remain nearly so long in Srinagar, but the continuity of the chain of entertainments proved too firm to break, and dances and dinners, bridge and golf, kept us bound from day to day, until the *fête* at the Residency on the 15th practically brought the Srinagar season to a close, and broke up the line of house-boats that had been moored along both banks of the river.

We had arranged to start with a party of three other boats up the river, visiting Atchibal with our friends, and then going up the Lidar Valley, while they retraced their way to Srinagar.

The most popular bachelor in Kashmir was appointed commodore, and deputed to set the pace and arrange rendezvous. He began by sending on his big house-boat, dragged by many coolies, to Pampur, a distance of some ten miles by water, and, following himself on horseback by road, instituted a sort of "Devil take the hindmost" race, for which we were not prepared.

On reaching Pampur we heard that the "Baltic Fleet" had sailed for Avantipura, so we followed on; but, alas! having made a forced march to this latter place, we found that Rodjestvenski Phelps had again escaped us and "gone before."

We consigned him and the elusive "chota resident," who was in command of the rest of the party, to perdition, and decided to pursue the even tenor of our way to the Lidar Valley.

The upper reaches of the Jhelum tire not wildly or excitingly lovely. The narrowed waters, like sweet Thames, run softly between quiet British banks, willow veiled. The wide level flats of the lower river give place to low sloping hills or "karewas," which fall in terraced undulations from the foothills of the higher ranges which close in the eastern extremity of the Kashmir Valley.

It was well into the evening, and the sun had just set, throwing a glorious rosy flush over the snows which surround the Lidar Valley, when we came to the picturesque bridge which crosses the stream at Bejbehara.

The scene here was charming—a grand festa or religious tamasha being toward; the whole river was swarming with boats—great doungas, with their festive crews yelling a monotonous chant, paddled uproariously by. Light shikaras darted in and out, making up for want of volume in their song by the piercing shrillness of their utterances. The banks and bridge teemed with swarming life, and all Kashmir seemed to have contributed its noisiest members to the revel.

Beyond the bridge we could see through the gathering dusk many house-boats of the sahibs clustering under a group of magnificent chenars, over whose dark masses the moon was just rising, full orbed. The piers of the bridge seemed to be set in foliage, large willows having grown up from their bases, giving a most curious effect. We marked with some apprehension the swiftness of the oily current which came swirling round the piers, and soon we found ourselves stuck fast about half-way under the bridge, apparently unable to force our boat another inch against the stream which boiled past. An appalling uproar was caused by the coolies and the unemployed upon the bridge, who all, as usual, gave unlimited advice to every one else as to the proper management of affairs under the existing circumstances, but did nothing whatever in support of their theories. The situation was becoming quite interesting, and the "mem-sahib" and I, sitting on the roof of our boat, were speculating as to what would happen next when the Gordian knot was cut by the unexpected energy and courage of the first-lieutenant, who boldly slapped an argumentative coolie in the face, while the admiral dashed promiscuously into the shikara, and—yelling "Hard-a-starboard!—Full speed ahead!—Sit on the safety—valve!"—boldly shot into an overhanging mulberry tree, wherein our tow-rope was much entangled. The rope was cleared, the crew poled like fury, the coolies hauled for all they were worth, every one yelled himself hoarse, and we forged ahead. We crashed under the mulberry tree, which swept us from stem to stern, nearly carrying the hen-coop overboard; while Jane and I lay flat under a perfect hail of squashy black fruit which covered the upper deck.

We went on shore for a moonlight stroll after dinner. The place was like a glorified English park; chenars of the first magnitude, taking the place of oaks, rose from the short crisp turf, while a band of stately poplars stood sentry on the river bank. Through blackest shadow and over patches of moonlit sward we rambled till we came upon the ruins of a temple, of which little was left but a crumbled heap of masonry in the middle of a rectangular grassy hollow which had evidently been a tank, small detached mounds, showing where the piers of a little bridge had stood, giving access to the building from the bank. An avenue of chenars led straight to the bridge, showing either the antiquity of the trees or the comparatively modern date of the temple.

June 19.—Yesterday afternoon we left Bejbehara, and went on to Kanbal, the port of Islamabad. A hot and sultry day, oppressive and enervating to all but the flies, which were remarkably energetic and lively. The river below Islamabad is quite narrow, and hemmed in between high mudbanks.

Here we found the "Baltic Fleet," but, knowing that our fugitive friends must have already reached Atchibal, we held to our intention of going up the Lidar.

Having tied up to a remarkably smelly bank, which was just lofty enough to screen our heated brows from any wandering breeze, we landed to explore. A hot walk of a mile or so along a dusty, poplar-lined road brought us to the town of Islamabad, which, however, concealed its beauties most effectually in a mass of foliage. Although it ranks as the second town in Kashmir, it can hardly be said to be more than a big village, even allowing for its 9000 inhabitants, its picturesque springs, and its boast of having been once upon a time the capital of the valley. The first hundred yards of "city," consisting of a highly-seasoned bazaar paved with the accumulated filth of ages, was enough to satisfy our thirst for sight-seeing, and after a visit to the post-office we trudged back through a most oppressive grey haze to the boat. Crowds of the *élite* of the neighbourhood were hastening into Islamabad, where the "tamasha," which we came upon at Bejbehara, is to be continued to-morrow.

We had a good deal of difficulty in getting transport for our expedition, as the Assistant Resident and his party had, apparently, cleared the place of available ponies and coolies. An appeal to the Tehsildhar was no use, as that dignitary had gone to Atchibal in the Court train. However, a little pressure applied to Lassoo, the local livery stablekeeper, produced eight baggage ponies and a good-looking cream-coloured steed, with man's saddle, for my wife.

The syce, a jovial-looking little flat-faced fellow, was a native of Ladakh.

We made a fairly early start, getting off about six, and, having skirted the town and passed the neat little Zenana Mission Hospital, we had a pretty but uneventful march of some six miles to Bawan, where, under a big chenar, we halted for the greater part of the day.

Here let me point out that life is but a series of neglected opportunities. We were within a couple of miles of Martand, the principal temple in Kashmir, and we did not go to see it! I blush as I write this, knowing that hereafter no well-conducted globe-trotter will own to my acquaintance, and, indeed, the case requires explanation. Well, then, it was excessively hot; we were both in bad condition, and I had ten miles more to march, so we decided to visit Martand on our way down the valley. Alas! we came this way no more.

Little knowing how much we were missing, we sat contented in the shade while the hot hours went by, merely strolling down to visit a sacred tank full of cool green water and swarming with holy carp, which scrambled in a solid mass for bits of the chupatty which Jane threw to them.

A clear stream gushed out of a bank overhung by a tangle of wild plants. To the left was a weird figure of the presiding deity, painted red, and frankly hideous.

We were truly sorry to feel obliged, at four o'clock, to leave Bawan with its massy trees and abundance of clear running water, and step out into the heat and glare of the afternoon.

I found it a trying march. The road led along a fairly good track among rice-fields, whence the sloping sun glinted its maddening reflection, but here and there clumps of walnuts—the fruit just at the pickling stage—cast a broad cool shadow, in which one lingered to pant and mop a heated brow e'er plunging out again into the grievous white sunlight.

The cavalcade was increased during the afternoon by the addition to our numbers of a dog—a distinctly ugly, red-haired native sort of dog, commonly called a pi-dog. He appeared, full of business—from nowhere in particular—and his business appeared to be to go to Eshmakam with us.

As we neared that place the road began to rise through the loveliest woodland scenery—white roses everywhere in great bushes of foamy white, and in climbing wreaths that drooped from the higher trees, wild indigo in purple patches reminding one not a little of heather. Above the still unseen village a big ziarat or monastery shone yellow in the sinking sunlight, and overhead rose a rugged grey wall of strangely pinnacled crags, outliers of the Wardwan, showing dusky blue in the clear-cut shadows, and rose grey where the low sun caught with dying glory the projecting peaks and bastions.

In a sort of orchard of walnut trees, on short, clean, green grass, we pitched our tents, and right glad was I to sit in a comfortable Roorkhee chair and admire the preparations for dinner after a stiff day, albeit we only "made good" some sixteen miles at most.

June 20.—A brilliant morning saw us off for Pahlgam, along a road which was simply a glorified garden. Roses white and roses pink in wild profusion, jasmin both white and yellow, wild indigo, a tall and very handsome spiraea, forget-me-not, a tiny sort of Michaelmas daisy, wild strawberry, and honeysuckle, among many a (to me unknown) blossom, clothed the hillside or drooped over the bank of the clear stream, by whose flower-spangled margin lay our path, where, as in Milton's description of Eden,

> "Each beauteous flower,
> Iris all hues, roses, and jessamine
> Reared high their flourished heads."

Soon the valley narrowed, and closer on our left roared the Lidar, foaming over its boulders in wild haste to find peace and tranquil flow in the broad bosom of Jhelum.

The road became somewhat hilly, and at one steep zigzag the nerves of Jane failed her slightly and she dismounted, rightly judging that a false step on the part of the cream-coloured courser would be followed by a hurried descent into the Lidar. I explained to her that I would certainly do what I could for her with a dredge in the Wular when I came down, but she preferred, she said, not to put me to any inconvenience in the matter. We were asked to subscribe, a few days later, at Pahlgam to provide the postman with a new pony, his late lamented "Tattoo" having been startled by a flash of lightning at that very spot, and having paid for the error with his life.

A halt was called for lunch under a blue pine, where we quickly discovered how paltry its shade is in comparison with the generous screen cast by a chenar; scarcely has the heated traveller picked out a seemingly umbrageous spot to recline upon when, lo! a flickering shaft of sunlight, broken into an irritating dazzle by a quivering bunch of pine needles, strikes him in the eye, and he sets to work to crawl vainly around in search of a better screen.

Nothing approaches the great circle of solid coolness thrown by a big chenar. The walnut does its best, and comes in a good second. Pines (especially blue ones) are, as I remarked before, unsatisfactory.

But if the pine is not all that can be wished as a shade-producer, he is in all his varieties a beautiful object to look upon. First, I think, in point of magnificence towers the Himalayan spruce, rearing his gaunt shaft,

"Like the mast of some tall ammiral,"

from the shelving steeps that overhang the torrents, and piercing high into the blue. In living majesty he shares the honours with the deodar, but he is merely good to look upon; his timber is useless and in his decay his fallen and lightning-blasted remains lie rotting on these wild hills, while the precious trunks of the deodar and the excelsa are laboriously collected, and floated and dragged to the lower valleys, producing much good money to Sir Amar Singh and the best of building timber to the purchaser.

The road towards Pahlgam is a charming woodland walk, where the wild strawberries, still hardly out of flower, grow thick amidst a tangle of chestnut, yew, wild cherry, and flowering shrubs. Overhead and to the right the rocky steeps rise abruptly until they culminate in the crags of Kohinar, and on the left the snow-fed Lidar roars "through the cloven ravine in cataract after cataract."

About four miles from Pahlgam, on turning a corner of the gorge, a splendid view bursts upon the wayfarer. The great twin brethren of Kolahoi come suddenly into sight, where they stand blocking the head of the valley, their double peaks shining with everlasting snow.

It needed all the beauty of the scene to make me forget that the thirteen miles from Eshmakam were long and hot, and that I was woefully out of condition, and we rejoiced to see the gleam of tents amid the pine-wood which constitutes the camping-ground of Pahlgam.

We sat peacefully on the thyme and clover-covered maiden, amongst a herd of happily browsing cattle, until our tents were up and the irritating but needful bustle of arrival was over, and the tea-table spread.

Pahlgam stands some 2000 feet above Srinagar, and although it is not supposed to be bracing, yet to us, jaded votaries of fashion in stuffy Srinagar, the fresh, clear, pine-scented air was purely delightful, and a couple of days saw us "like kidlings blythe and merry"—that is to say, as much so as a couple of sedate middle-aged people could reasonably be expected to appear. The camping-ground is in a wood of blue pines, which, extending from the steeper uplands, covers much of the leveller valley, and abuts with woody promontories on the flowery strath which borders the river. Here some dozen or so of visitors had already selected little clearings, and the flicker of white tents, the squealing of ponies, and the jabber of native servants banished all ideas of loneliness.

About half a mile below the camping-ground is the bungalow of Colonel Ward, clear of the wood and with Kolahoi just showing over the green shoulder which hides him from Pahlgam. I was fortunate enough to find the Colonel before he left for Datchgam to meet the Residency party, and to get, through his kindness, certain information which I wanted about the birds of Kashmir.

An enthusiast in natural history, Colonel Ward has given himself with heart-whole devotion for many years to the study of the beasts and birds of Kashmir, and he is practically the one and only authority on the subject.

We were very anxious to cross the high pass above Lidarwat over into the Sind Valley, having arranged to meet the Smithsons at Gangabal on their way back from Tilail. Knowing that Colonel Ward would be posted as to the state of the snow, I had written to him from Srinagar for information. His reply, which I got at Islamabad, was not encouraging, nor was his opinion altered now. The pass might be possible, but was certainly not advisable for ladies at present.

Friday, June 23.—We were detained here at Pahlgam until about one o'clock to-day, as Colonel Ward, as well as two minor potentates, had marched yesterday, employing every available coolie. The fifteen whom I required were sent back to me by the Colonel, and turned up about noon, so, after lunch, we set forth.

Camels are usually unwilling starters. I knew one who never could be induced to do his duty until a fire had been lit under him as a gentle stimulant. He lived in Suakin, and existence was one long grievance to him, but no other animal with which I am acquainted approaches a Pahlgam coolie in *vis inertiâ*.

Whether a too copious lunch had rendered my men torpid, or whether the attractions of their happy homes drew them, I know not, but after the loads (and these not heavy) had been, after much wrangling, bound upon their backs, and they had limped along for a few hundred yards or so, one fell sick, or said he was sick, and, peacefully squatting on a convenient stone, refused to budge.

We were still close to some of the scattered huts of Pahlgam, so an authority, in the shape of a lumbadhar or chowkidar, or some such, came to our help, and promptly collected for us an elderly gentleman who was tending his flocks and herds in the vicinity. Doubtless it was provoking, when he was looking forward to a comfortable afternoon tea in the bosom of his family, after a hard day's work of doing nothing, to be called upon to carry a nasty angular yakdan for seven miles along a distinctly uneven road;

but was he therefore justified in blubbering like a baby, and behaving like an ape being led to execution?

The first half-mile was dreadful. At every couple of hundred yards the coolies would sit down in a bunch, groaning and crying, and nothing less than a push or a thump would induce them to move. We felt like slave-drivers, and indeed Sabz Ali and the shikari behaved as such, although their prods and objurgations were not so hurtful as they appeared, being somewhat after the fashion of the tale told by an idiot,

"Full of sound and fury, signifying nothing."

Presently we became so much irritated by the ceaseless row that we decided to sit down and read and sketch by the roadside, in order to let the whole mournful train pass out of sight and earshot.

Now, I wish to maintain in all seriousness that I am not a Legree, and that, although I by no means hold the "man and brother" theory, yet I am perfectly prepared to respect the *droits de l'homme*.

This may appear a statement inconsistent with my acknowledgment that I permitted coolies to be beaten—the beating being no more than a technical "assault," and never a "thrashing!"—but my contention is that when you have to deal with people of so low an organisation that they can only be reached by elementary arguments, they must be treated absolutely as children, and judiciously whacked as such.

No Kashmiri without the impulsion of *force majeure* would ever do any work—no logical argument will enable him to see ultimate good in immediate irksomeness.

It is very difficult for the Western mind to give the Kashmiri credit for any virtues, his failings being so conspicuous and repellent; for not only is he an outrageous coward, but he feels no shame in admitting his cowardice. He is a most accomplished thief, and the truth is not in him. He and his are much fouler than Neapolitan lazzaroni, and his morals—well, let us give the Kashmiri his due, and turn to his virtues. He is, on the whole, cheerful and lively, devoted to children, and kind to animals.[1]

> [1] This is incorrect, the European Residents having frequently attempted, but hitherto vainly, to induce the native authorities to curb Kashmiri cruelty.

Here is a story which is fairly characteristic of the charming Kashmiri.

During the floods which nearly ruined Kashmir in 1901, a village near a certain colonel's bungalow was in danger of losing all its crops and half its houses, the neighbouring river being in spate. My friend, on going to see if anything could be done, found the water rising, and the adult male inhabitants of the village lying upon the ground, and beating their heads and hands upon it in woebegone impotence.

He walked about upon their stomachs a little to invigorate them, and, sending forthwith for a gang of coolies from an adjacent village which lay a little higher, he set the whole crowd to work to divert part of the stream by means of driftwood and damming, and was, in the end, able to save the houses and a good part of the crops.

When the hired coolies came to be paid for their labour, the villagers also put in a claim for wages, and were desperately vexed at my friend's refusal to grant it, complaining bitterly of having had to work hard for nothing!

You will find a good description of the Kashmiri in *All's Well that Ends Well*:—

> *Parolles*. He will steal, sir, an egg out of a cloister.... He professes not keeping of oaths, in breaking them, he is stronger than Hercules. He will lie, sir, with such volubility, that you would think truth were a fool: drunkenness is his best virtue; ... he has everything that an honest man should not have; what an honest man should have, he has nothing.
>
> He excels his brother for a coward, yet his brother is reputed one of the best that is: in a retreat he outruns any lackey; marry, in coming on he has the cramp.

We had not long sat sketching and basking in the genial glow of a summer afternoon among the mountains, when it began to be borne in upon us that the weather was going to change, and that the usual thunderstorm was meditating a descent upon us. Black clouds came boiling up over the mountain peaks, and the too familiar grumble of distant thunder sent us hurrying along the lovely ravine, through which the path leads to Aru. Only a seven miles' journey, but ere we had gone half-way the storm broke, and a thick veil of sweeping rain fell between us and the surrounding mountains.

Presently we found a serious solution of continuity in the track, which, after leading us along a precarious ledge by the side of the river, finished abruptly; sheared clean off by a recent landslip.

We were very wet, but the river looked wetter still, and it boiled round the rocky point, where the road should have been but was not, in a distinctly disagreeable manner.

However, Jane dismounting, I climbed upon the cream-coloured courser, and proceeded to ford the gap. The water swirled well above the syce's knees, but the noble steed picked his way with the greatest circumspection over and among the submerged boulders, till, after splashing through some hundred yards of water, he deposited me, not much wetter than before, on the continuation of the high-road, whence I had the satisfaction of watching Jane go through the same performance.

Hoping against hope that the coolies, by a little haste, might have got the tents pitched before the storm came on, we plodded on, until, wet to the very skin, we slopped into Aru, to behold a draggled party squatting round a central floppy heap in a wet field, which, as we gazed, slowly upreared itself into a drooping tent.

In dear old England this sort of experience would have spelt shocking colds, and probably rheumatism for life, but here—well, we crawled into our tent and found it, thanks to a couple of waterproof sheets spread on the ground, surprisingly dry. A change of clothes, a good dinner, produced under the most unfavourable circumstances from a wretched little cooking-tent, and a fire burning goodness knows how, in the open, showed the world to be quite a nice place after all.

After dinner a great camp-fire was lit in front of our tent, the rain cleared off, and I sat smoking with much content, while all our soaking garments were festooned on branches round the blaze, and Jane and I turned them like roasting joints, at intervals, until the steam rose like incense towards the stars.

The coolies, too, had quite got over their homesickness, and were extraordinarily cheerful, their incessant jabber falling as a lullaby on our ears as we dropped off to sleep.

Saturday, June 24.—We got away in good time for our short eight-mile march to Lidarwat. The coolies went off gaily—the day was warm and brilliant, and the views down the valley towards Pahlgam superb.

We had camped on the low ground at Aru, just across the bridge, but about half a mile on, and upon a grassy plateau there is an ideal camping-ground facing down the Lidar Valley, towards the peaks which rise behind Pahlgam. Want of water is the only drawback to this spot, but if mussiks are carried, water can easily be brought from a small nullah towards Lidarwat.

Tearing ourselves away from this spot, and turning our backs upon one of the most gorgeous views in Kashmir, we plunged into a beautiful wood. Maidenhair and many another fern grew in masses among the great roots which twined like snakes over the rocky slopes. Far below, with muffled roar, the unseen river tore its downward way.

By-and-by, the path emerging from the wood shelved along a green hillside, where bracken and golden spurge clothed the little hollows, while wild wall-flower, Jacob's Ladder, and a large purple cranes-bill brightened the slopes where happy cattle, but lately released from their winter's imprisonment, were feeding greedily on the young green grass.

I fancy the cattle have a remarkably poor time here in winter. Hay is not made, and very little winter forage seems to be collected. As the snows fall lower on the hills, the flocks and herds are driven down to the low ground, where they drag through the dark days as best they can, on maize-stalks and such like.

I noticed early in May the water buffaloes just turned out to graze in the Lolab, and more weakly, melancholy collections of skin—and—bone I have seldom seen.

Now, however, up high in every sunny grassy valley, the Gujars may be found camping with their flocks—cattle, ponies, buffaloes, and goats, working upwards hard on the track of the receding snow, where the primula and the gentian star the spring turf.

A series of grassy uplands brought us close to Lidarwat, when a sharp shower, arriving unexpectedly from nowhere in particular, sent us to eat our lunch under the shelter of some fairly waterproof trees in the company of a herd of water buffaloes of especially evil aspect.

One hoary brute in particular, with enormous horns and pale blue eyes, made me think of the legend concerning the origin of the buffalo.

When the Almighty was hard at work creating the animals, the devil came and looked on until he became filled with emulation, and begged the Deity to let him try his hand at creation. So the Almighty agreed, asking him what beast he would prefer to make, and he said, "A cow." So he went away and created a water buffalo, which so disgusted the Creator that the devil was not permitted to make any more experiments.

As soon as the rain held up and the thunder had rolled off up the valley, we packed the tiffin basket, had one more drink from an icy spring, and left the shelter of the friendly trees, followed by the glares of all the buffaloes, who appear to have a decided antipathy to the "sahib logue."

We soon came to Lidarwat, passing several tents there, pitched by the edge of a green lawn, and sheltered by a deep belt of trees. Crossing to the right bank of the river by the usual rickety bridge, we continued our way, as the farther up the glen we get to-night, the less shall we leave for to-morrow, when we intend to visit the Kolahoi Glacier.

The cream-coloured courser nearly wrecked my Kashmir holiday at this point, owing to the silly dislike of white folk which he possesses in common with the buffaloes. As I was incautiously handing Jane her beloved parasol, he whisked round and let out at me, and I was only saved from a nasty kick by my closeness to the beast, whose hock made such an impression upon my thigh as to cause me to go a bit short for a while.

We camped in rather a moist-looking place, where the wood begins to show signs of finishing, and the slopes fall steep and bare to the river.

A rather rank and weedy undergrowth was not inviting, and was strongly suggestive of dampness and rheumatism. It was fairly chilly, too, at night, as our camp was some 11,000 feet above the sea, and the little breezes that came sighing through the pines were straight from the snow.

Sunday, June 25. — A most glorious morning saw us start early for an expedition to the Kolahoi Glacier. The sombre ravine in which we were camped amid the pines lay still in a mysterious blue haze, but the sun had already caught the snow-streaked mountain-tops to our left, and gilded their rugged sides with a swiftly descending mantle of warmth and light.

A very fine waterfall came tumbling down a wooded chasm on our right, and as fine waterfalls are scarce in Kashmir we stopped for some time to admire it duly.

The track now led out into a wide and treeless valley, flanked by snow-crowned mountains, and we pushed on merrily until we arrived at the brink of a rascally torrent, which gave us some trouble to ford, being both exceeding swift and fairly deep. Luckily, it was greedy, and, not content with one channel, had spread itself out into four or five branches, and thus so squandered itself that Jane on her pony and I on coolie-back accomplished the passage without mishap. For some miles we held on along an easy path which curved to the right along the right bank of the river, which was spanned in many places by great snow bridges, often hundreds of yards in width. We lunched sitting on the trunk of a dead birch which had been carried by the snow down from its eyrie, and then left, a melancholy skeleton, bleaching on the slowly melting avalanche. Some two miles farther on we could see the end of the Kolahoi Glacier, its grey and rock-strewn snout standing abrupt above the white slopes of snow.

Behind rose the fine peak of Harbagwan, in as yet undisputed splendour, Kolahoi being still hidden behind the cliffs which towered on our right.

Distances seem short in this brilliant air, but we walked for a long while over the short turf, flushing crimson with primulas and golden with small buttercups, and then over snowy hillocks, before we reached the solid ice of the great glacier.

It was so completely covered with fragments of grey rock that Jane could hardly be persuaded that it really was an ice slope that we were scrambling up with such difficulty, until a peep into a cold mysterious cleft convinced her that she was really and truly standing upon 200 feet of solid ice.

The sight that now burst upon us was one to be remembered. Kolahoi towered ethereal—a sunlit wedge of sheer rock some six thousand feet above us—into the crystal air. From his feet the white frozen billows of the great glacier rolled, a glistering sea, to where we, atoms in the enormous loneliness, stood breathless in admiration. Around the head of the wide amphitheatre wherein we stood rose a circle of stately peaks, their bases flanged with rocky buttresses, dark amid the long sweeps of radiant snow, their shattered peaks reared high into the very heavens. A great silence reigned. There was no wind with us, and yet, even as we watched, a white cloud flitted past the virgin peak of Kolahoi—ghostly, intangible; and immediately, even as vultures assemble suddenly, no one knows whence, so did the clouds appear, surging over the gleaming shoulders of the mountain ridges, and up and round the grim precipices. We turned and hurried down the face of the glacier, and made for camp, as we knew from much experience that a thunderstorm was inevitable.

Over the beds of dirty snow, down by the side of the new-born torrent, which leaped full-grown to life from the womb of a green cavern below the glacier; over patches of pulpy turf just freed from its wintry bondage, and already carpeted with masses of rose-coloured primulas, we hastened, keeping to the left bank of the stream, in order to avoid the torrent which had so troubled us in the morning, which we knew would be deeper in the afternoon owing to the melting of the snows in the sunshine.

We had got but a bare half of our journey done when the storm burst, and in a very short time we were reduced to the recklessness which comes of being as wet as you can possibly be.

> "The thunder bellows far from snow to snow
> (Home, Rose and Home, Provence and La Palie),
>   And loud and louder roars the flood below.
> Heigho! But soon in shelter we shall be
> (Home, Rose and Home, Provence and La Palie)."

Crossing the river on a big snow-bridge below the point where our old enemy came thundering down the mountain-side, we tramped gaily through mud and mire and over slippery rocks until we were gladdened by the sight of our camp, dripping away peacefully in the midst of the weeping forest.

The rain, as usual, ceased in the evening. A great camp-fire was lit, and the neighbouring buffaloes of Gujar-Kote having kindly supplied us with milk, we dined wisely and well and dropped off to sleep, lulled by the roaring of the Kolahoi River, which raced through the darkness close by.

Tuesday, June 27.—Being still hopeful of achieving the pass over into the Sind, we struck camp early yesterday and marched down to Lidarwat, only to find that the party which we knew had camped there with a view to crossing, had given up the idea and retreated down the valley; so I sent a swift messenger to countermand the three days' supply of "rassad" which I had ordered from Pahlgam for my men, and we marched on to Aru. Upon the spur which overlooks Aru we found Dr. Neve encamped, and proceeded to discuss the possibility of crossing into the Sind Valley *viâ* Sekwas, Khem Sar, and Koolan. The Doctor, who is an enterprising mountaineer, was himself about to cross, but he did not encourage Jane to go and do likewise, as he said it would be very difficult owing to the late spring, and would probably entail a good deal of work with ropes and ice-axes.

This absolutely decided us, our valour being greatly tempered by discretion, and we camped quietly at Aru, and came on into Pahlgam this forenoon. The river, for some reason best known to itself, was so low that we got dry-shod past the corner which had worried us so much on the way up.

CHAPTER XI
GANGABAL

Friday, *June* 30.—The last few days have been somewhat uneventful. We left Pahlgam at early dawn on Wednesday, just as the first lemon-coloured light was spreading in the east over the pine-serrated heights above the camp.

The rapids below Colonel Ward's bungalow, which had been fierce and swollen as we passed them on our upward way, were now reduced to roaring after the subdued fashion of the sucking dove; so we hardly paused to contemplate either them or the big boulder, red-stained and holy, at Ganesbal, but hastened on to the point where, just before turning a high bluff which shuts him from sight for the last time, we got the view of Kolahoi, with the newly-risen sun glowing on his upper slopes. An hour flew by much too fast, and it was with great reluctance that we finally turned our back on the finest part of the Lidar Valley, and sadly resumed our march to Sellar, crossing the river and following a rather hot and dull road. Sellar itself is not nearly as pretty as Eshmakam, and we grew rather tired of it by evening, as we arrived soon after one o'clock, and found little to do or see.

Yesterday we left Sellar and marched to Bejbehara, the hottest and dullest march I know of in Kashmir. A shadeless road slopes gently down across the plains to the river. All along this road we overtook parties of coolies laden with creels of silk cocoons, whose destination is the big silk factory at Srinagar, small clouds of hot red dust rising into the still air, knocked up by the shuffling tread of their grass-shod feet.

In the fields, dry and burnt to our eyes after the green valleys, squatted the reapers, snipping the sparse ears, apparently one by one, with sickles like penknives. They seemed to get the work done somehow, as little sheafs laid in rows bore witness; but the patience of Job must have been upon them!

The chenars of Bejbehara threw a most welcome shade from the noonday sun, which was striking down with evil force as we panted across the steamy rice-fields which surround them.

Hither we came at noon, only to find that our boats were not awaiting us as we had directed. A messenger bearing bitter words was promptly despatched to root the lazy scoundrels out from Islamabad, while Jane and I camped out beneath a huge tree and lunched, worked, and sketched until four o'clock, when the Admiral brought the fleet in and fondly deemed his day's work done.

This was by no means our view of the case, and the usual trouble began—"No coolies"—"Very late"—"Plenty tired," &c. &c.

Of course Satarah was defeated, and was soon to be seen sulkily poling away in the stern-sheets, while his son-in-law still more sulkily paddled in the bow.

We made about eight or ten miles, having a swift current under us, before a strong squall came up the valley, making the old ark slue about prodigiously, and inducing us to tie up for the night.

This morning we slipped down stream to Srinagar, only halting for a short while to obtain some of the native bread for which Pampur is celebrated.

The river seemed exceedingly hot and stuffy after the lovely air which we have been breathing lately, and we quite determined that the sooner we get out of the valley the better for our pleasure, if not for our health.

We have been greatly exercised as to how best dispose of the time until September, for, during the months of July and August, the heat in the valley is very considerable, and every one seeks the higher summer retreats. The Smithsons suggested an expedition to Leh, which would, undoubtedly, have been a most interesting trip, but which would in no wise have spared us in the matter of heat. Had we started about this time for Leh we should have reached our destination towards the end of July, and would therefore have found ourselves setting out again across an arid and extremely hot country on the return journey somewhere about the middle of August.

The game did not seem to be worth the candle, and the Smithsons themselves shied at the idea when it was borne in upon them that there would be little or no shooting to be done *en route*.

The alternatives seemed to lie between Gulmarg, where most of the beauty and fashion of Kashmir disports itself during the hot weather, Sonamarg, and Pahlgam.

Sonamarg, from description, seemed likely to be quiet, not to say dull, as a residence for two months. One cannot live by scenery alone, and even the loveliest may become *toujours pâté de l'anguille.*

Pahlgam suffered in our eyes from the same failing, and our thoughts turned to Gulmarg. Here, however, a difficulty arose. It is a notoriously wet place. We heard horrid tales of golf enthusiasts playing in waders, and of revellers half drowned while returning from dinners in neighbouring tents.

We thought of rooms in Nedou's Hotel, but our memories of this hostelry in Srinagar were not altogether sweet, and we did not in the least hanker after a second edition; moreover, every available room had been engaged long ago, and it was extremely doubtful, to say the least of it, if the good Mr. Nedou could do anything for us. The prospect of a two-month sojourn in a wet tent wherein no fire could ever be lighted, and in which Jane pictured her frocks and smart hats lying in their boxes all crumpled and shorn of their dainty freshness, was far from enticing!

Tent existence, when one lives the simple life far from the madding crowd, clad in puttoo and shooting-boots, or grass shoes, is delightful; but tent life in the midst of a round of society functions—golf, polo, with their attendant teas and dinners—was not to be thought of without grave misgiving.

Sorely perplexed, and almost at our wits' end, the Gordian knot was cut by our being offered a small hut which had been occupied by a clerk in the State employ, now absent, and which the Resident most kindly placed at our disposal for a merely nominal rent. Needless to say we gratefully accepted the offer, in spite of the assurance that the hut was of very minute dimensions.

Sunday, July 2.—Yesterday we toiled hard in the heat to get everything in train for a move to Gulmarg. Subhana, that excellent tailor and embroiderer, arranged to have all our heavy luggage sent up to meet us on the 10th, and from him, too, we arranged for the hire of such furniture as we might require, for we knew that the hut was bare as the cupboard of nursery fame.

This morning we set off down the river to keep tryst with the Smithsons at Gangabal, where we hope to meet them about the 5th on their way back from Tilail. The usual struggle with the crew resulted, also as usual, in our favour, and we got right through to Gunderbal at the mouth of the Sind River, where we now lie amid a flotilla of boats whose occupiers have fled away from the sultriness and smelliness of Srinagar in search of the cool currents, both of air and water, which are popularly supposed to flow down the Sind.

As Jane and I returned from a visit to the post-office along a sweltering path among the rice-fields, from which warm waves of air rose steaming into the sunset, we failed to observe the celebrated and superior coolness of Gunderbal'

Thursday, July 6.— The lumbadhar of Gunderbal, in spite of his magnificent name, is a rascal of the deepest dye. He put much water in our milk, to the furious disgust of Sabz Ali, and he failed to provide the coolies I had ordered; I therefore reported him to Chattar Singh, and sent my messengers forth, like another Lars Porsena, to catch coolies.

This was early on Tuesday morning, and a sufficient number of ponies and coolies having been got together by 5.30, we started.

I may here note that, owing to a confusion between *Gunderbal* (the port, so to speak, of the Sind Valley, and route to Leh and Thibet) and *Gangabal*, a lake lying some 12,000 feet above the sea behind Haramok, our arrangement to meet the Smithsons at Gangabal was altered by a letter from them announcing their imminent arrival at Gunderbal! This was perturbing, but as the mistake was not ours, we decided not to allow ourselves to be baulked of a trip for which we had surrendered an expedition to Shisha Nag, beyond Pahlgam.

The lower part of the Sind Valley is in nowise interesting; the way was both tedious and hot, and we rejoiced greatly when, having crossed the Sind River, we found a lovely spring and halted for tiffin. After an hour's rest we followed the main road a little farther, and then, passing the mouth of the Chittagul Nullah, turned up the Wangat Valley. The scenery became finer, and the last hour's march along a steep mountain-side, with the Wangat River far below on our right, was a great improvement on what we had left behind us.

The little village of Wangat, perched upon a steep spur above the river, was woefully deficient of anything like a good camping-ground. We finally selected a small bare rice patch, which, though extremely "knubbly," had the merits of being almost level, moderately remote from the village and its smells, and quite close to a perfect spring.

Yesterday we achieved a really early start, leaving Wangat at 4.15, the path being weirdly illuminated by extempore torches made of pine-wood which the shikari had prepared. A moderately level march of some three miles brought us to the ruined temples of Vernag and the beginning of our work, for here the path, turning sharply to the left, led us inexorably up the almost precipitous face of the mountain by means of short zigzags.

It was a stiff pull. The sun was now peering triumphantly over the hills on the far side of the valley, and the path was (an extraordinary thing in Kashmir) excessively dusty. Up and on we panted, Jane partly supported by having the bight of the shikari's puggaree round her waist while he towed her by the ends.

There was no relaxation of the steep gradient, no water, and no shade, and the height to be surmounted was 4000 feet.

If the longest lane has a turning, so the highest hill has a top, and we came at last to the blissful point where the path deigned to assume an approach to the horizontal, and led us to the most delightful spring in Kashmir! The water, ice-cold and clear, gushes out of a crevice in the rock, and with the joy of wandering Israelites we threw ourselves on the ground, basked in the glorious mountain air, and shouted for the tiffin basket.

Only the faithful "Yellow Bag" was forthcoming, the tiffin coolie being still "hull down," and from its varied contents we extracted the only edibles, apricots and rock cakes.

Never have we enjoyed any meal more than that somewhat light breakfast, washed down by water which was a pure joy to drink.

Alas! There were but two rock cakes apiece! Another half-hour's clamber, along a pretty rough track, brought us to a point whence we looked down a long green slope to our destination, Tronkol—a few Gujar huts, indistinct amidst a clump of very ancient birch-trees, standing out as a sort of oasis among the bare and boulder-strewn slopes.

The view was superb. To the right, the mountain-side fell steeply to where, in the depths of the Wangat Nullah, a tiny white thread marked the river foaming 4000 feet below, and beyond rose a jagged range of spires and pinnacles, snow lying white at the bases of the dark precipices. "These are the savage wilds" which bar the route from the Wangat into Tilail and the Upper Sind.

Over Tronkol, bare uplands, rising wave above wave, shut out the view of Gangabal and the track over into the Erin Nullah and down to Bandipur.

On our left towered the bastions of Haramok, his snow-crowned head rising grimly into the clear blue sky.

We pitched our camp at Tronkol about two o'clock, on a green level some little way beyond the Gujar huts, and just above a stream which picked its riotous way along a bed of enormous boulders, sheltered to a certain extent by a fringe of hoary birches.

We had never beheld such great birches as these, many of them, alas! mere skeletons of former grandeur, whose whitening limbs speak eloquently of a hundred years of ceaseless struggle with storm and tempest.

I saw no young ones springing up to replace these dying warriors. The Gujars and their buffaloes probably prevent any youthful green thing from growing. It seems a pity.

Towards evening we observed baggage ponies approaching, and at the sight we felt aggrieved; for, in our colossal selfishness, we fancied that Tronkol was ours, and ours alone. A small tent was pitched, and presently to our surly eyes appeared a lonely lady, who proceeded solemnly to play Patience in front of it while her dinner was being got ready.

A visit of ceremony, and an invitation to share our "irishystoo" and camp-fire, brought Mrs. Locock across, and we made the acquaintance of a lady well known for her prowess as a shikari throughout Kashmir—

> "There hunted 'she' the walrus, the narwal, and the seal.
> Ah! 'twas a noble game,
> And, like the lightning's flame;
> Flew our harpoons of steel"

I cannot resist the quotation, but I do not really think Mrs. Locock hunts walruses in Kashmir, and I know she doesn't use a harpoon. No matter, she proved a cheery and delightful companion, and we entirely forgave her for coming to Tronkol and poaching on our preserves.

We were extremely amused at the surprise she expressed at Jane's feat in climbing from Wangat. Evidently Jane's reputation is not that of a bullock-workman in Srinagar!

This morning we all three went to see Lake Gangabal. An easy path leads over some three or four miles of rolling down to our destination, which is one of a whole chain of lakes—or rather tarns—which lie under the northern slopes of Haramok.

We came first upon a small piece of water, lying blue and still in the morning sun, and from which a noisy stream poured forth its glacier water. This we had a good deal of trouble in crossing, the ladies being borne on the broad backs of coolies, in attitudes more quaint than graceful. A second and deeper stream being safely forded, we climbed a low ridge to find Gangabad stretched before us—a smooth plane of turquoise blue and pale icy green, beneath the dark ramparts of Haramok, whose "eagle-baffling" crags and glittering glaciers rose six thousand sheer feet above. In the foreground the earth, still brown, and only just released from its long winter covering of snow, bore masses of small golden ranunculus and rose-hued primulas.

An extraordinary sense of silence and solitude filled one—no birds or beasts were visible, and only the tinkle of tiny rills running down to the lake, and the distant clamour of the infant river, broke, or rather accentuated, the loneliness of the scene.

We had brought breakfast with us, and after eating it we made haste to recross the two rivers, because, troublesome as they were to ford in the morning, they would certainly grow worse with every hour of ice-melting sunshine.

Once more on the camp side, however, we strolled along in leisurely mood, staying to lunch on top of the ridge overlooking Tronkol. I left the ladies then to find their leisurely way back among the flowery hollows, and made for a peak overlooking the head of the Chittagul Nullah. A sharp climb up broken rocks and over snow slopes brought me to the top, a point some 13,500 feet above the sea. In front of me Haramok, seamed with snow-filled gullies, still towered far above; immediately below, the saddle—brown, bare earth, snow-streaked—divided the Chittagul Nullah from Tronkol. Far away down the valley the Sind River gleamed like a silver thread in the afternoon light, and beyond, the Wular lay a pale haze in the distance.

To the northward rose the fantastic range of peaks that overhang the Wangat gorge, and almost below my feet, at a depth of some 1500 feet, lay a sombre lakelet, steely dark and still, in the shadow of the ridge upon which I sat.

The sun was going down fast into a fleecy bed of clouds, amid which I knew that Nanga Parbat lay swathed from sight. To see that mountain monarch had been the chief object of my climb, so, recognising that the sight of him was a hope deferred, I made haste to scramble down to the tarn below, stopping here and there to fill my pith hat with wild rhubarb, and to pick or admire the new and always fascinating wild flowers as I passed. Large-flowered, white anemones; tiny gentian, with vivid small blue blossoms; loose-flowered, purple primulas, and many strange and novel blossoms starred the grassy patches, or filled the rocky crevices with abundant beauty.

By the lake side the moisture-loving, rose-coloured primula reappeared in masses, and as I followed down its outgoing stream towards the camp, I waded through a tangle of columbine, white and blue; a great purple salvia, arnica, and a profusion of varied flowers in rampant bloom.

Saturday, July 8.—An early start homewards yesterday, in the cold dawn, rewarded us by the sight of the first beams of the rising sun lighting up the threefold head of Haramok with an unspeakable glory, as we crossed the open boulder-strewn uplands, before descending into the nullah, which lay below us still wrapped in a mysterious purple haze. The downward zigzags, with their uncompromising steepness, proved almost as tiring as the ascent had been, and we were more than ready for breakfast by the time we reached the ruined temples of Vernag.

These temples, built probably about the beginning of the eighth century, are, like all the others which I have seen in Kashmir, small, and somewhat uninteresting, except to the archaeologist. They consist, invariably, of a "cella" containing the object of veneration, the lingam, surmounted by a high-pitched conical stone roof. In structure they show apparently signs of Greek influence in the doorways, and the triangular pediments above them. Phallic worship would seem to have been always confined to these temples, with ophiolatry—the nagas or water-snake deities being accommodated in sacred tanks, in the midst of which the early Kashmir temples were usually placed.

Any one who wishes to study the temple architecture of Kashmir cannot do better than read Fergusson's *Indian Architecture*, wherein he will find all the information he wants.

To the ordinary "man in the street" the ancient buildings of Kashmir do not appeal, either by their aesthetic value or by the dignity of size. Martand, the greatest, and probably the finest, both in point of grandeur and of situation, I regret to say, I did not see; but the temples at Bhanyar, Pandrettan, and Wangat resemble one another closely in design and general insignificance. The position of the Wangat ruins, embosomed in the wild tangle

"Of a steep wilderness, whose airy sides
With thicket overgrown, grotesque and wild,
Access denied; and overhead up grew
Insuperable height of loftiest shade,
Cedar, and pine, and fir,"

and seated at the base of a solemn circle of mountains, gives the group of tottering shrines a picturesqueness and importance which I cannot concede that they would otherwise have had.

I do not remember ever to have seen it noted that all buildings which are impressive by the mere majesty of size are to be found in plains and not in mountainous countries. This is probably due to two causes. The one being the denser population of the fat plains, whereby a greater concourse of builders and of worshippers would be sustained, and the other being the—probably unconscious—instinct which debarred the architect from attempting to vie with nature in the mountains and impel him to work out his most majestic designs amid wide and level horizons.

The fact remains, whatever may be the cause, that architecture has never been advanced much beyond the mere domestic in very mountainous regions, with the exception of the mediaeval strongholds, which formed the nucleus of every town or village, where a *point d'appui* was required against invasion, for the protection of the community.

Breakfast, followed by a prowl among the ruins and a short space for sketching, gave the sun time to pour his beams with quite unpleasant insistence into the confined fold in the hills, where we began to gasp until the ladies mounted their ponies, and we took our way down the valley, crossing the river below Wangat, and keeping along the left bank to Vernaboug, where we camped, the only incident of any importance being the sad loss of Jane's field-glasses, which, carried by her syce in a boot-bag, were dropped in a stream by that idiot while crossing, he having lost his footing in a pool, and, clutching wildly at the pony's reins, let go the precious binoculars.

This morning we were up betimes, Mrs. Locock having ordained a bear "honk"! This was, to me, a new departure in shikar, and truly it was amusing to see the shikari, bursting with importance, mustering the forty half-naked coolies whom he had collected to beat. A couple of men with tom-toms slung round their necks completed the party, which marched in straggling procession out of the village at dawn.

A mile of easy walking brought us to the rough jungly cliffs, seamed with transverse nullahs, narrow and steep, which bordered the river. Here we were placed in passes, with great caution and mystery, by the shikari and his chief-of-the-staff—the "oldest inhabitant" of Vernaboug; and here we sat in the morning stillness until a distant clamour and the faint beating of tom-toms afar off made us sit up more warily, and watch eagerly for the expected bear.

The yells increase, and the tom-toms, vigorously banged, seem calculated to fuss any self-respecting bear into fits. We watch a narrow space between two bushes some dozen yards away, and see that the Mannlicher across our knees and the smooth-bore, ball loaded in the right and chokeless barrel, lie handy for instant use.

Hidden in the dense jungle, some hundred yards below, sits Mrs. Locock on the matted top of a hazel, while Jane, chittering with suppressed excitement, crouches a few paces behind me.

The beaters approach, and pandemonium reigns. A few scared birds dart past, but no bear comes; and when the first brown body shows among the brushwood we shout to stop the uproar, and all move on to another beat.

Four "honks" produced nothing, so far as I was concerned; but a bear—according to her shikari—passed close by Mrs. Locock, so thickly screened by jungle that she couldn't see it. This may be so, but Kashmir shikaris have remarkably vivid imaginations.

After a delightful morning to all parties concerned—for we were much amused, the coolies were adequately paid, and the bear wasn't worried—we returned to breakfast, and then marched fifteen hot miles into Gunderbal, where we found the Smithsons, with whom we dined. They have been in Gurais and the Tilail district ever since they left Srinagar on the 24th April, and have had an adventurous and difficult time, with plenty of snow and torrents and avalanches, but somewhat poor sport.

This is not according to one's preconceived ideas of shikar in Kashmir, as they went into a nullah which no sahib had penetrated for five years; they had the best shikari in Kashmir (he said it, and he ought to know); they worked very hard, and their bag consisted of one or two moderate ibex and a red bear.

Tuesday, July 11.—On Sunday morning the combined fleet sailed for Palhallan. The Smithsons had a "matted dounga," and she "walked away" from our heavier ark down the winding Sind at a great pace. We reached Shadipur at 11 A.M., but the Smithsons had "gone before," so, crossing the Jhelum, we made after them in hot pursuit, and reached them and Palhallan at sunset.

A narrow canal, bordered by low swampy marshland, allowed us to get within a mile of the village and tie up among the shallows, whereupon the mosquitoes gathered from far and near, and fell upon us.

The final packing, effected amid a hungry crowd of little piping fiends, was a veritable nightmare, and yesterday morning we rescued our mangled remains from the enemy, and, having paid off our boats, hurriedly clambered on to the ponies which had come—late, as usual—from Palhallan to convey what was left by the mosquitoes to Gulmarg.

The unfortunate Jane—always a popular person—is especially so with insects; and if there is a flea or a mosquito anywhere within range it immediately rushes to her.

She paid dearly for her fatal gift of attractiveness at Palhallan—her eyes, usually so keen, being what is vulgarly termed "bunged up," and every vulnerable spot in like piteous plight!

We quitted Palhallan as the Lot family quitted Sodom and Gomorrah, but with no lingering tendency to look backward; we cast our eyes unto the hills, and kicked the best pace we could out of our "tattoos," halting for breakfast soon after crossing the hot, white road which runs from Baramula to Srinagar.

As we left the steamy valley and wound up a rapidly ascending path among the lower fringes and outliers of the forest our spirits rose, and by the time we had clambered up the last stiff pull and emerged from the darkly-wooded track into the little clearing, where perches the village of Babamarishi, we were positively cheerful.

Once more the air was fresh and buoyant, the spring water was cool and "delicate to drink," and from our tents we could look out over the valley lying dim in a yellow heat-haze far below.

Babamarishi is a picturesquely-grouped collection of the usual rickety-looking wooden huts, no dirtier, but perhaps noisier than usual, owing to the presence of a very holy ziarat much frequented by loudly conversational devotees. We spent the crisp, warm afternoon peacefully stretched on the sloping sward in front of our tents, and making the acquaintance of the only good thing that came out of Palhallan—a charming quartette of young geese which Sabz Ali had bought and brought.

These delightful birds evinced the most perfect friendliness and confidence in us, and we became greatly attached to them. They and the fowls seemed excellent travellers, and after a long day's march would come up smiling, like the jackdaw of Rheims, "not a penny the worse."

This morning we had but a short and easy march from Babamarishi to Gulmarg, along a good road, through a fine forest of silver fir.

CHAPTER XII
GULMARG

Somehow one's preconceived ideas of a place are almost always quite wrong, and so Gulmarg seemed quite different from what I had expected. It seemed all twisted the wrong way, and was really quite unlike the place which my imagination had evolved.

Turning through a narrow gap, we found ourselves facing a wide, green, undulating valley completely surrounded by dense fir forest. Beyond, to the left, rose the sloping bulk of Apharwat, one of the range of the Pir Panjal; while to the right low, wooded hillocks bounded the valley and fell, on their outward flanks, to the Kashmir plain.

Immediately in front of us a small village or bazaar swarmed with native life, and sloped down to a stream which wound through the hollows.

All round the edge of the forest a continuous ring of wooden huts and white tents showed that the "sahib" on holiday intent had marked Gulmarg for his own.

As we rode through the bazaar the view expanded. Apharwat showed all his somewhat disappointing face; his upper slopes, streaked with dirty snow, looked remarkably dingy when contrasted with the dazzling white clouds which went sailing past his uninteresting summit. The absence of all variety in form or light and shade, and the dull lines of his foreshortened front, made it hard to realise that he stood some five thousand feet above us.

Near the centre of the marg, on a small hill, was a large wooden building surrounded by many satellite huts and tents: this we rightly guessed to be Nedou's Hotel. Below, on a spur, was the little church, and to the right, in the hollow, the club-house faced the level polo-ground.

A winding stream, which we subsequently found to be perfectly ubiquitous, and an insatiable devourer of errant golf-balls, ran deviously through the valley, which seemed to be rather over a mile long, and almost equally wide.

The Smithsons rode away vaguely in search of a camping-ground; while we, having found out where our hut was, turned back and climbed a knoll behind the bazaar, and found ourselves in front of our future home, a very plain and roughly-built rectangular wooden hut, containing a small square room opening upon a verandah, and having a bedroom and bathroom on each side.

Such was our palace, and we were well satisfied with it.

The cook-house and servants' quarters were in a hut close by, and I could summon my retainers or chide them for undue chatter from my bedroom window—a serviceable short cut for the dinner, too, in wet and stormy weather!

Life at Gulmarg is extremely apt to degenerate into the "trivial round" of the golf links varied by polo, or polo varied by golf, with occasional gymkhanas and picnics. There are, doubtless, many delightful excursions to be made, but upon the whole it seems difficult to break far beyond the "Circular Road," a fairly level and well-kept bridle-path, which for eight beautiful miles winds through the pine forest, giving marvellous glimpses of snowy peaks and sunlit valleys.

The "Circular Road" is always fine, whether seen after rain, when, far below in the Ferozepore Nullah, the

> "Swimming vapour slopes athwart the glen,
> Puts forth an arm, and creeps from pine to pine,"

or when in the evening sunlight the whole broad Valley of Kashmir lies glowing at our feet, ringed afar by the ethereal mountains whose pale snows stand faint in the golden light, until beneath the yellowing sky the clouds turn rosy, and from their midst Haramok and Kolahoi raise their proud heads towards the earliest star.

The expedition to the top of Apharwat is, in my opinion, hardly worth making, but then I was not very lucky in the weather. Major Cardew, R.F.A., and I arranged to do the climb together, and duly started one excessively damp and foggy morning towards the middle of July.

Taking our ponies, we scrambled up a rough path through the forest to Killanmarg, a boulder-strewn slope, some half a mile wide, which lies between the upper edge of the forest and the final slopes of the mountain.

Sending our ponies home, we set about the ascent of the 3500 feet that remained between us and our goal. The whole hillside was a perfect wild garden. Columbines, potentillas—yellow, bronze, and crimson—primulas, anemones, gentian, arnica, and quantities of unknown blossoms gave us ample excuse for lingering panting in the rarefied air, as we struggled through brushwood first, and then over loose rocks and finally slopes of shelving snow, before we found ourselves on the crest of the mountain, shivering slightly in the raw, foggy air.

Our view was narrowed down to the bleak slopes of rock and snow that immediately surrounded us, for our hope that we should get above the cloud belt was not fulfilled, and beyond a dismal tarn, lying just below us, in whose black waters forlorn little bergs of rotten snow floated, and a very much circumscribed view of dull tops swathed in flying mist, we saw nothing.

Had the sky been clear, I am told that the view would have been magnificent, but I should think probably no better than that from Killanmarg, as it is a mistake to suppose that a high, or at least too high, elevation "lends enchantment." As a rule the view is finer when seen half-way up a lofty mountain than that obtained from the summit.

We did not stay long upon the top of Apharwat discussing the best point of view, because Cardew sagaciously remarked that if it grew much thicker he wouldn't be answerable for finding the way down, and as I have a holy horror of rambling about strange (and possibly precipitous) mountains in a fog, we set about retracing our own footsteps in the snow until we regained the ridge we had come up by.

A remarkably wet couple we were when we presented ourselves at our respective front doors, just in time for a "rub down" before lunch!

The golf at Gulmarg is very good, the 18-hole course being exceedingly sporting, and tricky enough to defeat the very elect. Jane and I had conveyed our clubs out to Kashmir, knowing that they were likely to prove useful. I had also taken the precaution to pack up a box or two of balls, but I found my labour all in vain, as "Haskells" and "Kemshall-Arlingtons" were supplied by the club at precisely the same price as in England—viz., 1 r. 8 an., or two shillings.

New clubs are also cheap and in plenty, but repairs to old favourites are not always satisfactory. My pet driver, having been damaged, was very evilly treated by the native craftsman, who bound up its wounds with large screws!

The mountains of Kashmir have been a constant joy to us. Varying with every change of light and shade, custom cannot stale their infinite variety; but as yet I had not seen the great monarch of Chilas, Nanga Parbat.

In July and early August he is rarely visible from Gulmarg, owing to the haziness of the atmosphere. One clear morning, however, towards the end of July, after a night of rain and storm, I was strolling along the Circular Road when, lo! far away in the north-west, soaring ethereal above the blue ranges that overlook Gurais, above the cloud-banks floating beyond their summits, the great mountain, unapproachable in his glory, stood revealed.

The early morning sun struck full on his untrodden snows, making it hard to realise that eighty-five miles of air separated me from that clear-cut peak. Soon, very soon, a light cloud clung to his eastern face, and within ten minutes the whole vision had faded into an up-piled tower of seething clouds.

Later in the season, as the air grew clearer, Jane and I made almost daily pilgrimages to the point, only a few minutes' walk from our hut, whence, framed by a foreground of columnar pines, Nanga Parbat could generally be seen for a time in the morning.

Tuesday, August 1.—Society in Gulmarg is particularly cheery, as indeed might be expected where two or three hundred English men and women are gathered together to amuse themselves and lay in a fresh store of health and energy before returning to the routine of duty in the plains.

There have been many picnics lately, the little glades or margs, which are frequent in the forest slopes, being ideal places of rendezvous for merrymakers on horse or foot. Picnics of all sorts and sizes, from the little impromptu gatherings of half-a-dozen congenial young souls (always an even number, please), who ride off into the romantic shades to nibble biscuits and make tea, to the dainty repasts provided by a hospitable lady, whose official hut overlooks the Ferozepore Nullah, and who, in turn, overlooks her cook, to the great gratification of her guests.

How small a thing will upset the best-laid plans of hospitality! It is said that a most carefully planned picnic, where all the little tables, set for two, were discreetly screened apart among the bushes, was entirely ruined by a piratical damsel undertaking a cutting-out expedition for the capture of the hostess' best young man.

Our evenings are by no means dull. On many a starlit night has Jane mounted the noble steed which, through the kindness of the Resident, we have hired from the "State," and ridden across the marg attended by her slaves (her husband and the ancient shikari, to wit), to dine and play bridge in some hospitable hut, or dance or see theatricals at Nedou's Hotel.

Last week we tore ourselves away from our daily golf, and joined the Smithsons in a futile expedition to the foot of the Ferozepore Nullah for bear. Three days we spent in vain endeavour to find "baloo," and on the fourth we wended our toilsome way up the hill again to Gulmarg.

Monday, August 27.—There are drawbacks as well as advantages in being perched, as it were, just above the bazaar. Its proximity enables our good Sabz Ali to sally forth each morning and secure the earliest consignment of "butter and eggs and a pound of cheese," which has come up from Srinagar, and select the best of the fruit and vegetables. It affords also an interesting promenade for the geese, who solemnly march down the main street daily for recreation and such stray articles of food as may be found in the heterogeneous rubbish-heaps.

It possesses, however, a superabundance of pi-dogs, who gather together on the slope in front of our hut in the watches of the night, and serenade us to a maddening extent.

The natives, too, have a sinful habit of chattering and shouting at an hour when all well-conducted persons should be steeped in their beauty sleep.

A few nights ago this culminated in what Keats would have called a "purple riot." The sweeper and his friends were holding a meeting for the purpose of conversation and the consumption of apple brandy.

Having fruitlessly sent the shikari to try and stop the insufferable noise, I was fain to sally forth myself to investigate matters.

Then to a happy and light-hearted party seated chattering round a blazing fire there came suddenly the unwelcome apparition of an exceedingly irate sahib, in evening dress and pumps, brandishing a khudstick.

A wild scurry, in which the bonfire was scattered, a few remarks in forcible English, a whack which just missed the hindmost reveller, and the place became a deserted village.

Next morning Sabz Ali came to me in a towering rage to report that the sweeper—that unclean outcast—had dared to say most opprobrious things to him, being inspired thereto by the devil and apple brandy. Nothing less than the immediate execution of the culprit by hanging, drawing, and quartering would satisfy the outraged feelings of our henchman.

I promised a yet severer punishment. I said I would "cut" the wretched minion's pay that month to the amount of a rupee. Vengeance was satisfied, and the victim reduced to tears.

It is good to hear Jane—who for many years has been accustomed to having her own way in all household matters—ordering breakfast.

"Well, Sabz Ali—what shall we have for breakfast to-morrow?"

"Jessa mem-sahib arder!"—with a friendly grin.

"Then I shall have kidneys."'

"No kidney, mem-sahib! Kidney plenty money—two annas six pice ek. Oh, plenty dear!"

"I'm tired of eggs. Is there any cold chicken you could grill?"

"Chota murghi one egg lay, mem-sahib, anda poach. Sahib, chicken grill laike!"

"Oh, all right! But I thought of a mutton-chop for the major sahib."

"Muttony stup" (mutton's tough). "Sahib no laike!"

"Very well, that will do—a poached egg for me and grilled chicken for the sahib."

"No, mem-sahib—no 'nuf. Sahib plenty 'ungry—chicken grill, peechy ramble-tamble egg!"

"Have it your own way. I daresay the major sahib *would* like scrambled eggs, and we'll have coffee—not tea."

"No, mem-sahib. No coffee—coffee finish!"

"Send the shikari down to the bazaar, then, for a tin of coffee from Nusserwanjee."

"Shikari saaf kuro lakri ke major sahib" (cleaning the golf-clubs). "Tea breakfast, coffee kal" (to-morrow).

And, utterly routed on every point, Jane gives in gracefully, and makes an excellent breakfast as prearranged by Sabz Ali!

The news is spread that there will be an exhibition of pictures held in Srinagar in September. Every second person is a—more or less—heaven-born artist out here, so there promises to be no lack of exhibits. I dreamed a dream last night, and in my dream I was walking along the bund and came upon an elderly gentleman laying Naples yellow on a canvas with a trowel. The river was smooth and golden, and reflected the sensuous golden tones of the sky. Trees arose from golden puddles, half screening a ziarat which, upon the glowing canvas, appeared remarkably like a village church. "How beautiful!" I cried, "how gloriously oleographic!" and the painter, removing a brush from his mouth, smiled, well pleased, and said, "I am a Leader among Victorian artists and the public adores me!" and I left him vigorously painting pot-boilers. Then in a damp dell among the willows of the Dal I found a foreigner in spectacles, and the light upon his pictures was the light that never was on sea or land; but through a silvery mist the willows showed ghostly grey, and a shadowy group of classic nymphs were ringed in the dance, and I cried "O Corot! lend me your spectacles. I fain, like you, would see crude nature dimmed to a silvery perpetual twilight." And Corot replied: "Mon ami moi je ne vois jamais le soleil, je me plonge toujours, dans les ombres bleuâtres et les rayons pâles de l'aube."

Then upward I fared till, treading the clear heights, I found one frantically painting the peaks and pinnacles of the mountains in weird stipples of alternate red and blue.

"Great heavens!" I exclaimed, "what disordered manner is this!"

The artist glanced swiftly at me, and said disdainfully: "I am a modern of the moderns, and if you cannot see that mountains are like that, it is your fault—not mine. Go back, you stand too close."

And as I went back I looked over my shoulder, and, truly, the flaring rose-colour had blended amicably with the blue, and I admitted that perhaps Segantini was not so mad as he looked.

A little lower down a stout Scotchman painted a flowery valley. The flowers were many and bright, but not so garish as they appeared to him, and I hinted as much; but he scorned my criticism.

"Mon," he shouted, "I painted the Three Graces, an' they made me an Academeesian. I painted a flowery glen in the Tyrol (dearie me, but thae flowers cost me a fortune in blue paint), and it was coft for the Chantry Bequest, and hoo daur *you* talk to me?"

Then I departed hurriedly and came upon four men, two of them with long beards, and all with unkempt hair, laboriously depicting a blue pine, needle by needle, and every one in its proper place. I asked them if theirs was not a very troublesome way of painting.

They looked at one another with earnest blue eyes, and remarked that here was evidently a Philistine who knew not Cimabue and cared not a jot for Giotto; and the first said: "Sir, methinks he who would climb the golden stairs should do so step by step;" and the second said, sadly: "We are but scapegoats, truly, being cast forth by the vindictive Victorians of our day."

The third murmured in somewhat broken English.

"Victoria Victrix,
Beata Beatrix,"

whereby I recognised him to be a poet, if not a painter.

But the fourth—an energetic-looking man with a somewhat arrogant manner—said briskly: "Perchance the ass is right; these pine needles are becoming monotonous, and I have seventeen million four hundred and sixty-two thousand five hundred and eleven more to do. Beshrew me if I do not take to pot-boiling!"

Down by the water-side a lady sat, sketching in water-colours for dear life; around her lay a litter of half-finished works, scattered like autumn leaves in Vallombrosa. I approached her, quite friendly, and offered to gather them up for her—at least some of them, saying soothingly, for I saw she was in a temper—

"Dear, dear, Clara, why, what *is* the matter?"

"I am painting the Venice of the East," she cried petulantly, "but for the life of me I can't see a campanile, and how can I possibly paint a picture without a campanile?"

I understood that, of course, she couldn't, so I stole away softly on tip-toe, leaving her turning doungas into gondolas for all she was worth.

A dark, dapper man, with an alert air and an eyeglass, sat near the seventh bridge, writing. Beside him stood an easel and other painting-gear. I asked him what he was doing, and he answered, with a fine smile, "I am gently making enemies;" so, to turn the subject, I picked up a large canvas, smeared over with invisible grey, like the broadside of a modern battleship, and sprinkled here and there with pale yellow blobs.

"What have we here, James?" I inquired cheerfully, and he, staying his claw-like hand in mid-air, made reply—

"A chromatic in tones of sad colour, with golden accidentals—Kashmir night-lights."

"Ah! quite so," I exclaimed; "but have I got it right side up?"

He looked at it doubtfully for a moment, then, pointing to a remarkable butterfly (*Vanessa Sifflerius*) depicted in the corner, cried: "It's all right; you'll never make a mistake if you keep this insect in the *right bottom corner*. It is put there on purpose."

Lastly, on an eminence I saw a man like an eagle, sitting facing full the sun, and upon his glowing canvas was portrayed the heavens above and the earth beneath and the waters under the earth, and behind him sat one who patted him upon the back, and looked at intervals over his shoulder at the glorious work, and then wrote in a book a eulogy thereof; and I, too, came and looked over the painter's shoulder, and I muttered, with Oliver Wendell Holmes,

> "The foreground golden dirt,
> The sunshine painted with a squirt."

Then the man who patted the painter on the back turned upon me aggressively, and said: "This is the only painter who ever was, or will be, and if you don't agree with me you are a fool." The painter, smiling a sly

Monna-Lisan smile of triumph, remarked: "Right you are, John. I rather think this *will* knock that rascal Claude," and I laughed so that I awoke; but the memory of the dream remained with me, and it seemed to me that, perhaps, we poor amateurs might not be any better able to compass aught but caricatures of this marvellous scenery than the ghostly limners of my dream!

The hut just above ours was tenanted by a party of three young Lancers on leave from Rawal Pindi, a gramophone, and a few dogs.

One of the soldiers was laid up with a bad ankle, and it soon became a daily custom for Jane or me to play a game of chess or piquet with the invalid.

Later on, when leave had expired for the hale, when the dogs had departed, and the voice of the gramophone was no more heard in the land, we came to see a great deal of the wounded warrior, and finally arranged to personally conduct him off the premises, and return him, in time for medical survey, to Rawal Pindi.

Many years ago I read a delightful poem called *The Paradise of Birds* — I believe it was by Mortimer Collins,[1] but I am not sure. Now the Poet (who, together with Windbag, sailed to this very paradise of birds) deemed that this happy asylum of the feathered fowls was somewhere at the back of the North Pole. He cannot have known of Kashmir, or he would assuredly have sent the persecuted birds thither, and placed the "Roc's Egg" as janitor, somewhere by the portals of the Jhelum Valley. Kashmir is truly and indeed the paradise of birds, for there no man molests them, and no schoolboy collects eggs, and the result is a fascinating fearlessness, the result of perpetual peace and plenty.

[1] It is by Courthope, not Collins.

I regret exceedingly that my ornithological knowledge is extremely limited. I could find no books to help me,[2] and, as I did not care to kill any birds merely to enable me to identify their species, my notes were merely "popular" and not "scientific."

[2] See Appendix II.

Shall I confess that I began an erudite work on the birds of Kashmir, but got no further than the Hoopoe? It began as follows: —

THE HOOPOE

Early history of. — Tereus, King of Thrace, annoyed his wife Procne so much by the very marked attention which he paid to her sister Philomela, that she lost her temper so far as to chop up her son Itylus, and present him to his papa in the form of a ragoût.

This, naturally, disgusted Tereus very much, and he "fell upon" the ladies with a sword, but, just as he was about to stab them to the heart, he was changed into a Hoopoe, Philomela into a nightingale, Procne into a swallow, while Itylus became a pheasant.

> "Vertitur in volucrem, cui stant in vertice cristæ
> Prominet immodicum pro longa cuspide rostrum;
> N epops volucri."

OVID, Metam. lib. vi.

His crest and patent of nobility.—Once upon a time, King Solomon, while making a royal progress, was much, incommoded by the powerful rays of the sun, and as he had ascendency over the birds, and knew their language, he called upon the vultures to come and fly betwixt the sun and his nobility, but the vultures refused. Then the kindly Hoopoes assembled, and flew in close mass above his head, thus forming a shade under which he proceeded on his journey in ease and comfort.

At sundown the monarch sent for the King of the Hoopoes, and desired him to name a reward for the service which he and his followers had rendered.

Then the King of the Hoopoes answered that nothing could be more glorious than the golden crown of King Solomon; and so Solomon decreed that the Hoopoes should thenceforward wear golden crowns as a mark of his favour. But alas! when men found the Hoopoes all adorned with golden crowns, they pursued and slew them in great multitudes for greed of the precious metal, until the King of the Hoopoes, in heavy sorrow, hied hastily to King Solomon, and begged that the gift of the golden crowns might be rescinded, ere every Hoopoe was slain.

Then Solomon, seeing the misery they had brought upon themselves by their presumption, transformed their crowns of gold to crowns of feathers, which no man coveted (for the Eastern ladies didn't wear hats), and the Hoopoes wear them to this day as a mark of royal favour, but all the feathers fell off the necks of the disobliging vultures.

His amazing talent.—In those dark ages ... the Hoopoe was considered as prodigiously skilful in defeating the machinations of witches, wizards, and hobgoblins. The female, in consequence of this art, could preserve her offspring from these dreaded injuries.

She knew all the plants which defeat fascinations, those which give sight to the blind; and, more wondrous still, those which open gates or doors, locked, bolted, or barred.

Aelian relates that a man having three times successively closed the nest of a Hoopoe, and having remarked the herb with which the bird, as often, opened it, applied the same herb, and *with the same success*, to charm the locks off the strongest coffer.—*Naturalists' Magazine* (about 1805).

His personal appearance.—The beak is bent, convex and sub-compressed, and in some degree obtuse; the tongue is obtuse, triangular and very short, and the feet are ambulatory. As this bird has a great abundance of feathers, it appears considerably thicker than it is. It is, in fact, about the size of a mistletoe thrush, but looks, while in its feathers, to be as large as a common pigeon.—*Naturalists' Magazine.*

I had got *no* further in my *magnum opus*, when I unfortunately showed my notes to Colonel—well, I will not mention his name, but he is the greatest authority on the birds and beasts of Kashmir. He besought me to spare him, pathetically remarking that I should cut the ground from under his feet, and take the bread out of his mouth, and the wind out of his sails, if I went any further with my monograph on the Hoopoe. He saw at a glance that I was conversant with authorities whom he had never consulted, and possessed a knowledge of my subject to which he could hardly aspire, so I gracefully agreed to leave the field to him, and relinquished my *magnum opus* in its very inception.

One of the chiefest charms of Kashmir, and one which is apt to be overlooked, is the entirely unspoilt freshness of its scenery. No locust horde of personally-conducted "trippers" pollutes its ways and byways, nor has the khansamah of the dâk bungalow as yet felt constrained to add sauerkraut and German sausage to his bill of fare—for which Allah be praised!

The world is growing very small, and the globe-trotter rushes round it in eighty days. The trail of the cheap excursionist is all over Europe, from the North Cape to Tarifa, from the highest Alpine summit (which he attains in comfort by a funicular railway) to the deepest mines of Cornwall. Egypt has become his footstool, and the shores of the Mediterranean his wash-pot. Niagara is mapped and labelled for his benefit, and the Yosemite is his happy hunting-ground. He "does" the West Indies in "sixty days for sixty pounds," and he is now arranging a special cheap excursion from the Cape to Cairo. "But," it may be remarked, "what were Jane and I but globe-trotters'? and am I not trying to sing the praises of Kashmir with the avowed object of inducing people to go out and see it for themselves?"

By all manner of means let us travel. Far be it from me to wish folks to stay dully at home, while the wonders and beauties of the wide world lie open for the admiration and education of its inhabitants.

But there are globe-trotters and globe-trotters. My objection is only to those—alas! too numerous—vagrants who cannot go abroad without casting shame on the country which bred them; whose vulgarity causes offence in church and picture-gallery; who cannot see a monument or a statue without desiring to chip off a fragment, or at least scrawl their insignificant names upon it.

From these, and such as these, Kashmir is as yet free; but some day, I suppose, it will be "opened up," when the railway, which is already contemplated, is in going order between Pindi and Srinagar, and cheap excursion tickets are issued from Berlin and Birmingham.

Here is a specimen page of the Guide Book (bound in red) for 19—(?):

"Ascend Apharwat by the funicular railway. The neat little station, with its red corrugated-iron roof, makes a picturesque spot of colour near the Dobie's Ghât. Fares, 4 an. 6 pi., all the way."

"A local guide should on no account be omitted (several are always to be found near the station leaning on their khudsticks, and discussing controversial theology in the sweet low tones so noticeable in the Kashmiri). See that he be provided with a horn, to the hooting of which the Echo Lake will be found responsive."

"From the balcony of the * Hôtel Baloo an unrivalled view of Nanga Parbat should be obtained. Glasses can be procured from the anna-in-the-slot machines which are dotted about."

"This veritable king of the Himal—" (here follows a pageful of regulation guide-book gush).

"Good sport is to be obtained from the obliging and enterprising manager of the hotel, Herr Baer. A few rupees will purchase the privilege of shooting at that monarch of the mountains, the markhor. Start not, fair tourist, for no danger lurks in the sport. No icy precipices need be scaled, no giddy gulfs explored, and the only danger which menaces the bold hunter in the mimic stalk, is that which menaces his shins in the broken soda-water bottles and sharp-edged sardine tins with which the summit of Apharwat is strewn."

"As a matter of fact, the consumption of mutton is considerable in the Hôtel Baloo in the tourist season, and the worthy Baer conceived the brilliant and financially sound scheme of attaching some old ibex and markhor horns (bought cheap when the old library at Srinagar was swept away in the last flood) to his live stock, and turning his decorated flock loose on the mountain's brow, where the sportsman saves him the trouble of slaughter while enjoying all the excitement and none of the difficulty of a veritable stalk."

"Another brilliant invention of the good Baer is his 'sunset spectacles.' These are made with the glasses in two halves—the upper part orange and the lower one purple. These are simply invaluable to those who have only a brief half-hour in which to 'do' Apharwat before darting down to catch the 3.15 express for Leh (*viâ* the newly opened Zoji La tunnel), since for the modest sum of 8 a. a superb sunset can be enjoyed at any time of the day."

"Should, however, the leisured globe-trotter have unlimited time at his disposal, he would do well to lunch at the Hôtel Baloo, in order to taste the celebrated Kashmir sauerkraut (made of wild rhubarb) and Gujar pie (composed of the most tempting tit-bits of the water buffalo), before returning to the 'Savoy' at Srinagar by the turbine tram from Tangmarg, or by the pneumatic launch which leaves Palhallan Pier every ten minutes, weather permitting."

"Should the tourist be a naturalist he can hardly fail to observe, and be interested in, the mosquitoes of this charming and picturesque locality. He will note that they rival the song-thrush in magnitude and the Bengal tiger in ferocity. A coating of tar laid with a trowel over the exposed parts of the body will be found the best protection, especially as the new Armour Company's patent hermetically sealed bear-proof visor will be found too hot for comfort in summer."

"The environs of Srinagar are charming. Notice the picturesque 'furnished apartments' for paying guests all along the water-side, and the mixed bathing establishments, crowded daily by the Smart Set, whose jewelled pyjamas flash in rivalry of the heliographic oil-tins which deck the neighbouring temples."

"By a visit to the Museum, and an inspection by eye and nose of the quaint specimens of antique clothing exhibited there, the intelligent and imaginative traveller may conjure up a mental picture of the unpolished appearance of the old-time Mangi and his lady before he adopted the tall hat and frock coat of civilisation, or she had discovered the 'swanbill'!"

CHAPTER XIII
THE FLOOD

Tuesday, *September* 12.—A second edition of the Noachian deluge is upon us! It began to rain on Saturday, at the close of a hot and stuffy week, and, having succeeded in thoroughly soaking the unfortunate ladies who were engaged in a golf competition that day, it proceeded to rain abundantly all through Sunday and Monday.

The outlook from our hut is dispiriting; through a thick grey veil of vapour the gleam of water shines over the swamp that was the polo-ground. The little muddy stream in which so many erring golf-balls lie low is up and out for a ramble over its banks. The lower golf-greens resemble paddy-fields, and round the marg the spires of dull grey pines stand dripping in a steadfast shower-bath.

Sometimes the heavy cloud folds everything in its leaden wing, blotting out even the streaming village at our feet, and reducing our view to the immediate slope below us where the wilted ragwort and rank weeds bend before the tiny torrents which trickle everywhere. Then comes a break, falsely suggestive of an improvement, and lo! soaring above the cloudy boil, the lofty shoulders of Apharwat sheeted in new-fallen snow!

After the somewhat oppressive heat of last week, the sudden raw cold strikes home, and Jane and I take a great interest in the fire, the "Old Snake"[1] is an accomplished fire-master, and it is pleasant to watch him squatting like an ungainly frog in front of the hearth, and sagaciously feeding the flame with damp and spitting logs.

[1] Our pet name for Shikari Mark II., who reigns in the stead of Ahmed Bot, sacked for expensive inefficiency.

It is amazing what lavish expenditure of fuel one will indulge in when it costs nothing a ton!

We are just beginning to find out the exact spots where chairs may be planted so as to avoid the searching draughts which go far to make our happy home like a very airy sort of bird-cage.

Well! we might have been worrying through all this in a sodden tent, where even a boarded floor would barely have kept out rheumatism, and where one would have been liable to alarms and excursions at all sorts of untoward times when drains wanted deepening and guys slackening. The mere thought of such things sent us into a truly thankful state of mind, and we discussed from our cosy chairs the probable condition of the party from the Residency which set forth, full of high hope, on Saturday morning to attack the markhor of Poonch.

Here it has rained with vehemence ever since they left; up in the high ground it has doubtless snowed; and although they were well armed with cards and whisky, yet it would appear but a poor business to play bridge all day in a snow-bound tent on the top of the Pir Panjal! Nothing short of a hundred aces every few minutes could make the game worth the candle!

This spell of bad weather has greatly interfered with the movements of a large number of the folks who were to leave Gulmarg early this week. Many got away betimes on Saturday, and a few faced the elements on Sunday, and a painful experience they must have had.

We had intended to leave next Thursday, and had ordered boats to meet us at Parana Chauni, but the road will be so bad that I wired this morning to put off our transport till further orders.

The end of the season at Gulmarg sees the bazaar stock at low water. Eggs, fowls, cherry brandy, and spirits of wine are "off," also butter, but the latter scarcity does not affect us, as we make our own in a pickle jar. The bazaar butter became very bad, probably because the large numbers of visitors to Gulmarg caused an additional supply to be got from uncleanly Gujars, so we, by the kindness of the Assistant Resident, had a special cow detailed to supply us daily with milk at our own door.

That cow was very friendly; I first made its acquaintance one forenoon. While I was sitting below the verandah sketching, with a dozen lovely peaches spread by me on the hoards to obtain their final touch of perfection in the sun before lunch, the cow strolled up. I was much interested in the sketch, and believed that the cow was too; but when I looked up at last, expecting to see its eye fixed upon the work in silent approbation,

"The 'cow' was still there, but the 'peaches' were gone."

In the afternoon the weather showed signs of a desire to amend its ways. The clouds broke here and there, and, though it still rained heavily, it became apparent that the clerk of the weather had done his worst, and the supply of rain was running short. Clad in aquascutic garments, and surmounted by an ungainly two-rupee bazaar umbrella (my dapper British one having been annexed by a covetous Mangi)—

> "Ombrifuge, Lord love you, case o' rain,
> I flopped forth 'sbuddikins on my own ten toes."

The whole slope in front of the hut was a trickle of water, threading the dying stalks of dock and ragwort, and hurrying down to add its dirty pittance to the small yellow torrent rushing along the greasy strip of clay that in happier days was the path.

The whole marg was become lake or stream—lake over the polo-ground and half the golf-links—fed by the weeping slopes on every side, whence innumerable rills rioted over the grass, emulating in ferocity and haste, if not in size, the tawny torrents which drained the sides of Apharwat.

The road from the bazaar to the club was all but impassable, but as it had still a few inches of freeboard, I followed it to the foot of the church slope, and, skirting the hill, inspected the desolation which had been wrought at the Kotal hole, where the stream had torn through its banks and wrecked the green.

During a visit of condolence to Mrs. Smithson, whose unfortunate husband is pursuing markhor in Poonch, the sky cleared—a splendid effort in the way of a "clearing shower" being followed by a decided break-up of the pall of wet cloud in which we have been too long immersed. Not without a severe struggle did Jupiter Pluvius consent to turn off the tap, but at length the sun broke through the hanging clouds and sent their sodden grey fragments swirling up the Ferozepore Nullah to break in foamy wreaths round the ragged cliffs of Kulan.

Finding the road across to the post-office altogether under water for some distance—a lake extending from the twelfth hole for nearly a quarter of a mile to the main road—I wandered back towards the higher ground, joining a waterproof figure, a member of the Green Committee, who was sadly regarding the water-logged links with the disconsolate air of the raven let loose from the ark! We agreed that this was a remarkably good opportunity for observing the drainage system, and taking notes for future guidance, and in company we went over as much of the links as possible, finishing below the second hole, where the cross stream which comes down from the higher ground had torn away the bridge and cut off the huts beyond from civilisation.

The homeward stroll at sunset was perfectly beautiful, and showed Gulmarg in an absolutely new guise. The lower part of the marg, being all lake, reflected the lustrous golden sky and rich dark pine-woods in a faithful mirror. Flying fragments of cloud, fleeces of gold and crimson, clung to the mountain-sides or sailed above the forests, while beyond Apharwat, coldly clad in a pure white mantle of snow, new fallen, rose silhouetted against the darkening sky.

Saturday, September 16. — After the Deluge came the Exodus, everybody trying to leave Gulmarg at once. We had always intended to go down to Srinagar about the 15th, but, finding that the Residency party meant to move on that day, we arranged to migrate a day earlier in order to avoid the pony and coolie famine which a Residential progress entails on the ordinary traveller.

On Wednesday afternoon the ten ponies, carefully ordered a week before from the outlying villages, were congregated on the weedy slope which falls away from our verandah, picking up a scanty sustenance from decaying ragwort and such like.

Secure in the possession of the necessary transport, Jane and I strolled forth for a last look at Nanga Parbat, should he haply deign to be on view. He did not deign, however, preferring to remain, like Achilles, when bereft of Briseis, sulking in his cloudy tent. So we consoled ourselves with an exceedingly fine view of the snow-crowned heights at the head of the Ferozepore Nullah. Upon returning to our beloved log cabin we were met by Sabz Ali—almost speechless with wrath—who broke to us the distressing news that six of our ten weight-carriers had departed from the compound. The entire staff, with the exception of our factotum, were away in pursuit, and there was nothing for it but to possess our souls in what patience we might until they returned.

As we had arranged for a four o'clock start next morning, it was most disconcerting to have all our transport desert so late in the evening. An urgent note to the Assistant Resident, and some pressure on the Tehsildhar, produced promise of assistance.

Early on Thursday morning came an indignant chit from an irate General, complaining that my servants were trying to seize his ponies, for which he had paid an advance of two rupees, and would I be good enough to investigate the affair. Here was the murder out. His chuprassie had obviously bribed my pony wallahs, and a letter, stating my case pretty clearly, produced the ponies and an apology.

This delay kept us till after midday, when, stowing our invalid snugly in a dandy, we left Gulmarg and began the descent to Srinagar. I remained behind to see the hut clear and make a sketch, and then hurried down the direct path, which drops some 2000 feet to Tangmarg. Here I found Jane and the invalid comfortably disposed in a landau, but the baggage spread about anywhere, and the usual clamour of coolies uprising in the heated and dust-laden air.

No ekka—the one which had been ordered with the landau having apparently got another job and departed. Presently a stray ekka, drawn by a sorely weary-looking mule, appeared on the scene, and we seized upon it instantly, loaded it up with most of the baggage, and despatched coolies with the rest.

After the storm came a holy calm, and we settled down to a light but welcome lunch before starting down the long slope into the valley.

We had heard most disquieting tales of floods; the water had burst the bund at Srinagar, and there was said to be ten feet over the polo-ground. The occupants of Nedou's Hotel were going in and out by boat, and Srinagar itself was said to be quite cut off from all access by road.

The Residency party have countermanded their intended move to-morrow.

At the post-office I was told that only a small part of the mail had been brought into Srinagar, the road being "bund" between Baramula and that place, while an unusual number of landslips and bridges have come down in the Jhelum Valley.

Nevertheless, we had made a push to get on; things in Kashmir are often less gloomy than their reports would make one believe, and so we bowled quite cheerfully down the road from Tangmarg, basking in the hot and sunny air, which seemed to us really delicious after the raw cheerlessness of the last few days at Gulmarg.

From Tangmarg to the dâk bungalow at Margam, a steady descent is maintained by an excellent road over the sloping Karewa, for about ten miles, of which we had just about travelled half when a series of yells from the syce behind, a wild swerve, and a heavy plump brought us up just on the edge of the steep and rocky bank, which fell sharply from the roadside.

Alas! the axle of the off hind wheel had snapped, and the wheel itself was hopelessly lying in the thick white dust, and our landau looked like an ancient three-decker in a squall.

The horses being unharnessed, we sent the drivers with one of them forward to look for help, and Hesketh and Jane proceeded to make tea while I sat by the roadside and sketched.

Presently an empty dandy came "dribbling by" on its return journey to Gulmarg, and it was immediately impressed for the benefit of the lame.

Hardly had we packed him in, when a wandering tonga hove in sight, and, being promptly requisitioned, we rattled off the five miles which lay between us and Margam in no time.

Here we found a large party assembled in the little rest-house. Colonel and Mrs. Maxwell (who had kindly sent us back the tonga on hearing of the breakdown); Mr. and Mrs. Allen Baines, whose dandy had been the means of bringing Hesketh along; and Sadleir-Jackson, and Edwards of the 9th Lancers.

The bungalow was full, but I found out that one room was appropriated by a coming event, who had cast his shadow before him in the guise of a bearer. This being contrary to the etiquette as observed in dâk bungalows, I gently but firmly cleared out the neatly arranged toilet things and ready-made bed; while Hesketh was taken over, somewhat shattered by his tedious though exciting day, by his fellow Lancers.

The resources of the little place were severely strained; dinner was a scanty meal, and soda-water gave out almost immediately: nevertheless, a cheroot and a rubber of bridge sent us contented to bed.

Yesterday (Friday) the question of how to proceed arose. The road was reported to be impassable after about five miles, the remaining ten being under water.

We set out after breakfast, Jane perched on a pony which Sabz Ali had raised or stolen, Hesketh in the dandy, and I on foot. After a warm five miles' march we came upon signs of a block. Vehicles of many and strange sorts were drawn up in the shade of a chenar, under whose wide branches the Baines family was faring sumptuously on biscuits and brandy and water.

Horses, goats, and cattle strayed around, and a chattering mob of natives, busily engaged, as usual, in doing nothing, completed the picture.

Hesketh was reduced to despair; after two months in bed, this could not but be a trying journey under the most favourable circumstances, and the prospect as held out by his pessimistic bearer was pretty gloomy—no boats available, and no signs of our doungas.

I pushed on to the break in search of my shikari, whom I had sent on by pony early in the morning, and soon found that estimable person, who is not really the blithering idiot he looks!

In the first place, he had appropriated the only two shikaras he could find, and our baggage was already being stowed in them; secondly, he had discovered both Juma and Ismala, our Mangis, who reported the doungas moored below Parana Chaum, about four miles away over the flooded fields.

This was good news, and we ate a cheerful lunch under a tree densely populated by jackdaws.

The Maxwells got away somehow in search of their house-boat, which was supposed to have left Baramula some days ago. They started cheerfully, but vaguely, down the Spill Canal, and we trust they found their ark somewhere!

Promising to send back a boat for the Baines, we paid and dismissed coolies and ponies, and paddled away over the flood water. The country was simply a vast lake, the main road merely marked by a dense row of poplars. Trees rose promiscuously out of the calm and sunlit water, wisps of maize and wreckage clinging to their lower boughs. Presently the road showed in patches, a broad waterfall breaking it every here and there as the imprisoned waters from above sought the slightly lower channel of the Jhelum.

We passed a party of natives bivouacking near the roof and upper storey of their wooden hut, which, floating from above, was held up by the Baramula road. Sounding now and then with our khudsticks, we found no bottom over the submerged rice crops, though we could see plainly the laden ears waving dismally down below. This is nothing less than a great calamity for the owners, as the rice was just ready for gathering.

Towards dusk we arrived at our ships, calmly lying moored to poplar trees by the roadside, and right gladly did we clamber on board, for our invalid was pretty well fagged out.

This morning we cast loose from our poplars, and brought the fleet up to within half a mile of the seventh bridge, or, rather, of the spot where the seventh bridge used to be, for all but a fragment has been washed away! The strong current prevented us from getting any higher up the river in our doungas. Jane and I, however, were anxious to see what appearance Srinagar presented, so we manned the shikara with five able-bodied paddlers and pushed our way upwards. Turning into a side canal we passed a demolished bridge, and tried to force our way up a small but swift stream.

Failing to make anything of it, we landed and had the boat carried over into a wider channel. Three times we were obliged to get out and leave our stalwart crew to force the boat on somehow, and they did it well—hauling, paddling, and shouting invocations to various saints, particularly the one whose name sounds like "jam paws!"

The water had already fallen some four or five feet, but there was plenty left. A great break in the bund between Nusserwanjee's shop and the Punjab Bank allowed us to paddle into the flooded European quarter, past the telegraph office, standing knee-deep in muddy water, up over the main road to Nedou's Hotel, where boats lay moored outside the dining-room windows, then across the lagoon, lightly rippled by a tiny breeze, beneath which lay the polo-ground, to the Residency, where we landed to inspect damages.

The water had been all over the lower storey, but a muddy deposit on the wooden floor, and a brown slimy high-water mark on the door jambs, alone remained to show what had happened. The piano had been hoisted upon a table, carpets and curtains bundled upstairs, and everything, apparently, saved. The poor garden, with its slime-daubed shrubs, broken palings and torn creepers, trailing wisps of draggled foliage in the oozy brown pools, was a sad and pitiful sight, especially when mentally contrasted with the glowing glory of asters and zinneas which it should have been.

The flood has been nearly as bad as the great one of 1903. Fortunately the Spill Canal, cut above Srinagar to carry off the flood water, took off some of the pressure; the bund, also, is three feet higher than it was then, but it gave way in two places—one somewhere near the top, and the other just below the Bank, letting in the river to a depth of ten feet over the low-lying quarter. The stream is now falling fast, and, after doing a little shopping and visiting the post-office, which is temporarily established on the bund in the midst of an amazing litter of desks, boxes, and queer pigeon-holes admirably adapted to lose letters by the score, we spun swiftly down the rushing stream to tea and our cosy dounga.

Monday, September 18.—It was impossible to get our boats up the river yesterday, so I spent the day sketching amidst the most picturesque, but horribly smelly, part of the town; much quinine in the evening seemed desirable as a counterblast to possible malaria.

The sunsets lately have been really magnificent; the poplars and chenars, darkly olive, reflected in the flooded fields against a red gold sky, in the foreground the black silhouettes of the armada.

The days are almost too hot, but the nights are cool and delicious, and the mosquitoes are only noticeable for a brief period of sinful activity about sundown, after which the wicked cease from troubling and the weary are at rest.

At half-past ten this morning we set sail; that is to say, we hired nine extra coolies and a second shikara to tow, and advanced on Srinagar. Hesketh's boat, being the lighter, kept well ahead (here let me note that "bow" in that boat is quite the prettiest girl we have seen in Kashmir, and the minx knows it!), but we had good men, and worked along slowly and steadily up the main river, the side canals being all choked by broken bridges and such like. We crept past the Amira Kadal, or first bridge, about two o'clock, and tied up for lunch, revelling in the most perfect pears, peaches, and walnuts. As a rule the Kashmir fruit is disappointing; abundant and cheap certainly, but not by any means of first-rate quality.

Strawberries, cherries, apricots, melons, and grapes might all be far better if properly cultivated, and scientifically improved from European stock.

The pears alone defy criticism, and the apples, I am told, are excellent also.

Vegetables are in great plenty, but, like the fruit, would be much improved by good cultivation.

Wednesday, September 25.—The abomination of desolation wrought by the flood is borne in upon one more and more as an inspection of the town reveals the damage done more fully—the houses standing empty, their lower storeys dank and slimy, the ruined gardens, and muddy, slippery roads. The wrecked garden of the Punjab Bank is one of the saddest sights, and must be a painful spectacle to Mr. Harrison, whose joy it was to spend time and money on importing exotic and improving indigenous plants.

One cannot help reflecting how desperately depressed Noah, and the probably more impressionable Mrs. Noah, must have been when, discarding their aquascutums for the first time, they sallied forth, a primeval party, to observe the emerging country.

Mrs. Noah, tucking up the curious straight garment that is a memory of our childhood, went ahead with feminine curiosity; Noah, bare-legged, slithering along in the rear and beseeching the ladies to note the slipperiness of the alluvial deposit, and for goodness' sake not to make a glissade down the side of Ararat.

I feel confident they must have taken great precautions, for Sabz Ali slipped up on the shelving bank of the Jhelum, and, had he not caught the gunwale of our dounga in his descent, would most certainly have had to swim for his life—which I doubt if he can do!

Now, Shem and Co. were as valuable to Noah as Sabz Ali is to us, and I should not be surprised if he made them travel on all-fours in the risky places. Fathers were very dictatorial in those days, and there was nobody about to make them consider their dignity.

One can imagine the scene. Ararat, a muddy pyramid dotted here and there with olive trees—curious, by the way, to find olives so high!—in the receding waters the vagrant raven cheerfully picking out the eye of a defunct pterodactyl. The heavy clouds rolling off the sodden world—they must have indeed been heavy clouds, nimbus of the first water—as they had raised the world's water-level 250 feet per day during "the flood" ... surely a record output!

The primeval family party, sadly poking about along the expanding margin of the world, noting how Abel Brown's tall chimney was beginning to show, and how Cain Jones' wigwam was clean gone. Mrs. Shem said she knew it would, the mortar work had been so terribly scamped.

And Naboth Robinson's vineyard—well, *it* was in a pretty mess, to be sure, and serve him right, for Mrs. Noah had frequently offered him two of her (second) best milch mammoths for it; yet he had held on to his nasty sour grapes, like the mean old curmudgeon that he was.

And now Hammy must set to work and tidy it up; and oh! what lots of nice manure was floating about, all for nothing the cartload ... And so the primeval family felt better, and went back to the ark to tea, feeling almost cheerful, but rather lonesome.

Fortunately this great flood did little injury to life or limb. A certain amount of destruction of crops and other property was inevitable, but on the whole the loss was not so great as was at one time feared, and much was saved that at first seemed irreparable.

A well-known lady artist came near to giving the note of tragedy to the British community, and losing the number of her mess (to use a nautical, and therefore appropriate expression) by reason of a big willow tree, beneath whose shady boughs she had moored her floating studio. This hapless tree, having all its sustenance swept from beneath by the greedy water, came down with a crash in the night upon the confiding house-boat, and all but swamped it.

The cook-boat, occupied as usual by a pair of prolific Mangis and their large small family, was saved by the proverbial "acid drop"—the children crawling out somehow or anyhow from among the branches of the fallen tree.

The fair artist, having with shrieks invoked the aid of a neighbour, he promptly descended from his roof or other temporary camp, and helped her with basins and chatties to bale out the half-swamped boat. The lady is now safely moored to the mudbank on the other side of the river where willow trees do not grow.

The whole bund is in a very unsafe state: it was raised three feet after the last flood, but its width was not increased correspondingly. Now that the water has fallen, great fissures and subsidences have appeared, and in many places large portions of the bank have fallen away, carrying big trees with them.

CHAPTER XIV
THE MACHIPURA

Wednesday, *September* 27.—We left Srinagar yesterday, very sorry indeed to part from the many good friends we have made and left there. Truly Kashmir is a hospitable country, and we have met with more kind friendliness in the last six months than we could have believed possible, coming as we did, strangers and pilgrims into a strange land. Our consolation is that every one comes "Home" sooner or later, so that we can look forward to meeting most of our friends again ere very long, and recalling with them memories of this happy summer with those who have done so much to make it so.

Farewell, Srinagar! Your foulness and inward evilness were lost in the background behind your picturesque and tumble-down houses as we floated for the last time down Jhelum's olive waters, where the sharp-nosed boats lay moored along the margin or, poled by their sturdy Mangis and guided by the chappars of their wives and daughters, shot athwart the eddying flood, breaking the long reflections of the storeyed banks.

Past the Palace of the Maharajah, its fantastic mixture of ancient fairness and modern ugliness blending into a homogeneous beauty as distance lent it enchantment.

Past the temples, their tin-coated roofs refulgent in the brilliant sunlight; under the queer wooden bridges, their solid stone piers parting the suave flow of water into noisy swirl and gurgle.

Past the familiar groups of grave, white-robed men solemnly washing themselves, then scooping up and drinking the noisome fluid; past their ladies squatting like frogs by the river-side, washing away at clothes which never seem a whit the cleanlier for all their talk and trouble.

Past the children and fowls, and cows and crows, all hob-nobbing together as usual.

Past all these sights—so strange to us at first and now so strangely familiar—we floated, till the broken remnant of the seventh bridge lay behind us, and the lofty poplars that hem in the Baramula road stood stark and solemn in their endless perspective.

Here a jangling note, out of tune and harsh, was struck by the dobie, with whom we had a grave difference of opinion regarding the washing.

That gentleman having "lost by neglect" certain articles of my kit—to wit sundry shirts and other garments—and having rendered others completely *hors de combat* by reason of his sinful method of washing, I decided to "cut" three rupees off his remuneration.

This decision seemed to have taken from him all that life held of worth, and he implored me to spare his wife, children, and home, all of whom would be broken up and ruined if I were cruel enough, to enforce my awful threat. Seeing that I was obdurate, being well backed by the infuriated Jane, whose underwear showed far more lace and open work than nature intended, the wretched dobie melted into loud and tearful lamentation, and perched himself howling in the prow. This soon became so boresome that I deported him to Hesketh's boat, where he underwent another defeat at the hands of that irate Lancer, whose shirts and temper had suffered together; finally the woeful washerman, still howling lugubriously, was landed on the river bank, and we saw and heard him no more!

Down the gentle river we swiftly glided all day, while the Takht and Hari Parbat grew smaller and bluer, and Srinagar lay below them invisible in its swathing greenery.

Reaching Sumbal at sunset, we turned to the left down a narrow canal, and soon the Wular lay—a sheet of molten gold—upon our right; and by the time we had moored alongside a low strip of reedy bank, the glorious rosy lights had faded from the snows of the Pir Panjal, and their royal purple and gold had turned to soft ebony against the primrose of the sky.

A few hungry mosquitoes worried us somewhat before sunset, promising worse to follow; but the sharp little breeze that came flickering over the Wular after dark seemed to upset their plans, and send them shivering and hungry to shelter among the reeds and rushes.

This morning we crossed the Wular, starting as the first pale dawn showed over the eastern hills.

Before the sun rose over Apharwat, his shafts struck the higher snows and turned them rosy; while the lower slopes, their distant pines suffused with strong purple, stood reflected in the placid mirror of the lake.

> "Full many a glorious morning have I seen
> Flatter the mountain tops with sovran eye,"

but seldom a more lovely one than this—our last on the Wular Lake.

The active figures of the propellent Mangis, and the quiet ones of their ladies at the helm, completed a picture to be recalled with a sigh when we are parted by thousands of miles from this entrancing valley.

Sopor we had understood to be but an uninteresting place, but we were, perhaps, inclined to regard things Kashmirian through somewhat rosy spectacles. Anyhow, we rather liked Sopor. Mooring close alongside a remarkably picturesque building standing in the midst of a smooth green lawn, which was once, I believe, a dâk bungalow, we halted to make arrangements for the hire of coolies and ponies to take us inland, and I went off to the post-office for letters and to make inquiries as to the probable depth of water in the river Pohru.

Our skipper, Juma, affirmed that there was no water to speak of; but Juma probably—nay, certainly—prefers the *otium* of a sojourn at Sopor to the toil of punting up the Pohru.

The postmaster declared that there was lots of water, but qualified his optimism by saying that it was falling fast. So we arranged for our land transport of ponies for ourselves, and a dandy for Hesketh, to meet us one march up the river at Nopura, while we ourselves set forward in our boats to Dubgam, three or four miles down the Jhelum, where the Pohru joins it. At the entrance are large stores of timber, principally deodar, which is floated down from the Lolab, stored at Dubgam, and sent thence down country and otherwhere for sale. The great boom across the river to catch the floating logs had been carried away in the flood, and merely showed a few melancholy and ineffectual spikes of wood sticking up above the now calm and sluggish river.

We towed up easily enough, through a quiet and peaceful country, which only became gorgeous under the alchemy of sunset, reaching Nopura in good time to tie up before dinner.

Friday, September 29.—On Thursday morning we started, as usual, at dawn, and proceeded to pole and haul our way up the devious channel of the Pohru. Some four or five miles we accomplished successfully, although there were ominous signs of a gradual lack of water, until we came upon a hopeless shallow, where the river, instead of concentrating its energies on one deep and narrow channel, had run to waste over a wide bed, where the wrinkling wavelets showed the golden brown of the gravel just below the surface. Our big dounga stuck hard and fast at once, and Captain Jurna promptly gave up all hope of getting farther. He was, in fact, greatly gratified to find his prophesies come true, and an insufferable air of "I told you so" overspread his face as he wagged his head with mock sorrow, and gently poked the bottom with his pole to show how firmly fixed we were.

Having an invalid with us, however, it was important to gain every easy mile we could, and it was not until all the fleet in turn had attempted to cross the shallow, and failed, that we made up our minds to take to our land transport. It was uncommonly hot in the full glare of the sun as Hesketh in his dandy, Jane on her "tattoo," and I on foot set forward for the forest house at Harwan, which lay some five miles away across the fields, where the rice is now being busily cut.

At the foot of a very brown and parched-looking hill stood the little wooden hut, facing the valley of the Pohru and the Kaj-nag range. Hot and thirsty, we blessed the good Mr. Blunt, the kindly forest officer, who had so courteously given us permission to use the forest huts of the Lolab and the Machipura. Our blessings of Blunt turned swiftly to curses directed towards the chowkidar, who was not to be seen, and who had left the hut firmly fastened from within. An attempt to force the door brought upon us the resentment of a highly irritable swarm of big red wasps, who plainly regarded us as objectionable intruders; and Jane was really getting quite cross (she says—she always does—that it was I who lost my temper)—before the bold sweeper, prying round the back premises, found an unbarred window, and the joy bells rang once more.

The Colonel turned up from the Malingam direction, and pitched his tent in the rest-house compound; and, as the afternoon grew cooler, he and I sallied forth to select a few chikor for the pot.

The chikor is extremely like the ordinary European redleg or Barbary partridge, not only in colouring, but in habit, loving the same dry, scrub-covered country, and preferring, like him, to run rather than fly when pursued. The chikor, however, is certainly far superior in the capacity of what fowl fanciers call "a table bird," being, in fact, truly excellent eating.

He is not an altogether easy bird to shoot, owing to his annoying predilection for the steepest and rockiest hillsides, and those most densely clothed in spiny jungle, wherein lurking, he chooses the inopportune moment when the sportsman is hopelessly entangled, like Isaac's ram, to rise chuckling and flee away to another hiding-place.

Without dogs, he would be often extremely hard to find; but unluckily for himself, being a true Kashmiri bird, he cannot help making a noise, and thereby betraying his presence. His corpse, when dead, is hard to find in the jungle, and a runner is, of course, hopeless without canine help. It is well, therefore, to kill him as dead as possible, and to that end I used No. 4 shot, with, I think, a certain advantage over Walter, who shot with No. 6, and who, in consequence, lost several birds.

The friendliness and sociability of the beasts and birds of Kashmir has been a great joy to us. The thing can be overdone, though, and both the wasps and the rats of Harwan were inclined to overstep the bounds of decorum.

The latter were obviously overjoyed to see visitors, and visions of unlimited plunder from our festive board would, of course, put them somewhat above themselves. Still, they should have refrained from rioting so openly around our beds as soon as the lights were out, and Jane was naturally indignant when a large one ran over her feet!

On Friday morning we left Harwan, pretty early, as usual, for it is still somewhat too warm to travel comfortably in the middle of the day. The Colonel (always an early bird) got away first, followed by our invalid in his dandy, while Jane and I remained to hunt the loiterers out of camp. A glorious morning, and the cheering knowledge that breakfast was in front of us, sent us merrily along for a mile or two, until branching paths led us to inquire of an intelligent Kashmiri, who appeared to be busily engaged in reaping rice with a penknife, as to the road taken by our precursors, especially the tiffin coolie!

The industrious one had seen no sahibs at all pass by. This was a blow, and Jane and I sat down to review the situation. We finally decided that the son of the soil was indulging in what the great and good Winston Churchill has called a "terminological inexactitude," as the others must have gone by one of the two roads; so, putting our fortunes to the touch, we took the left-hand path, and were in due time rewarded by reaching Sogul, and there finding our pioneers peacefully seated under a tree, and breakfast ready.

Leaving Sogul, we skirted for some miles a bare ridge which rose on the right, and which looked an ideal ground for chikor, and then turned into a beautiful valley drained by the Pohru, now quite a small and insignificant stream.

Drogmulla, our objective, lies about fourteen miles from Harwan, and the forest house is a full mile beyond the village, at the end of a somewhat steep and winding path.

A welcome sight was the snug rest-house, perched upon a hillock above a fussy little stream and surrounded by a fine clump of deodars.

A tiny lawn in front was decorated with an artificial tank full of water-plants, and through the opening, among the trees, we saw the snowy crest of Shambrywa and the Kaj-nag rising over the deeply-wooded foothills.

Drogmulla was so fascinating a spot, and the weather was so remarkably fine, that we made up our minds to remain here for a few days. That old red-bearded snake, the shikari, has sent the Colonel into a seventh heaven of anticipation by pointing to the encircling forest with promise of "pul-lenty baloo, sahib, this pul-lace." We straightway ordained a honk.

Our sick soldier is so much better since leaving Gulmarg that he is able to hop "around" with considerable activity on his crutches.

Saturday, September 30, 4 P.M.—Walter and I have been bear-honking all day in a district reputed to be simply crawling with bears. I love bear-honking; it is such a peaceful occupation.

After a stiff and very hot scramble up a rugged hillside covered with the infuriating scrub through which nothing but a reptile could crawl easily, the spot is reached within short range of which (in the opinion of the "oldest inhabitant," backed up by the "Snake") the bear *must* pass.

Here the battery of rifles and guns is carefully arranged, and I proceed to wipe my heated brow and settle down to the calm enjoyment of the honk. Drawing forth my cigar-case, I am soon wreathed in the fragrant clouds engendered by the incineration of a halfpenny cheroot, and, with a sigh of satisfaction, I spread out my writing or sketching materials and proceed to scribble or paint, calm in the knowledge that nothing on earth is in the least likely to disturb the flow of ideas, or interrupt the laying on of a broad flat wash. Now and again, lazily, I lean back to watch the witless hoverings of a big butterfly, or sleepily listen to the increasing sound of the tom-toms and the yells of the beaters, whose voices, as those of demons of the pit, rend the peaceful air and add to my sense of Olympian aloofness!

A feeling of drowsiness steals over me; that succulent cold chikor, followed by a generous slice of cake upon which I so nobly lunched, clouds somewhat my active faculties, and the article—"A Bear Battue in the Himalayas"—which I am engaged in writing for the *Field*—seems to flag a little.

Come, come! Begone dull sloth—let me continue—

"As the sound of the beaters swells upon the ear, and the thunder of the tom-toms grows more insistent, the keen-eyed sportsman grasps more firmly the lever of his four-barrelled Nordenfeldt and prepares to play upon the bears his hail of stinging missiles. Hark! The plot is thickening, behind yon dense screen at the end of the cover the ph—— bears are beginning to crowd, the pattering of their feet upon the dead leaves sends a thrill through the beating heart of the expectant sportsman. A few bears break back amid wild yells from the coolies. One or two odd ones dart out here and there at angles of the covert. Steady! Steady! Here they are, following the lead of yon fine old cock; with a whirr and a rush the bouquet is upon us. The shikari, mad with excitement, presses the second Gatling and the light Howitzer into our hands as he screams: 'Bear to right, sahib!—Bear over!!—Bear behind!!! Bang—bang!'"

"Eh? What? Oh, all right, shikari. Honk finished? Is it? Saw nothing? Dear me! how very odd. Very well, then gather up my guns and things, and we'll go on to the next beat."

Sunday, October 1.—To-day being Sunday, we have been idle and happy—sketching, loafing, and enjoying the scenery and the glorious weather. Our bear-honk yesterday was only productive of annas to the beaters, but we picked up some chikor on the way home, and we have found mushrooms growing close to the hut, so that our lower natures are also satisfied. After lunch I mustered up energy sufficient to take me down to the village to sketch a native hut which, surrounded by a patch of flaming millet, had struck me on Friday as an extraordinary bit of colour. Jane and Walter, after many "prave 'orts" about climbing the ridge behind Drogmulla, contented themselves with a minor ascent of a knoll about fifty feet high, while the Lancer, reckless in his increasing activity, managed to trip over his crutches and give himself an extremely unfortunate fall.

Monday, October 2.—There was a man who, during our bear-honk on Saturday, rendered himself conspicuous, partly by reason of his likeness to my shikari, and also because of his complete knowledge of the whereabouts of all bears for many miles around. He was quite glad to impart much information to us, and so won upon the sporting but too trustful heart of the brave Colonel, that he was retained by that officer in order that he might show sport to the Philistines, and annas and even rupees were bestowed upon him; and he and the old original "Snake" were sent forward on Saturday evening, as Joshua and Caleb, to spy out the promised land in the neighbourhood of Tregam.

Lured by rumours of many bears, Walter and I set forth at daylight for Tregam, leaving Jane and the youthful Lancer (once more, alas! reduced to stiff bandages and a painful relapse) in possession of the hut. We "hadna gane a mile—a mile but barely twa," when the old shikari met us with the painful intelligence that two sahibs were already at Tregam, and had killed many bears there, grievously wounding the rest; so we altered course eight points to port, crossed the Pohru, and made for Rainawari.

A sharp climb over a wooded ridge (on the top of which we halted for breakfast), followed by a steep descent, brought us into a flat and well-cultivated plain, which sloped gently from the foothills of the Kaj-nag to the bed of the Pohru. Everywhere, in the glowing sunlight, the villagers were busily engaged in reaping the rice, which lay in ripe brown swathes along the little fields. The walnuts, of which there are a great plenty in this district, have been lately gathered, some few trees only still remaining, loaded with a heavy crop, but the main produce lay drying in heaps in the villages as we rode through.

The road to Rainawari seemed curiously devious. A Kashmiri track seldom shies at a hill, but pursues its way, heedless of gradient, for its objective; but this path imitated a corkscrew in its windings, and reduced us to the utmost limit of our patience before, passing through a small village whose dull-coloured houses were enlivened with gorgeous festoons of scarlet chilies, we climbed a steep little hill and found ourselves upon a park-like lawn or clearing, and facing the cluster of rough wooden shanties which compose the Rainawari forest bungalow and its outhouses. Behind the huts the densely-wooded hill drops sharply to where a stream of good and pure water riots among the maidenhair and mosses.

A large and inquisitive company of apes came up from the wood to take stock of us, and I sat for a long time watching them as they played about quite close to me, feeding, chattering, and quarrelling, entirely unconcerned by the presence of their human spectator.

Friday, October 6.—All Tuesday was spent in honking bear in the lower woods which stretch far towards the Pohru. The high hills which rise above, covered with jungle, are said to be too large to work, and I can well believe it! For the first drive I was posted on a steep bank overlooking a most lovely little hollow, where the shafts of sunlight fell athwart the grey trunks and heavy green masses of the pines, lighting up the yellow leaves of the sumachs till they glowed like gold, and casting a flickering network of strong lights and shadows among the tangled mazes of undergrowth. A happy family of magpies, grey-blue above, with barred tails and yellow beaks, flitted about in restless quest, their constant cries being the only sound which broke the peaceful stillness, until the faint and distant sound of shouts and tom-toms showed that the first act of the farce had begun.

Towards the end of the third beat, while I was drowsily digesting tiffin, and, truly, not far from napping, I was electrified by the report of a rifle, followed by yells and a second shot! The beaters redoubled their shouts, and the tom-tommers seemed like to burst their drums.

My shikari, writhing with extreme excitement, hissed, "Baloo, sahib, baloo!" and began aimlessly running to and fro, apparently hoping to meet the bear somewhere. It was truly gay for a few minutes, but as nothing further occurred, and the beaters grew very hoarse with their prodigious efforts, I hurried on to Walter's post to learn what had happened.

A bear had suddenly come out of the cover some 40 yards off, and stood to look. The Colonel missed it, whereupon it dashed forward, passing within a few yards of him, and he missed it again. It departed at top speed across some open ground behind him, and gained the great woods which stretch away to the Kaj-nag, and never shall we see that bear again! The Colonel was much disgusted, and if language—hot, strong, and plenty of it—could have slain that bear, he would have dropped dead in his tracks.

The beaters brought up a wonderful tale of how another bear, badly wounded in the leg, had charged through their lines and gone back. They stuck to their story, and either a second bear actually existed or they are colossal liars. I incline to the latter theory.

We had wasted all our luck. No more bears came to look at us, and so, late in the afternoon, we sought the rest-house and consolation from Jane and Hesketh, who had arrived from Drogmulla.

I had occasion to deplore the bad manners of the rats at Harwan, but their conduct was exemplary compared with that of the rats of Rainawari! I had been writing my journal, according to my custom, before going to sleep, and hardly had "lights out" been sounded than a rat went off with my candle, literally from below my very nose. Then, from the inadequately partitioned chamber where the invalid vainly sought repose, came sounds of strife—boots and curses flying—followed by an extraordinary scraping and scuffling. A large rat, having fallen into the big tin bath, was making bids for freedom by ineffectually leaping up the slippery sides. At last he contrived to get out, and peace reigned until we managed to get to sleep.

Wednesday was spent honking in the forlorn hope of a bear, I have now spent more than fourteen days in pursuit of black bear, and I have only seen one. Every one said to me in spring, "Oh, go to the Lolab, it's full of bear," I went, and was informed that it was a late season and I was too early—the bears were not yet awake. I was consoled by learning that later on, when the mulberries were ripe, the berry-loving beasts jostled one another in the pursuit of the delicacy so much, that they were no sport I went down from Gulmarg for three days, honking among the mulberries, but saw none. Then I was told the maize season was undoubtedly the best. Now the maize is full ripe; the maize fields are tempting in their golden glory, and the only thing wanting to complete the picture is a big, black bear.

Either my luck has been particularly bad (and I think it has, as the Colonel got a fine bear below Gulmarg, and had another chance at Rainawari), or else there are not so many bears in real life as exist in the imaginations of those who know. My own theory is, that, unless he has remarkable luck, a stranger, in the hands of an ignorant shikari, and knowing nothing of the language, has but a remote chance of sport. If the shikari does not happen to know the district thoroughly, he is necessarily in the hands of the villagers, and has to trust to them to arrange the beats and place the guns. The villagers want their four annas for a day's shouting, but do not know or care if a bear is in the neighbourhood, so, having planted the gun (and shikari with him), they proceed to beat after their own fashion, in other words to stroll, in Indian file, like geese across a common, along the line of least resistance, instead of spreading out and searching all the thickest jungle.

Much yelling serves both to cheer the sahib, and frighten away any bear which might otherwise haply frighten them.

I cannot say I regret the time I have spent looking for bear. The scenery has always been fine—sometimes magnificent, and there has always been a certain cheering hope, which sustained me as I lay hour after hour in the Malingam Nullah, or sat expectant amid ever varying and always beautiful glades and passes, watching the bird life, and storing up scenes and memories which I know I shall never forget.

Alas! we have but a very few days yet before us in Kashmir, and it is lamentable, for now the climate is simply perfect, the air clear and clean, and without the haze of summer; the first crispness of coming autumn making itself felt most distinctly in the early hours of morning ere

> "Nor dim nor red, like God's own head,
> The glorious sun uprist;"

and each dawn saw us up and out to watch these sunrises, whose splendour cannot be expressed on paper. This morning it was more than usually wonderful, the whole flank of Nanga Parbat and his lesser peaks, turning from clear lemon to softest rose, stood radiant above the purple shades of the great range which lies around Gurais. In the middle distance, rising above the level yellow of the plain, still dim and shadowy below the morning light, rolled wave upon wave of the blue hills which hold in their embrace the fruitful Lolab. At our feet the deodars, still dark with the shadow of night, crept up the dewy slope upon whose top we stood. Then suddenly

> "The sanguine sunrise, with his meteor eyes,"

flamed over the eastern ridges, and in a flood of glory the soft shadows and pallid lights of the dawn became merged in the brilliance of a Kashmir autumn day.

Our march yesterday from Rainawari to Kitardaji was charming. I had no idea that this Machipura country, which is not much visited by summer sojourners in Kashmir, was so fine. The district lies along the lower shoulders and foothills of the Kaj-nag, and, while lacking the savage grandeur of the Lidar or Upper Sind, yet possesses the charm of infinite variety and, in this early autumn, a climate in which it is a pure joy to live. On leaving Rainawari we followed up a river valley for some distance, and then wound through richly cultivated hollows and past well-wooded hills, where the dark silver firs and the deodars were lit up by splashes of scarlet and orange, and the deciduous sumach and thorn-bushes hung out their autumn flags. Walnuts—the trees in many places turning yellow—were being gathered into heaps, and the apple trees, reddening in the autumn glow, hung heavy with abundant fruit.

Turning into a narrow gorge, where the trees overhung the path and shaded the wanderer with many an interlaced bough; where ferns grew in great green clumps, and the friendly magpies chattered in the luminous shade, I hurried on, having stayed behind the others to sketch. Up and up, till only pines waved over me, and the track, leading along the edge of a deep khud, opened out at last upon a plateau, hot and sunlit; here an entrancing panorama of Nanga Parbat and the whole range of mountains round Haramok caused me to stop "at gaze" until a mundane desire for breakfast sent me scurrying down the dusty and slippery descent to Larch, where I found, as I had hoped, the rest of the party assembled expectant around the tiffin basket, while the necromancer, Sabz Ali, had just succeeded in producing the most delightful stew, omelette, and coffee from the usual native toy kitchen, made, apparently, in a few minutes with a couple of stones and a dab of mud!

It has been an unfailing marvel to us how, in storm or calm, rain or fine, the native cook seems always able to produce a hot meal with such apparently inadequate materials as he has at his command. Give him a fire in the open, screened by stones and a mud wall, a *batterie de cuisine* limited to one or two war-worn "degchies," and let him have a village fowl and half-a-dozen tiny eggs, and he will in due time serve up, with modest pride, a most excellent repast.

The remaining half of our twelve-mile march lay along a continually rising track, which finally brought us to Kitardaji, a cosy pine-built hut, perched upon a hill clothed with deodars, at the foot of which ran the inevitable stream.

This, alas! is our last Kashmir camping-ground, and it is one of the most charming of all.

At 8.15 this morning we bade farewell to Kitardaji. We had got up before dawn to see the sunrise, but afterwards took things leisurely, as the march is short to Baramula, and our boats were to be in waiting there, and we had made all arrangements for a landau and ekkas to be in readiness to take us down to Rawal Pindi, while the Colonel returned up the Jhelum for more shooting before rejoining his wife at Bandipur.

The march of about thirteen miles from Kitardaji to Baramula is fine—the views of Nanga Parbat in the early hours, before the sun's full strength cast a golden glow over the distance, were magnificent, and long we lingered upon the last ridge, gazing over the great valley, ringed with its guardian mountains, ere we sadly turned our backs for the last time on the scene, and wended our way downward to Baramula and our boats.

Kashmir seems to be as difficult to get out of as to get into! What was our amazement and disgust to find neither landau nor ekkas, nor, apparently, any chance of getting them!

Baramula was in a ferment, and wild confusion reigned because the Viceroy, having somewhat suddenly determined to come to Jammu, the Maharajah and all his suite, together with the Resident and his belongings, were to start down the road at once, and all transport was commandeered by the State. Here was a coil! Officers innumerable, who had stayed in Kashmir until the limit of their leave, were struggling vainly to get on, and had got to Baramula only to find all transport in the hands of the State officials. Some few had, by fair means or foul, got hold of an ekka or two and hidden them; others had seized ponies, but nothing to harness them to. A few of the younger men set forth on foot, and others had their servants out in ambush on the roads to try and collect transport.

It was most important that we should get on, as Hesketh had to be in Pindi to go before a medical board on the 14th, in order to be invalided home to England; and as he was most anxious to catch a steamer sailing on the 25th, he had no time to spare.

I telegraphed to Sir Amar Singh for authority to engage ekkas, and I sent for the Tehsildhar of Baramulla to complain of my ekkas being taken. He appeared in due course—a somewhat pert little person—who promised to do what he could, which I knew would be nothing. A farewell dinner on board Walter's ship concluded a fairly busy day.

Saturday, October 7.—A strenuous day, to say the least of it. Sir Amar Singh most courteously met my wishes, and himself directed the local authorities to assist me. Armed with this power, I again sent for the Tehsildhar, who promised many ekkas, but appeared to have some difficulty in fulfilling his promises. I spent the forenoon in hunting transport, sending out my servants also in pursuit. The Tehsildhar produced one ekka with great pomp, as earnest of what he could and would do later on.

During the afternoon the landau turned up from Srinagar, and at 6 P.M. one of my myrmidons rushed in to say that two ekkas had arrived at the dâk bungalow.

It was but a few yards away, and in a couple of minutes I was on the spot. The ekkas had come up from Pindi, and the sahib who had lured them to Baramula seemed astonished at my method of taking them over. In an uncommonly short while the ekkas were parked, with the landau, close to the boats and under strict watch, while all harness was brought on board my dounga, just in time, as native officials of some sort romped up and claimed the ekkas, and threatened to beat my servants. It was explained to them gently, but firmly, that if they touched my ekkas or landau they would taste the waters of the Jhelum. We were then left in peaceful possession.

Tuesday, October 10.—On Sunday morning we really saw our way to making a start. We had three ekkas collected, and the Tehsildhar produced a fourth with a great flourish, as though in expectation of a heavy tip. The landau was being piled with odds and ends while the last bits of business were being got through. Juma and his crew were paid and tipped (grumbling, of course, for the Kashmiri is a lineal descendant of the horse-leech). The shikari went to Smithson, and the sweeper and permanent coolie were transferred to the assistant forest officer, while Ayata (in charge of Freddie, the blackbird) scrambled into the leading ekka.

By noon all was ready, and amid the rattle and jingle of many harness bells and the salaams of the domestics, we bowled out of Baramula, and set forward down the valley of the Jhelum.

CHAPTER XV
DELHI AND AGRA

The journey down was uneventful, and quite unlike the journey up, when we had been briskly occupied in dodging landslips for days. A good road, white and dry, and sloping steadily downward; a good pair of ponies, strong and willing; a roomy landau, wherein Hesketh—still suffering from his fall at Drogmulla—could stretch himself in comparative comfort, combined to bring us to Kohala this afternoon in a state of excellent preservation. Here we crossed the bridge, which brought us to the right bank of the river—from Kashmir to British territory.

Kohala is the proud possessor of one of the very worst dâk bungalows yet discovered. This seems disappointing when stepping under the folds of the Union Jack full of high hope and confidence.

Climbing up through a particularly noisome bazaar to the bungalow, I was met with the information that it was already full. I said that was a pity, but that room must be found for my party.

Room was got somehow, a dâk bungalow being an extraordinarily elastic dwelling. Hesketh was stored in a little tent. I lodged in the dining-room, and Jane took up her quarters in a sort of dressing-room kindly given up by a lady, who bravely sought asylum with a sister-in-law and a remarkably strong-lunged baby. I believe more travellers arrived later, for—although, thanks to Sir Amax Singh and good luck, we gained a good start at Baramula—now the tongas are beginning to roll in and the plot to thicken.

I cannot think where the last arrivals bestowed themselves—not on the roof, I trust, for a thunderstorm, accompanied by the usual vigorous squall of wind, fell upon us during the night, and raged so furiously that I was greatly relieved to see the Lancer's little tent still braving the battle and the breeze in the morning.

We had a long day before us, so started in good time to make the tedious ascent to Murree. It rained steadily, and a cold wind swept down the river valley as we began to make our slow way up the long, long hill.

I never knew milestones so extraordinarily far apart as those which mark the distance between Kohala and Murree. There are twenty-five of them, distributed along a weary winding road which extends without an apparent variation of gradient from Kohala to the Murree cemetery. The rise from the river level to Murree is 5000 feet, and this, in a heavy landau over a road often deep in red mud, is a heavy strain on equine endurance and human patience.

We had a fresh pair of horses waiting for us half-way up the hill, but they proved absolutely useless, being obviously already dead tired and quite unable to drag the carriage through any of the muddier places even with every one but the invalid on foot. So we apologetically put the gallant greys in again, poor beasties, and they took us up well.

From the cemetery the road runs fairly level to where, upon rounding a sharp corner, the hill station of Murree comes into sight, clinging to its hill-tops and overlooking the far flat plains beyond Pindi.

I cannot imagine how anybody would willingly abide in Murree who could go anywhere else for the hot weather. There being no level ground, there is no polo, no cricket, and no golf. There is no river to fish in, and I do not think that there is anything at all to shoot. Doubtless, however, it has its compensations. Probably it abounds in pretty mem-sahibs, who with bridge and Badminton combine to oil the wheels of life, and make it merry on the Murree hills.

Leaving the station high on the left, we dipped in a most puzzling manner down a slope through a fine wood giving magnificent views towards the hills of our beloved Kashmir, and presently came to "Sunny Bank," whence a steep road seemed to run sharply hack and up to Murree itself. It was late, and both we and our unfortunate horses were tired, but a hasty peep into the little inn showed it to be quite impossible as a lodging, and a biting wind sent us shivering down the hill as fast as might be to seek rest and warmth at Tret.

The good greys took us down the eleven miles in a very short time, and we pulled up at the dâk bungalow at 7.30, having been just twelve hours doing the forty miles from Kohala.

The dâk bungalow and all the compound in front was crowded, detachments *en route*, from Murree to Pindi having halted here for the night. Hesketh was lucky enough to share a room with a brother Lancer, and a mixed bag of Gunners and Hussars made up a cheery dinner-table.

The only member of the party showing signs of collapse was the unfortunate Freddie, who, shaken up in his small cage for three days in an ekka, seemed in piteous plight, feathers (what there were of them) ruffled and unkempt, and eyes dim and half closed. Poor dear, it was only sleep he wanted, for next morning he showed up, as his fond owner remarked, "bright as a button!"

12th.—The road from Tret to Pindi seemed tame to us, but probably charming to the horses, first down a few gently sloping hills, and then for the remainder of its six-and-twenty miles it wound its dull and dusty length along the level.

We halted for our last picnic lunch in a roadside garden full of loquat trees and big purple hibiscus. The only curious thing here was a pi-dog which refused to eat cold duck! Certainly it was a *very* tough duck, but still, I do not think a pi-dog should be so fastidious.

A few more level dusty miles, and we rattled into Rawal Pindi, where, after depositing our sick man safely in his own mess precincts, we proceeded to ensconce ourselves in Flashman's Hotel, which is certainly far better than the Lime Tree, where we stayed before. Indian hotels are about the worst in the world. We have sampled rough dens in Spain, in Tetuan, and in Corsica—especially in Corsica, but then they are unpretentious inns in unfrequented villages, whereas in India you find in world-famous cities such as Agra or Delhi the most comfortless dens calling themselves hotels— hotels where you hardly dare eat half the food for fear of typhoid, and will not eat the rest because it is so unsavoury!

It may be argued that the hotels, if bad, are cheap, and that one cannot reasonably expect much in return for five or six rupees per day; it seems, however, that in a country where food and labour cost next to nothing, a good landlord should be able to "do" his customers well upon five rupees, and make a substantial profit into the bargain.

Probably, as the facilities for travel are rapidly increasing, and India is now as easy to reach as Italy was in days not so long by, the hotels will soon improve. Hospitality, which is still to-day greater in the East than in our more selfish Western regions, and which has, until quite recently, obviated for strangers and pilgrims the necessity for hotels, is now unable to cope with the increasing flood of visitors and wanderers; as the need becomes more pressing, so will the supply, consequent upon the demand, improve both in quality and quantity; and we have already heard of the new Taj Mahal Hotel at Bombay, the fame of which has been trumpeted through India, and which is said to rival in luxury the palaces of Ritz!

The real and serious difficulty, and one which at present seems insurmountable, is to secure cleanliness and safety in that Augean stable—the cook-house. Until the native can be brought to understand the inadvisability of using tainted water and unclean utensils, and of permitting the ubiquitous fly to pervade the larder—until, I say, that millennium can be attained, the danger of enteric and other ills will always be very great in Indian hotels.

Friday, October 13.—Lunch with Dr. Munro, who surprised us somewhat by having married a wife since we played golf and bridge together at Gulmarg only a few weeks ago. Tea, a farewell repast with our invalid—who goes before a medical board in a few days, and who will then be doubtless sent home on long sick leave—and the despatch of our heavy luggage direct to Bombay, occupied us pretty fully for the day; and in the evening, after dinner, we took up our residence in a carriage drawn up in a siding to be attached to the 6.30 mail in the morning. Our last recollection of Pindi was a vision of the faithful Ayata, paid, tipped, and provided with a flaming "chit," flapping along the road in the bright moonlight, with all his worldly possessions, *en route* for Abbotabad and home.

Saturday, October 14.—A prodigious amount of banging, whistling, and yelling seemed to be necessary before we could be coupled up to the early train, and sent flying towards Lahore. It was impossible to sleep, and I was peacefully watching the landscape as it slid past, first in the pink flush of early dawn, and gradually losing colour as the sun, gaining in strength, reduced everything to a white hot glow, when, scraping and bumping into a wayside station, we were suddenly informed that, owing to hot bearings or heated axles or something, we must quit our carriage at once, and so, half dressed and wholly wrathful, we were shot out on a hot and exceedingly gritty platform, with our hand luggage and bedding all of a heap, and with the whole length of the train to traverse to attain our new carriage. Sabz Ali being curled up asleep in an "intermediate," was all unwitting of this upheaval. The officials were impatient, and so Jane and I were in a thoroughly unchristian frame of mind by the time we were stowed, hot and greatly fussed, into a stifling compartment, whose dust-begrimed windows long withstood all endeavours to open them.

We reached Lahore about noon, and, having some six hours to dispose of there, we spent them in calm contemplation, sitting on the verandah of Nedou's Hotel. It was really too hot to think of sight-seeing.

Thursday, October 19.—Another night in the train brought us to Delhi at dawn, and we drove up to the execrable caravansary of Mr. Maiden. I do not propose to write much about Delhi. Every one who has been in India has visited the capital of the Moguls, whose wealth of splendid buildings would alone have rendered it a supreme attraction for the sight-seer, even had it not played the part it did in the Mutiny, and been memorable as the scene of the storming of the Kashmir Gate and the death of John Nicholson.

We, personally, carried away from Delhi an uncomfortable sense of disappointment. It was very hot, and Jane fell a victim to the heat or something, and took to her bed in the comfortless hotel, while I prowled sadly about the baking streets, and tried to work up an enthusiasm which I did not feel.

As soon as Jane was fit, we joined forces with a young fellow-countryman and his sister, who were the only other English people in the hotel, and drove out to see the Kutab Minar. On arrival we found a comfortable dâk bungalow, and, having made an excellent breakfast, sallied forth to view the Kutab. May I confess that I was again a little disappointed? I do not really know exactly why, but the great tower, whose fluted shaft, dark red in the sunglow, shoots up some 270 feet into the air, did not appeal to me. It is like no other column—it is unique, marvellous,—but it leaves me cold.

The splendid arch of the screen of the old temple, and the lovely columns of the Jain temple opposite, attracted me far more than the Kutab Minar.

Jane and young Buxton went off to see a native jump down a well fifty feet deep for four annas. The performance sounded curious, but unpleasant. The sightseers were much impressed! Meanwhile, Miss Buxton and I discovered a very modern and exceedingly hideous little Hindu temple, painted in the most appalling manner—altogether a gem of grotesqueness, and truly delightful and refreshing.

Tea in front of the dâk bungalow, in a corner blazing with "gold mohurs" and rosy oleanders, while the driver and the syce harnessed the lean pair of horses, a final visit to the Kutab and the great arch, and we fared back over the eleven bumpy miles that lay between us and Delhi.

A good deal of my spare time, while Jane was *hors de combat*, was spent in the jewellers' shops of the Chandni chowk, the principal merchants' quarter of Delhi. I do not think that anything very special in the way of a "bargain" is to be obtained by the amateur, although stones are undoubtedly cheaper than in London. I saw little really fine jewellery, probably because I was obviously unlikely to be a big buyer, but many good spinels, dark topaz, and rough emeralds. The stones I wanted I failed to get. Alexandrites were not, and pink topaz scarce and dear. The dealers generally tried to sell pale spinels as pink topaz. Peridot are cheaper, I think, at home, and certainly in Cairo, and the only amethysts worth looking at are sent out from Germany. The pale ones of the country come from Jaipur. By-the-bye, the best-coloured amethysts I ever remember seeing were in Clermont Ferrand.

Delhi has always been connected with gems in my mind. I am not certain why. Partly, perhaps, because the famous Peacock Throne of Shah Jehan stood in the Palace here. I cannot resist giving the description of it in the words of Tavernier, who saw it about 1655, and who describes it as follows: —

"This is the largest throne; it is in form like one of our field-beds, six foot long and four broad. The cushion at the back is round like a bolster; the cushions on the sides are flat. I counted about a hundred and eight pale rubies in collets about this throne, the least whereof weighed a hundred carats. Emeralds I counted about a hundred and forty."

"The under part of the canopy is all embroidered with pearls and diamonds, with a fringe of pearls round about. Upon the top of the canopy, which is made like an arch with four paws, stands a peacock with his tail spread, consisting entirely of sapphires and other proper-coloured stones;[1] the body is of beaten gold enchased with several jewels; and a great RUBY upon his breast, to which hangs a pearl that weighs fifty carats. On each aide of the peacock stand two nosegays as high as the bird, consisting of various sorts of flowers, all of beaten gold enamelled."

[1] "Au dessus du ciel qui est faite en voûte à quatre pans on voit un Paon, qui a la queue relevée fait de Saphirs bleus et autres pierres de couleur." —TAVERNIER, livre ii. chap. viii.

"When the king seats himself upon the throne there is a transparent jewel, with a diamond appendant of eighty or ninety carats weight, encompassed with rubies and emeralds, so hung that it is always in his eye. The twelve pillars also, that uphold the canopy, are set with rows of fair pearl, round, and of an excellent water, that weigh from six to ten carats apiece."

"At the distance of four feet, upon each side of the throne, are placed two umbrellas, the handles of which are about eight feet high, covered with diamonds, the umbrellas themselves being of crimson velvet, embroidered and fringed with pearl."

"This is the famous throne which Tamerlane began and Shah Jehan finished; and is really reported to have cost a hundred and sixty millions and five hundred thousand livres of our money."

One can picture the enraptured diamond merchant examining this masterpiece of Oriental luxury with awe-struck eye, appraising the size and lustre of each gem, and taking the fullest notes with which to dazzle his countrymen on returning to the more prosaic Europe from what was then indeed the "Gorgeous East!" This world-famous throne was seized by Nadir

Shah, when he sacked Delhi in 1739, and carried away (together with our Koh-i-noor diamond) into Persia. Dow, who saw the famous throne some twenty years before Tavernier, describes *two* peacocks standing behind it with their tails expanded, which were studded with jewels. Between the peacocks stood a parrot, life size, cut out of a single emerald!

Friday, October 20.—Yesterday at 6 A.M. we spurned the dust of Delhi, hot and blinding, from our feet and clambered into the train, which whirled us across the sun-baked plain to Agra.

There has been a woeful shortage of rain in the Punjab and Rajputana, and a famine seems imminent—not a great and universal famine, as, the monsoon having been irregular, only some districts have suffered to a serious extent, and they can be supplied from elsewhere, whereas in the great famine of 1901 the drought parched the whole land, and no help could be given by one State to another, all lying equally under the sun's curse. Not a great famine, perhaps; yet, to one accustomed to the genial juiciness of the West, the miles and miles of waterless hot plains, stretching away to where the horizon flickered in the glare, the brown and parched vegetation, the lean and hungry-looking cattle, tended by equally lean and famished herds, caused the monotonous view from the carriage windows to be strangely depressing.

This is the very battle-ground of Nature and the British Raj. We have given peace and, to a certain extent, prosperity to the teeming millions of India, and they have increased and multiplied until the land is overburthened, and Nature, with relentless will, bids Famine and Pestilence lay waste the cities and the plains. Then Science, with irrigation works and improved hygiene, strives hard to gain a victory, but still the struggle rages doubtfully.

Agra we liked as much as we disliked Delhi. To begin with creature comforts (and the well-being of the body produces a pair of *couleur de rose* spectacles for the mental eye), Laurie's Hotel at Agra is very much more comfortable than the den we abode in at Delhi, and after a good tiffin we set forth with light hearts to see the Fort.

This, the accumulated achievement of the greatest of the Mogul Emperors, is a magnificent monument of their power and pride. The earliest part, built by Akbar, is all of rich red sandstone. The great hall of audience and other portions show his broad-minded tolerance and catholicity of taste in being almost pure Hindu in style and decoration. Later, with Jehangir and Shah Jehan, the high-water mark of sumptuousness was attained in the use of pure white marble, lavishly inlaid with coloured stones.

As we wandered through halls and corridors of marble most richly wrought, while the sun-glare outside did but emphasise the cool shade within, or filter softly through the lace-like tracery of pierced white-marble screens, one longed to reclothe these glorious skeletons with all the pomp of their dead magnificence—for one magic moment replace the Great Mogul upon his peacock throne, surround him with a glittering crowd of courtiers and attendants, clothe the wide marble floors upon which they stand with richest carpets from the looms of Persia and the North, and drape the tall white columns with rustling canopies of silk.

Before the great audience hall let the bare garden-court again glow with a million blooms; there let the peacocks sun themselves, their living jewels putting to shame the gems that burn back from aigrette and from sword-hilt; see and hear the cool waters sparkling once again from their long-dried founts, flashing in the white sunlight, and flowing over ducts cunningly inlaid with zigzag bands to imitate the ripple of the mountain stream.

The dead frame alone is left of all this gorgeous picture. The imperishable marble glows white in the sunlight as it did in the days of Shah Jehan. The great red bastions of the Fort frown over the same placid Jumna, and watch each morning the pearly dome of the Taj Mahal rise like a moon in the dawn-glow, shimmer through the parching glare of an Indian day, and at eve sink, rosy, into the purple shadows of swiftly-falling night, as they did when Shah Jehan sat "in the sunset-lighted balcony with his eyes fixed on the snow-white pile at the bend of the river, and his heart full of consolation of having wrought for her he loved, through the span of twenty years, a work that she had surely accepted at the last."[2]

[2] *The Web of Indian Life*

We spent a long afternoon in the Fort, and drove out finally through the monstrous gateway in a little Victoria, feeling all the time that none but elephants in all their glory of barbaric caparison could pass through such a portal worthily.

The moon was full almost a week ago, unfortunately, so we determined that, failing moonlight, our first visit to the Taj should be at sunset.

The two miles' drive along an excellent road was delightful, and the approach to the Taj has been laid out with much skill as a beautiful bit of landscape garden. This care is due to Lord Curzon, who has taken Agra and its monuments into his especial keeping.

A very small golf-course has been laid out, and the familiar form of the enthusiast could be seen, blind to everything but the flight of time and his Haskell, hurrying round to save the last of the daylight.

Beneath a tree was laid out a tea equipage, and a few ladies indolently putting showed that, after all, the game was not taken too seriously.

I have no intention of trying to describe the Taj Mahal. The attempt has already been made a thousand times. I may merely remark that the detestable Indian miniatures, and little ivory or marble models that are, alas! so common, are incapable of giving an idea, otherwise than misleading, of this wonderful building, which is not—as they would vainly show it— glaring, staring, and hard, nor does its formality seem other than just what it should be.

As we saw it first—opalescent in the soft, clear light of sunset—the chief impression it made upon us was that of size; for this we were quite unprepared.

As we approached it from the great red entrance arch, along a smooth path bordering the central stretch of still, translucent water, the lovely dome rose fairy-like from the masses of trees that, in their turn, formed a background of solemn green for gorgeous patches of colour, in bloom and leaf, which glowed on either side as we advanced.

Ascending a flight of steps to the wide terrace, all of whitest marble, upon which the Taj is raised, we realised that the detail of carving and of inlay was as perfect as the general effect of the whole.

High as my expectations had been raised, I was not disappointed in the Taj, and that is saying much, for one's pre-formed ideas are apt to soar beyond bounds and to suffer the fate of Icarus. At the same time, I cannot agree with Fergusson that the Taj Mahal is the most beautiful building in the world. I do not admit that it is possible to compare structures of such widely divergent types as the Parthenon, the Cathedral of Chartres, the Campanile of Giotto, and the Taj Mahal, and pronounce in favour of any one of them. It is as vain as to contend that the "Rime of the Ancient Mariner" is a finer poem than Keats' "Eve of St. Agnes," or that the "Erl Konig" is better music than "The Moonlight Sonata."

Perhaps it is not too much to say that it is the loveliest tomb in the world, and the finest specimen of Mohammedan architecture in existence. If I dared to criticise what would appear to be faultless, I should humbly suggest that the four corner minarets are not worthy of the centre building, reminding one rather of lighthouses.

We spent a second day in Agra, revisiting the Fort and the Taj rather than seeing anything new. We could have hired a motor and rushed out for a hurried visit to Fatehpur-Sighri, and there was temptation in the idea; but we decided to content ourselves with the abundant food for eye and mind which we had in these two wonderful buildings, and in the evening we took the train for Jaipur.

Saturday, October 21.—One is apt to be cross and fussed and generally upset on being landed on a strange platform in the dark at 5.30 A.M., as we were at Jaipur, but much solace lay in the fact that a comfortable carriage stood waiting us and a most kind and genial host received us on the broad verandah of his bungalow, and the cheering fact was borne in upon us that we shall have henceforward but little to do with Indian hotels.

How one appreciates a large, cool room, good servants, good food, and last, but not least, the society of one's kind, after two or three weeks of racket and discomfort by road and rail.

A restful morning enlivened us sufficiently to enjoy a garden party at the Residency in the afternoon, where not only the English society, but a large number of native gentlemen, were playing lawn-tennis with laudable energy.

After Kashmir, where Sir Amar Singh is the only native who mixes at all with the English, it was interesting to see and meet on terms of good-fellowship these Rajput aristocrats.

Sunday, October 22.—The city of Jaipur is, I think, principally interesting as being modern and enlightened among those of the native states.

When the ancient city of Ambér was abandoned, principally on account of its scanty water-supply, Jaipur was built upon a regular and prearranged plan, having a great wide street down the centre, crossed by two large thoroughfares at right angles, thus dividing the town into six rectangular blocks.

We drove into the city in the afternoon, and were much impressed by its airiness and cleanliness. The houses are all coated with pink stucco, picked out with white, which, in the bright atmosphere, has, at a little distance, a charming effect. On closer inspection the real tawdriness and want of solidity of the work become painfully apparent, and the designs in white upon the pink, in which the wayward fancy of each householder runs riot, generally leave much to be desired, both in design and execution.

The broad, clean main streets were a perfect kaleidoscope of colour and movement. Men in pink pugarees—in lemon-coloured—in emerald green; women in blood-red saris, bearing shining brass pots upon their heads, all talking, shouting, jostling—a large family of monkeys on a neighbouring roof added their quota of conversation—calm oxen, often with red-painted horns and pink-streaked bodies, camels, asses, horses, strolled about or pushed their way through the throng. No Hindu cow would ever dream of making way for anybody. Yes, though! Here comes an elephant rolling along, and the holy ones with humps discreetly retire aside, covering their retreat before a *force majeure* by stepping up to the nearest greengrocer's stall and abstracting a generous mouthful of the most succulent of his wares.

Rising in the midst of a lovely garden, just outside the city, is the Albert Hall, a remarkably fine structure, built in accordance with the best traditions of Mohammedan architecture adapted to modern requirements by our host, the designer. It contains both a museum of the products of Rajputana, and also an instructive collection of objects of art and science, gathered together for the edification of the intelligent native.

We would willingly have spent hours examining the pottery and brass work for which Jaipur is famous, or in making friends with the denizens of the great aviary in the garden, but time is short, and even the baby panther could only claim a few minutes of our devotion.

The Palace of the Maharajah is neither particularly interesting nor beautiful, and we did not visit it further than to inspect the ancient observatory built by Jey Singh, with its huge sundial, whose gnomon stands 80 feet above the ground! What we are pleased to call a superstitious attention to times lucky or unlucky has given to astronomical observations in the East an unscientific importance which they have not had for centuries in Europe.[3] A slight attack of fever prevented me from going to Ambér; so I stayed at home, peacefully absorbing quinine, subsequently extracting the following from Jane's diary:—

> [3] I fear this is somewhat misleading. Jey Singh was, *par excellence*, an astronomer, not an astrologer,—T. R. S.

"'Tea ready, mem-sahib.' The familiar and somewhat plaintive sound of Sabz Ali's voice roused me, as it so often has in tent, forest hut, or matted dounga;"

but this time I was really puzzled for a moment, on awaking, to find myself in a real comfortable spring bed, white-enamelled and mosquito-netted, while for roof I only saw the clear, pale, Indian sky. Then it was I remembered that, at my host's suggestion, my bed had been carried out into the shrubbery, and that I had fallen asleep, lulled by the howling of the jackals and the rustle of the flying squirrels in the gold mohur-tree overhead.

"Springing on to the cool, grassy carpet, and dressing quickly, to gain as much time as possible before the rising of the hot October sun, I was soon ready for breakfast, which Miss Macgregor and I had in the garden among the parrots and the pigeons, and the dear little squirrels. We were ready for the road before seven, and were soon trotting along between dusty hedges of gaunt-fingered cactus, shaded here and there by neem trees and peepuls."

"Our smart victoria was lent by a Rajput friend of Sir Swinton's, and he had also sent us his private secretary as guide and escort—a very thin young man in a black sateen coat and gay-flowered waistcoat."

"Through the pink-stuccoed streets of Jaipur we threaded our way—slowly, on account of the holy pigeons breakfasting in thousands on the road, and the sacred bulls, who barely deigned to move aside to let us pass."

"It appears to be the custom, when a man dies, for his relatives to let loose a bull *in memoriam*, and the happy beast forthwith sets out to live a life of sloth and luxury. The city is his, and every green-grocer in it is only too much honoured if the fastidious animal will condescend to make free with his cabbages."

"Once clear of the crowded streets, we got on quicker, and about six miles out we found the elephant which had been sent out from the royal stable to carry us to Ambér. We climbed upon her (it was a lady elephant) in a great hurry, by means of a rickety sort of ladder, as we were told that an elephant, if 'fresh,' was apt to rise up suddenly, to the great detriment of the passenger who had 'not arrived.' She was a very friendly-looking creature though, and her little eyes twinkled most affably; her face was decorated in a scheme of red and green, and her saddle was a sort of big mattress surrounded by a railing."

"I am no judge of the paces of elephants, but this one seemed uncommonly rough; and we held on vigorously to the railing until we reached a ridge and saw the dead city of Ambér before us, dominated by the white marble palace, standing on a steep cliff, and reflected in the water of the lake which laps its base."

"Up a steep and narrow path we mounted until we reached the courtyard of the ancient palace of the ruler of Ambér, and there we alighted from our steed, and set out to explore the ruins. First we came to a small temple, ugly enough, but interesting, for here a goat is sacrificed every morning to Kali—a particularly hideous goddess, if the frescoes on the walls and the golden image in the sanctuary are in any way truthful! Formerly a human sacrifice was customary, but the unfortunate goat is found to fulfil modern requirements, since goddesses are more easily pleased or less pampered than of yore."

"The Palace, which dates from the seventeenth century, is chiefly remarkable for its magnificent situation, and for its court and hall of audience of marble and red sandstone."

"This work was so fine as to excite the jealousy of the Mogul Emperor, so the Prince of Ambér had it promptly whitewashed—and whitewashed it remains to this day. Some of the brazen doors are remarkably fine, as also those of sandal-wood, inlaid with ivory, in the women's quarters."

"We climbed to the marble court on the roof, where, canopied only by the sky and lighted by the moon, nocturnal durbars were held. Now, in the glare of the noonday sun, we fully appreciated the value of an evening sitting, for it was impossible to remain grilling there, even though the view of the silent city below, falling in tier after tier to the lake—the glare only broken here and there by patches of green garden—was superb. On either side rose the bare, rocky ridges, fort-crowned and looking formidable even in decay, while in front the dusty road stretched away into the haze of the dusty plains below. Of course, we should have visited the great Jain temples and other things worthy of note; but, alas! a green garden, whose palms overhung the lake, proved more attractive than even Jain temples, and a charming picnic on fruits and cool drinks strengthened us sufficiently to enable us to face the hot road home, buoyed up each mile by the nearer prospect of a tub."

Jaipur is celebrated for its enamelling on gold, so our host kindly sent for an eminent jeweller to come and show us some trifles. Expectant of a humble native carrying the usual bundle, we were much impressed when, in due time, a dignitary drove up in a remarkably well turned out carriage and pair. His servants were clad in a smart livery, and he himself was resplendent, with uncut emerald earrings, and the general appearance of a certain Savoy favourite as the "Rajah of Bong"!

Our spirits sank as he spread himself and his goods out upon the drawing-room floor, which speedily became a glittering chaos of gold and jewelled cups, umbrella handles, boxes, scent-bottles, and necklaces. Jane divided her admiration between a rope of fat pearls and a necklace of uncut emeralds, either of which might have been hers at the trifling price of some 7000 rupees, but we finally restricted our acquisitions to very modest proportions, and the stout jeweller departed, apparently no whit less cheerful than when he came.

The modern brass-work of Jaipur is somewhat attractive, and we bought various articles—a tall lamp-stand, an elephant bell, and a few ordinary bowls of excellent shape.

I have remarked before on the extreme tameness of, and the confidence shown by, wild creatures out here. A titmouse came and perched on the arm of my chair while sitting reading on the verandah at Gulmarg.

The rats and mice, who own the forest houses in the Machipura, have to be kicked off the beds at night. But the little grey squirrels in Sir Swinton Jacob's garden are—*facile princeps*—the boldest wild-fowl we have yet encountered.

Every afternoon about three, when tea was toward, the squirrels gathered on the gravel path, and prepared to receive bread and butter.

After a few nervous darts and tail whiskings, a bold squirrel would skip up close, and, after eating a little ground bait, would boldly come up and nibble out of a motionless hand. In two minutes half-a-dozen pretty little creatures would be fidgeting round, eating bread and butter daintily, neatly holding the morsel in their little forepaws and nuzzling into one's fingers for more.

A handsome magpie, and, of course, a contingent of crows, made up the fascinating party; while in the background, among the neem trees and the flaming "gold mohurs," the minahs and green parrots sustained an incessant and riotous conversation.

Wednesday, October 25.—Gladly would we have accepted the Jacobs' invitation to stay longer at Jaipur. We would have liked nothing better, but time was flying, and the 5th November—our day of departure from Bombay—was drawing rapidly near. So yesterday evening we took the 6.30 train for Ajmere, and, reaching there at 10.30, changed into the narrow-gauge railway for Chitor. We are becoming well accustomed to sleeping in an Indian train, and Sabz Ali had our beds unrolled and our innumerable hand luggage stowed away in no time, including four bottles of soda-water, which he has carefully garnered in the washstand, and which no hints, however broad, will induce him to relinquish.

CHAPTER XVI
UDAIPUR

We arrived, very sleepy and gritty, at Chitor at 5.30 A.M., to find an unprecedented mob of first-class passengers *en route* for Udaipur, and only one very minute compartment in which to stow them.

The station-master—a solemn Baboo, full of his own importance, becomingly clad in a waving white petticoat, with bare legs and elastic-sided boots, surmounted by a long cutaway frock-coat, topped by a black skull-cap, and finally decorated by a pen behind his ear—seemed totally unable to cope with the terrible problem he was set to solve.

I suggested that another carriage should be put on, but he had none, nor any solution to offer; so we cleared a second-class compartment and divided the party out, and then, with five people in our tiny compartment, we set out on the fifty-mile run to Udaipur.

Five people in a carriage in Europe is nowise unusual, but five people in an Indian one (and that a narrow, very narrow gauge), accompanied by rolls of bedding, tiffin-baskets, and all the quantity of personal luggage which is absolutely necessary, not to speak of a large-sized bird-cage (which cannot, strictly speaking, be classed as a necessary), requires the ingenuity of a professional packer of herrings or figs to adjust nicely!

By cramming the toilet place with bedding, khudsticks, a five-foot brass lamp-stand, and the four soda-water bottles, we made shift to stow portmanteaux, bags, tiffin-baskets, &c., under the seats and ourselves upon them, and then arranged a sort of centre-piece of Jane's big tin bonnet-box, surmounted by Freddy in his cage. The other passengers were very amiably disposed, and not fat, and they even went so far as to pretend to admire Freddy—a feat of some difficulty, as he is still very bald and of an altogether forbidding aspect. This admiration so won upon the heart of Jane, that in the fulness thereof she served out biscuits and a little tinned butter all round, while Freddy cheerfully spattered food and water upon all indiscriminately.

About eighteen miles from Udaipur we passed the ruins of Ontala. Here, in the stormy time when Jehangir had seized Chitor, there happened a desperate deed.

The Rana of Mewar, expelled from his capital, determined to attack and retake Ontala. Now, the Rajputs were divided into clans as fiery as any of those whose fatal pride went far to ruin Bonnie Prince Charlie at Culloden. The Chondawats and the Saktawats both claimed the right of forming the vanguard, and the Rana, unable to pronounce in favour of either, subtly decided that the van should be given to the clan which should first enter Ontala.

The Saktawats then made straight for the one and only gateway to the fortress, and, reaching it as day broke, almost surprised the place, but the walls were quickly manned and defended. Foiled for a moment, the leader of the Saktawats threw himself from his elephant, and, placing himself before the great spikes with which the gate was protected against the assault of the beast, ordered the mahout to charge; and so a crushed and mangled corpse was forced into the city on the brow of the living battering-ram, in whose wake the assailants rushed to battle.

Alas! his sacrifice was in vain. The Chondawat chief was already in Ontala. First of the stormers with scaling-ladders, he was shot dead by the defenders ere reaching the top of the rampart, and his corpse fell back among his dismayed followers. Then the chief of Deogurh, rolling the body in his scarf, tied it upon his back, fought his way to the crest of the battlements, and hurled the gory body of his chieftain into the city, shouting, "The vanguard to the Chondawat!"

It is further told how, when the attack began, two Mogul chiefs of note were engaged within upon a game of chess. Confident of the strength of the defence, they continued their game, unheeding the din of battle. Suddenly the foe broke in upon them, upon which they calmly asked for leave to finish their interesting match. The request was granted by the courtly Rajputs, but upon its termination they were both put to death.

Udaipur lies in a well-cultivated basin, shut in by a ring of arid hills. After skirting the flanks of some of the outlying spurs, we bustled through a tunnel and drew up at a bright little station, draped with great blue and pink convolvulus. And this was Udaipur.

We were picked out of the usual jabbering, jostling, gibbering crowd of natives by our host, who, looking most enviably cool and clean, took his heated, dishevelled, and unbarbered guests off to a comfortable carriage, and we were quickly sped towards tiffin and a bath.

The station is a long way from the town, as the Maharana, a most staunch conservative of the old school, having the railway more or less forced upon him, drew the line at three miles from his capital, and fixed the terminus there. One cannot help being glad that the prosaic steam-engine, crowned with foul smoke and heralded by ear-piercing whistles, has not been allowed to trespass in Udaipur, wherein no discordant note is struck by train line or factory chimney, and where everything and every one is as when the city was newly built on the final abandonment of Chitor, the ancient capital of Mewar.

Here in the heart of the most conservative of native States, whose ruler, the Maharana, Sir Fateh Singh, claims descent from that ancient luminary the Sun, we found novelty and interest in every yard of the three miles that stretch between the station and the capital. The scrub-covered desert has given place to a wooded and cultivated valley, ringed by a chain of hills, sterile and steep. The white ribbon of the road, through whose dust plough stolid buffaloes and strings of creaking bullock-carts, is bordered by tall cactus and yellow-flowered mimosa on either side. Among the trees rise countless half-ruined temples and chatries; on whose whitewashed walls are frequent frescoes of tigers or elephants rampant, and of wonderful Rajput heroes wearing the curious bell-shaped skirt, which was their distinctive dress.

The people too, their descendants, who crowd the road to-day, are remarkable—the men fine-looking, with beards brushed ferociously upwards, and all but the mere peasants carrying swords; the women, dark-eyed, and singularly graceful in their red or orange saris, and very full bell-shaped petticoats. Upright as darts, they walk with slightly swaying gesture, a slender brown arm upraised to support the big brass chatties on their heads, revealing an incredible collection of bangles on arms and ankles. These women are the descendants of those who, in the stormy days of the sixteenth century, while the Rajput princes still struggled heroically with the all-powerful Mogul emperors, preferred death to shame, and, led by Kurnavati (mother of Oodi Singh, the founder of Udaipur), accepted the "Johur," or death by fire and suffocation, to the number of 13,000, while their husbands and brothers threw open the city gates and went forth to fight and fall.

As we drew near our destination the towers of the Maharana's Palace rose up above the trees, gleaming snowy in the cloudless blue. The brown crenellated walls of the city appeared on our left, and, suddenly sweeping round a curve, we found ourselves by the border of a lovely lake, whose blue-rippled waters lapped the very walls of the town. In the foreground a glorious note of colour was struck by a group of "scarlet women" washing themselves and their clothes by the margin.

Up a steep incline, and we found ourselves before a verandah, blazing overhead with bougainvillea, and our hostess waiting to receive us beneath its cool shade.

In the afternoon, refreshed and rested, we went down to the shore, where our host had arranged for a state-owned boat and four rowers to be in waiting. Armed with rods and fishing tackle, we proceeded to see Udaipur from the lake which washes its northern side. First crossing a small landlocked bay bordered on the left by a long and picturesque crenellated wall, and passing through a narrow opening, we found ourselves in a second division of the water; on the left, still the wall, with a delightful-looking summer-house perched at a salient angle; on the right, small wooded islands, the haunt of innumerable cormorants, who, with snaky necks outstretched, watched us suspiciously from their eyrie.

A curious white bridge, very high in the centre, barred the view of the main lake till, passing through the central arch, we found ourselves in a scene of perfect enchantment. Before us the level sheet of molten silver lay spread, reflecting the snowy palaces and summer-houses that stood amid the palms and greenery of many tiny islands. On the left the city rose from the water in a succession of temples and wide-terraced buildings, culminating in the lofty pile of the Palace of the Maharana. Here, on this enchanted lake, we rowed to and fro until the sun sank swiftly in the west and the red gold glowed on temple and turret.

Then, with our catch, about 15 lbs. weight of most excellent fish, we rowed back past the white city to the landing-place, and, in the gathering dark, climbed the hillock upon which stood our host's bungalow.

We spent a week at Udaipur—a happy week, whose short days flew by far too quickly. The weather was splendid; hot in the middle of the day—for the season is late, and the monsoon has greatly failed in its cooling duty—but delightful in morning and evening.

Rising one morning at early dawn, before the sun leaped above the eastern hills, we took boat and rowed to one of the island palaces, where, after fishing for mahseer, we breakfasted on a marble balcony overlooking the ripples of the Pichola Lake, which lapped the feet of a group of great marble elephants.

Not the least interesting expedition was to the south end of the lake one afternoon to see the wild pigs fed. Traversing the whole length of the Pichola, past the marble ghâts where the crimson-clad women washed and chattered, while above them rose the roofs and temple domes of the fairy city culminating in the walls and pinnacles of the palace—past the fleet of queer green barges wherein the Maharana disports himself when aquatically inclined, we left the many islands marble-crowned on our right; and finally landed at a little jutting ledge of rock, whence a jungle track led us in a few minutes to a terrace overlooking a rocky and steep slope which fell away from the building near which we stood. The scene was surprising! Hundreds of swine of all sorts and sizes, from grim slab-sided, gaunt-headed old boars, whose ancient tusks showed menacing, to the liveliest and sprightliest of little pigs playing hide-and-seek among their staid relatives, were collected from the neighbouring jungle to scramble for the daily dole of grain spread for them by the Maharana.

A cloud of dust rose thick in the air, stirred up by the busy feet and snouts of the multitude, and grunts and squeals were loud and frequent as a frisky party of younglings in their play would heedlessly bump up against some short-tempered old boar, who in his turn would angrily butt a too venturesome rival in the wind and send him, expostulating noisily, down the hill!

Beyond the crowd of swine on the edge of the clearing, a few peacocks, attracted by the prospect of a meal, held themselves strictly aloof from the vulgar herd.

The whole city of Udaipur is a paradise for the artist—not a corner, not a creature which does not seem to cry aloud to be painted. The only difficulty in such *embarras de richesses* of subject and such scantiness of time, is to decide what not to do.

Hardly has the enthusiastic amateur sat down to delineate the stately pile of the palace, soaring aloft amid its enveloping greenery, than he is attracted by a fascinating glimpse of the lake, where, perhaps, a royal elephant comes down to drink, or a crimson-clad bevy of Rajputni lasses stoop to fill their brazen chatties with much chatter and laughter.

Bewildered by such wealth of subject, one is but too apt to sit at gaze, and finally go home with merely a dozen pages of scribbles added to the little canvas jotting-book!

The Palace of the Maharana is a very splendid pile of buildings, as seen from some little distance crowning the ridge which rises to the south of the lake, but it loses much of its beauty when closely viewed. It is, of course, not to be compared architecturally with the master-works of Agra and Delhi, and the internal decorations are usually tawdry and uninteresting. The entrance is fine; the visitor ascends the steep street to the principal gate, a massive portal, strengthened against the battering of elephants by huge spikes, and decorated by a pair of these animals in fresco-rampant. Beyond the first gate rises a second or inner gate. On the right are huge stables where the royal elephants are kept, and on the left stand a row of curious arches, beneath one of which the Maharanas of old were wont to be weighed against bullion after a victory, the equivalent to the royal avoirdupois being distributed as largesse to his people!

Within the gates, a long and wide terrace stretches along the entire front of the Palace, on the face of which is emblazoned the Sun of Mewar, the emblem of the Sesodias. This terrace was evidently the happy home of a great number of cows, peacocks, geese, and pigeons, which stalked calmly enough, among the motley crowd of natives, and gave one the impression of a glorified farmyard. The building itself, like most Indian palaces, is composed of a heterogeneous agglomeration in all sorts of sizes and styles. Each successive Maharana having apparently added a bit here and a bit there as his capricious fancy prompted.

Jane visited the armoury to-day with the Resident, who went to choose a shield to be presented by the Maharana to the Victoria Museum at Calcutta. I chose to go sketching, and was derided by Jane for missing such a chance of seeing what is not shown to visitors as a rule. She whisked away in great pomp in the Residential chariot, preceded by two prancing sowars on horseback, and subsequently thus related her experiences:—

"We really drove up far too fast to the Palace, I was so much interested in the delightful streets; and we just whizzed past the innumerable shrines and queer shops, and frescoed walls, where extraordinary lions and tigers, and Rajput warriors, riding in wide petticoats on prancing steeds, were depicted in flaming colours. I wanted, too, to gaze at the native women, in their accordion-pleated, dancing frocks of crimson or dark blue; but it seemed to be the correct thing for a 'Personage' to drive as fast as possible, and try to run over a few people just to show them what unconsidered trifles they were. Well, we were received at the entrance to the Palace by one of the Prime Ministers. There are two Prime Ministers—one to criticise and frustrate the schemes of the other; the result being, as the Resident remarked, that it is not easy to get any business done. Our Prime Minister was dressed in a coat of royal purple velvet, on his head was wound a big green turban, and round his neck hung a lovely necklet of pearls and emeralds, with a pendant of the same, he had also earrings to match. It was truly pitiful to see such ornaments wasted on a fat old man."

"Going up a narrow and rather steep staircase, we came to a small hall full of retainers of his Highness, waiting until it should please him to appear and breakfast with them, for it is the custom of the Maharana to make that meal a sort of public function. In the middle of the hall reposed a big bull, evidently very much at ease and quite at home!"

"A few more steps brought us to the door of the armoury. This is small and badly arranged, which seems a pity, as there were some lovely things. Chain armour and inlaid suits lay about the floor in heaps; and we were shown the saddle used by Akbar during the last siege of Chitor. The most remarkable things, however, were the Rajput shields, of which there were some beautiful specimens. They are circular, not large, and made, some of tortoiseshell, some of polished hippo hide, &c. One was inlaid with great emeralds, a second had bosses of turquoise, and a really lovely one was inlaid with fine Jaipur enamel in blue and green. There were swords simply encrusted with jewels—one with a hilt of carved crystal; another was a curiously-modelled dog's head in smooth silver, and I noticed a beauty in pale jade. Altogether it was a most fascinating collection, different from, but in its way quite as interesting, as the fine armoury at Madrid."

Thus did Jane triumph over me with her description of what she had seen and what I had missed; and I had been trying to delineate the Temple of Jagganath, and had been disastrously defeated, for it is indeed a complicated piece of drawing, and the children, both large and small, crowded round me to my great hindrance. Therefore, it was not until I had been soothed with an excellent lunch, and the contents of a very long tumbler, that I felt strong enough to take an intelligent interest in the contents of the Maharana's curiosity-shop!

Monday, October 30.—The more we see of Udaipur the more we are charmed with it. The whole place is so absolutely unspoilt by modernism, is so purely Eastern—and ancient Eastern at that—that we feel as though we were in a little world far apart from the great one where steam and electricity shatter the nerves, and drive their victims through life at high pressure.

Ringed in by a rampart of arid hills, beyond which the scrub-covered desert stretches for miles, the peaceful city of Udaipur lies secluded in an oasis, whose centre is a turquoise lake. High in his palace the Maharana rules in feudal state, and, like Aytoun's Scottish Cavalier,

> "A thousand vassals dwelt around—all of his kindred they,
> And not a man of all that clan has ever ceased to pray
> For the royal race he loves so well."

For to his subjects the Maharana is little less than a divinity, for is he not a direct descendant of the Sun? Likewise is he not the chief of the only royal house of Rajputana, who disdained to purchase Mogul friendship at the price of giving a daughter in marriage to the Mohammedan?

There are greater personages among the ruling Princes of India, according to British ruling—Hyderabad, for instance. And in the matter of precedence and the number of guns for ceremonial salutation, the Chief of Mewar—like other poor but proud nobles—is treated rather according to his actual power than the cloudless blue of his blood. Hence he is extremely unwilling to put himself in a position where he might fail to obtain the honour which he considers due to him. He was most averse from attending the Delhi Durbar, but such pressure was put upon him that he was induced to proceed thither in his special train running, as far as Chitorgarh, upon his own special railway. He reached Delhi, and his sponsors rejoiced that they had indeed got him to the water, although they had not exactly induced him to drink. As a matter of fact, the Maharana, having gone to Delhi to please the British authorities, promptly returned to Udaipur to please himself, alleging a terrific headache as reason for instant departure from the capital, without his having left his very own specially reserved first-class compartment!

He may not be a willing guest, but he is evidently disposed to be an excellent host, for great preparations are toward for the reception of the Prince of Wales, who is expected in the course of a fortnight or so.

The Residency, too, is being swept and garnished, the garden already looking like a miniature camp, with tents for the suite all among the flower-beds.

Tuesday, October 31.—A day or two ago we arose betimes, and before sunrise embarked in the State gig (which was always, apparently, placed at our host's disposal on demand), and set forth to catch fish for our breakfast, and then proceed to eat the same on one of the island palaces on the lake. We did not catch many fish—the mahseer were shy that morning—but fortunately we did not entirely depend on the caprices of the mahseer for our sustenance, and a remarkably well-fed and contented quartette we were when we got into the gig while the day was yet young, and rowed home as quickly as might be in order to escape the heat which at noonday is still great.

This afternoon we went for a (to us) novel tea picnic. A State elephant appeared by request, and we climbed upon him with ladders, and he proceeded to roll leisurely along at the rate of about two and a half miles an hour towards the foot of a hill, on the top of which stood a small summer palace.

The afternoon was warm, and the rhythmic pace drowsy, but our steed was determined to amuse us and benefit himself. So he blew great blasts of spray at his own forelegs and chest to cool himself, and now and then made shocking bad shots at so large a target, and, getting a trifle too much elevation, nearly swept us from our lofty perch.

Fortunately his stock of spray gave out ere long, or he found that the increasing gradient of the hill took all his breath, for we were left at leisure to admire the widening view until we reached the top.

Here we had tea in one of the cool halls, and then sat watching the sun sink towards the hills that stretch to Mount Aboo.

To the south-east lay Udaipur, milk-white along the margin of its "marléd" waters.

On our way home we met with an adventure. While prattling to my hostess, I observed that our toes were rising unduly, the saddle or howdah being seated somewhat after the fashion of an outside car. Glancing over my shoulder I descried Jane and her partner far below their proper level. The howdah was coming round, and our steed was eleven feet high! Agonised yells to the gentleman who guided the deliberate steps of the pachyderm from a coign of vantage on the back of his neck, awoke him to an appreciation of the situation. The elephant was "hove to" with all possible despatch, and we crawled off his back with the greatest celerity. We then sat down by the roadside and superintended the righting of the saddle and the tautening of the girths by several natives, who "took in the slack" with an energy that must have made the poor elephant very "uncomfy" about the waist! I secretly hoped it was hurting him horribly, as I had not forgiven him for his practical jokes on the way up.

We had no more thrills. Resuming our motor 'bus, in due course, we were landed opposite the top of our host's verandah, whereupon the beast shut himself up like a three-foot rule, and we got to ground.

The inexorable flight of time brought us all too soon to the limit of our stay at Udaipur. Early on Wednesday the 1st November, therefore, we bade adieu to the capital of the State of Mewar, and, accompanied by our kind host and hostess, set out to spend a day in exploring the ruined city of Chitor before taking train for Bombay.

As we drove to the station, we passed the group of ancient "chatries" or tombs of dead and gone Ranas of Mewar, and halted for a short inspection, as, the train by which we were to travel to Chitorgarh being a "special," we were not bound to a precise moment for our appearance on the platform.

Jane, who is perfectly Athenian in her passion for novelty, decided to travel on the engine, and proceeded to do so; until, at the first halting-place, a grimy and somewhat dishevelled female climbed into our carriage, and the next half-hour was fully occupied in scooping smuts out of her eyes with teaspoons.

It had been arranged that an elephant should await our arrival at Chitorgarh to take us up to the ancient city, but a careful search into every nook and cranny failed to reveal the missing animal.

So my host and I set out on foot to cross a mile or so of plain which spread in deceptive smoothness between us and the ascent to the city. What seemed a serene and level track became quickly entangled in a maze of rough little knobs and nullahs, and we took a vast amount of exercise before arriving at the old bridge which spans the Gamberi River.

Meanwhile, towering over the scrubby bushes and surrounded by a dusty halo, the dilatory pachyderm bore down upon us, and, after the mahout had been interviewed in unmeasured terms by my host, went rolling slowly to the station to pick up the ladies.

The ancient city of Chitor lies crumbling and desolate on the back of a long, level-topped hill, which rises solitary to the height of some five hundred feet above the far-stretching plain. Kipling likens it to a great ship, up the sides of which the steep road slopes like a gangway. At the foot lies the modern village, squalid but picturesque.

As we toil, perspiring, up the long ramp which for a weary mile slopes sidelong up the scarped flank of the mountain, and pass through the seven gates which guarded the way, and every one of which was the scene of many a grim and bloody struggle, I will try to sketch the outline of the history of the famous fort, for many centuries the headquarters of the royal race of Mewar.

The Gehlotes, or (as they were afterwards styled) the Sesodias, claim descent from the Sun through Manu, Icshwaca, and Rama Chandra, as indeed do the other Rajput potentates of Jaipur, Marwar, and Bikanir, the Rana of Mewar, however, taking precedence owing to his descent from Lava, the eldest son of Rama.

The ancient dynasty of Mewar has fallen from its high estate, but the history of its rise is lost in the mists of grey antiquity.

"We can trace the losses of Mewar, but with difficulty her acquisitions.... She was an old-established dynasty when all the other States were in embryo." Long before Richard of the Lion-heart fared to Palestine to wrest the Holy City from the infidel, "a hundred kings, its (Mewar's) allies and dependants, had their thrones raised in Chitor," to defend it against the sword of the Mohammedan; while overhead floated the banner displaying the golden sun of Mewar on a crimson field.

Some centuries later the Crusaders brought to Europe from the plains of Palestine the novel device of armorial bearings.

Chitor itself appears to have been in possession of the Mori princes until, in A.D. 728, it was taken by Bappa, who, though of royal race, was brought up in obscurity by the Bhils as an attendant on the sacred kine. This shepherd prince, ancestor of the present Rana of Mewar, became a national hero, and many legends are still current concerning him and his romantic deeds. The story of his "amazing marriage," by which he succeeded in wedding six hundred damsels all at once, is one of the most curious. Bappa, while still a youth, was appealed to, one holiday, by the frolicsome maidens of a neighbouring village, who, led by the daughter of the Solankini chief of Nagda, in accordance with the custom upon this particular saint's day, had come out to indulge in swinging, but who had forgotten to supply themselves with a swinging-rope. Bappa agreed to get them one if they would play his game first. This the young ladies readily agreed to do; whereupon, all joining hands, he danced with them a certain mystic number of times round a sacred tree.

"Regardless of their doom, the little victims played,"

and finally dispersed to their homes, entirely unconscious that they were all as securely married to Bappa as though they had visited Gretna Green with him.

Some time afterwards, upon the engagement of the Solankini maiden to an eligible young man, the soothsayer, to whom application had been made with regard to fixing a favourable and auspicious wedding-day, discovered from certain lines in her hand that the girl was already married! Thus the whole story came out, and no less than six hundred brides assumed the title of Mrs. Bappa.

He seems to have had a passion for matrimony, for when an old man he left his children and his country, and carried his arms west to Khorassan, where he wedded new wives and had a numerous offspring. He died at the age of a hundred!

From the days of the very much married Bappa, until the time of Samarsi, who was Prince of Chitor in the thirteenth century, the city continued to flourish and increase in power and importance. Samarsi, having married Pirtha, sister of Prithi Raj, the lord of Delhi, joined his brother-in-law against Shabudin. For three days the battle raged, until the scale fell finally in favour of Shabudin, and the combined forces of Delhi and Chitor were almost annihilated. "Pirtha, on hearing of the loss of the battle, her husband slain, her brother captive, and all the heroes of Delhi and Cheetore 'asleep on the banks of the Caggar in a wave of the steel,' joined her lord through the flames."

From that time forward the history of Chitor is but a tale of sack and slaughter, relieved in its murkiest days by flashes of brilliant heroism and self-sacrificing devotion while the chivalrous Rajputs struggled vainly against the successive waves of the Mohammedan invasions, which in a fierce flood for centuries swept over India, and deluged it with blood.

In the year 1275 Lakumsi became Rana of Chitor. His uncle Bheemsi had married Padmani, a fair daughter of Ceylon, and her beauty was such that the fame of it came to the ears of Alla-o-din, the Pathan Emperor.

He promptly attacked the fortress, but without success for a long period, until he agreed to a compromise, declaring that if he could merely see the Lady Padmani in a mirror he would be contented and raise the siege.

His request was granted, and, trusting to the honour of a Rajput, he entered the city unattended, and was rewarded by a sight of this Eastern Helen reflected in a mirror. Desirous of showing equal faith in a noble enemy, Bheemsi accompanied Alla back to his lines, but there he was captured and held to ransom, Padmani being the price.

Word was now sent to the Emperor that Padmani would be delivered to him, and seven hundred covered litters were prepared to convey her and her ladies to Delhi, but each litter was borne by six armed bearers, and contained no "silver-bodied damsels with musky tresses," but only steel-clad warriors, who, upon arrival in the Moslem camp, sprang from their concealment as surprisingly as Pallas from the head of Zeus.

Alla-o-din was, however, not to be caught napping, and, being prepared for all contingencies, a fierce combat took place, and the warriors of Chitor were hard put to it to stand their ground until Bheemsi had escaped to the stronghold on a fleet horse. Then the devoted remnant retreated, pursued to the very gates by their foes. The flower of Chitor had perished, but they had achieved their object. This was called the "half sack" of Chitor.[1]

> [1] These notes on the history of Chitor are taken, it need hardly be said, from Tod's *Rajast'han*, he being *the* authority on Rajputana. An account of the above incident is given somewhat differently by Maurice in his *Modern History of Hindostan* (1803), who also relates that Akbar used the same trick to enter Rhotas in Behar, after being long baffled by the apparent impregnability of that fortress.

Fifteen years later, Alla-o-din once more attacked Chitor, and this time the assaults were so deadly that the garrison was decimated and utter annihilation stared the survivors in the face. Then to the Rana appeared the guardian goddess of the city, who warned him that "if twelve who wear the diadem bleed not for Chitor, the land will pass from the line." Now the prince had twelve sons, and, in obedience to the goddess and in hope of eventually saving their dynasty, eleven of them cheerfully headed sorties on eleven following days, and were slain, until only Ajeysi, the youngest, was left alive. Then the Kana prepared for the end. He sent the boy Ajeysi with a small band by a secret way, and he escaped to Kailwarra, so that the royal race of Chitor should not become extinct. Then the women of the city, with the noble Padmani at their head, accepted the Johur; "the funeral pyre being lighted within the great subterranean retreat," they steadfastly marched into the living grave rather than yield themselves to the will of the conqueror. All being now ready for the last act of the hideous drama, the Rana caused the gates to be opened, and with his valiant remnant of an army fell upon the foe only to perish to a man, and then, and not till then, did the victorious Alla set foot of a conqueror within Chitor, where now no living thing remained to stay him from razing her deserted temples to the ground. The palace of Padmani alone was spared in this, the first "saka" of Chitor.[2]

[2] The Jain Tower of Fame was also left standing, it dates from about A.D. 900.

The wrecked stronghold remained an appanage of the Mogul until Hamir, who, though not the direct heir of Ajeysi, had gained the chieftainship through his valour, and who, having married a ward of the Hindu governor of Chitor, by her help regained possession of the fortress.

Defeating the Emperor Mahmoud, Hamir entered Chitor in triumph, and once again the standard of the Sun floated over its blood-stained rocks. The Emperor Mahmoud himself was led captive into Chitor, and kept prisoner there for three months until he regained his liberty by surrendering Ajmere, Rinthumbore, Nagore, and Sooe Sopoor, with fifty lacs of rupees and a hundred elephants. By this victory Hamir became the sole Hindu prince of power in India; and the ancestors of the present lords of Marwar and Jaipur brought their levies and paid homage, together with the chiefs of Boondi, Abu, and Gwalior.

Then ensued for Chitor a period of splendid prosperity, during which rose many noble buildings, amongst the ruins of which the great Tower of Victory still soars supreme. This splendid monument[3] was raised to commemorate the victory gained by Koombho over Mahmoud, King of Malwa, and the Prince of Guzzerat, who in A.D. 1440 had formed a league against Chitor. The Rana met them at the head of 100,000 troops and 1400 elephants, and overthrew them, and the commemorative tower was begun in 1451 and finished in ten years.

[3] It is also attributed to Lakha Rana, A.D. 1373.

The State of Mewar reached the zenith of her glory in 1509, when 80,000 horse, seven rajas of the highest rank, nine raos, and 104 chiefs bearing titles of rawul or sawut, with 500 elephants, followed Rana Sanga of Chitor into the field.

The Mogul Baber, who captured Delhi in 1527, was yet unwilling to face the ordeal of battle with the warlike Rajputs, but in the following year Sanga marched against him at the head of the princes of Rajast'han. A terrible battle ensued, which long inclined in favour of the Rajputs, until, through the treachery of a Tuar chief, they were defeated, and the star of Mewar began to decline, although so severe had been the struggle that Baber dared not follow up his victory.

In 1533 Chitor suffered her second "saka" at the hands of Buhadoor or Bajazet, Sultan of Guzzerat, who, after a grim struggle, obtained a footing at the "Beeka" rock, and, springing a mine there, blew up 45 cubits of rampart and killed the Prince of the Haras, with five hundred of his kin. Then the Queen-Mother, Jowahir Bae, clad in armour, headed a sally, and was slain before the eyes of all.

The entrance to the city being forced, the heir of the Sesodias, the infant Oodi Singh, son of Sanga, was placed in safety, while Bagh-ji, Prince of Deola, assuming royalty, prepared to die, for Chitor could only be retained by the Rajput princes while guarded by royalty.

The horrible Johur was decreed, and 13,000 women, headed by Kurnavati, the mother of Oodi Singh,[4] marched to death and honour through the "Gau Mukh," or entrance to the subterranean tomb; while the city gates were thrown open, and the defenders sallied forth. "Every clan lost its chief," and 32,000 Rajputs were slain during the siege and storm.

[4] And sister of the Rahtore queen, Jowahir Bae.

Now Kurnavati had bound Hamayoun, the son of Baber, to her cause by a curious ceremony: she having sent him the Rakhi (bracelet), and he having bestowed on her the Katchli (corselet), he was bound, in consequence of this bond, to assist the lady in any time of need. Too late to save Chitor, he retook it, and restored Bikramajit to the throne; but the guardian goddess had turned her face from the doomed city, and its final fall was at hand. The Emperor Akbar, having laid almost all India at his feet, determined to bring the proud princes of Rajputana into subjection. He attacked Chitor, but was foiled by the masculine courage of the Rana's concubine queen.

Again, in 1568, the Emperor Akbar attacked, and this time he found the fated city in evil case, for Oodi Singh,[5] the Rana, for whom in infancy his nurse had sacrificed her own child, was a degenerate son of his race. He left Chitor to be defended by his lieutenants Jeimul and Putta.

> [5] The infant Oodi Singh being threatened with death by conspirators, his Rajputni nurse hid him in a fruit-basket, and, covering it with leaves, had it conveyed out of the fort, substituting her own child just as Bimbir, the usurper, entered the room and asked for the prince. Her pallid lips refused to utter sound, but she pointed to the cradle and saw the swift steel plunged into the heart of her child.

In the first "saka" by Alla, twelve crowned heads defended the "crimson banner" to the death. In the second, when conquest, at the hand of Bahadur, came from the south, the chieftain of Deola, a noble scion of Mewar, claimed the crown of glory and of martyrdom. But on this, the third and greatest struggle, no royal victim appeared to appease the Cybele of Chitor and win her to retain its battlements as her coronet.

When Jeimul fell at the Gate of the Sun, the command devolved upon Putta of Kailwa, a lad of sixteen. His mother commanded him to don "the saffron robe," then, with him and his young bride, she fell full armed upon the foe, and the heroic trio died before the eyes of the war-worn garrison.

Once more was the Johur commanded, while 8000 Rajputs ate the last "beera" together, and put on their saffron robes. The gates were thrown open, "and few survived to stain the yellow mantle by inglorious surrender."

Thus in the blood-red cloud of battle sank for ever the Sun of Chitor; for from this, the third and last "saka," the ruined city never rose. Her doom has been as the doom of Babylon, of which Isaiah declared: "It shall never be inhabited, neither shall it be dwelt in from generation to generation … but wild beasts of the desert shall lie there; and their houses shall be full of doleful creatures; and owls shall dwell there…. And the wild beasts … shall cry in their desolate houses, and … in their pleasant palaces:… Her days shall not be prolonged."

The top of the long ascent being reached, the last gate, the Hathi Pol, is passed, and the wayfarer finds himself in the midst of the great dead city, which lies in ruins for three miles along the bastioned brow of the mountain.

Just beyond the first group of stately ruins, we came on the building which was probably the palace built by Lakha Rana in 1373. Here we sat and rested until the elephant, bearing the ladies and the lunch, stalked sedately round the jutting angle of a decayed fort, and then we wended our way along a road lined with many a half-fallen temple, until we reached the ancient palace where, six hundred years ago, dwelt the ill-starred Padmani, whose loveliness brought such woe upon Chitor. Here, in a cool chamber overlooking the tank, upon the brink of which the palace stands, we lunched; afterwards threading our way among the fallen fragments of many a stately shrine and palace towards the high point on which the great Jain Tower of Fame rears its deeply-sculptured shaft into the sky.

For a thousand years the innumerable stone gods which encircle the tower in endless profusion have watched with sightless eyes over the city. Grey already with age were they when they saw, raised in pristine beauty, the shattered domes and broken columns which now lie prone in the brushwood far beneath their feet. What ghastly scenes those stony faces have surveyed, when, swept by the scathing steel, the city has run red with blood, and her defenders have fallen to the last man. One crowning horror, though, they have been always spared, for no maid or matron of Chitor ever deigned to bow her neck beneath the yoke of the Mogul, but rather dared to face a fiery death in the bowels of the great cavern beneath the city than yield her honour to the conqueror.

The Tower of Fame is being repaired by the present Rana, under the superintendence of our host and a party of native workmen. Masons and most skilful carvers in stone were busily engaged in the restoration of parts that had fallen into dangerous decay—an extremely flimsy-looking scaffolding, made apparently of light bamboos, tied together in wisps, and forming a fragile-looking ramp, wound spirally up the outside of the tower. My host seemed to consider it a perfectly safe means of ascent, and as the workmen did not appear to slip off in any appreciable numbers I felt constrained to go up. I should like to have done it on all fours! The climb was well worth undertaking, as it enabled one to inspect the astonishing and finely-carved figures which encrust the whole exterior of the column.

From the Tower of Fame we made our way to the other great landmark of Chitor—the Tower of Victory.

Passing and examining *en route* many elaborately-carved temples, whose domes rose amid the strangling masses of desert tree and shrub, we came to the base of the red tower, whose shaft, four-square and in perfect preservation, has, with its more venerable brother of Fame, watched for so many centuries over the fallen fortress of Chitor.

Not far away, the rocky wall on which the city stands is shattered into a gloomy chasm, half-hidden in rank vegetation, which, clinging with knotted root to ledge and crevice, hangs darkly over a stagnant pool. Here was the awful portal, "the Gau Mukh," or "cow's mouth," by which, when all was lost to Chitor save honour, her women entered the subterranean cavern while the fuel was heaped high, and an honourable death by suffocation awaited them.

The burning Indian day was over, and the sun blazed red in the west, as we mounted our elephant and paced along the road towards the Hathi Pol. Darker grew the ghostly domes and shattered battlements against a golden sky, and the swift southern night fell, dark yet luminous, as we turned down the hill and left the dead city, splendid in its loneliness and isolation, asleep within its crumbling walls.

Our dinner-table was set out on the platform of the station at Chitorgarh, and our bedrooms were close by, our host and hostess sleeping in the "special" by which they were to return to Udaipur in the morning, while we slept in a siding, ready to be coupled up to the early train from Bombay.

Late into the warm and balmy night we paced the platform; for there seemed to be always something still to say, and we found it hard to part from our charming friends; realising, too, that this was the end of our holiday, and that before us lay merely the toil and bustle of a return to commonplace, everyday life. At last, though, the final fag-end of a cheroot was thrown away, the last hand-grips given, and the parting came.

There is little more to say.

All Thursday we rushed through the wide landscape; saw the parched plains stretch far into the dusty horizon; saw the lean men and leaner cattle, to whom the grim spectre of famine is already foreshadowed; flew past populous villages and creaking water-wheels, noting every phase of a scene now familiar, yet always delightful.

Late in the evening we changed at Baroda, and dawn next morning saw us speeding across the swamps and inlets, which gave place ere long to the palm groves and clustering houses which marked the farther limits of the suburbs of Bombay.

We found the heat—damp and oppressive—very trying after the drier air of Rajputana, and the Taj Mahal Hotel below our expectations in all respects save price. It is undoubtedly better than most Indian hotels, but yet it is not good!

Bombay is chiefly connected in our minds with the inevitable fuss and worry of packing and departure.

As we left the Taj Mahal Hotel, in a conveyance piled high with miscellaneous baggage, we saw the last of our faithful and indispensable Sabz Ali, as he hurriedly quitted the hostelry in our wake, fearful lest undue delay should jeopardise the possession of the spoils he was carrying off, wrapped in bulging bundles of goodly size.

Jane and I were sorrier, I think, to part with him than he with us. After all, we were but troublesome charges, for whose well-being he had to answer to "General 'Oon Sahib," — charges who had not been quite so lavish with their incalculable riches as they should have been, and who doled out rupees, and even annas, with a sorely grudging hand; still I think Sabz Ali, as he made his way to the station, with many rupees lining his inmost garments, and a flaming "chit" carefully stowed away, felt a certain regret at parting from the "sahibs," who had really shown a very fine appreciation of his merit, and were sending him back with much honour to his own country.

Late in the afternoon, as the spires and roofs of the city stood dark against the sky, and the many steamers and native dhows showed black upon a flood of liquid gold, the *Persia* got under way, and we slowly left the anchorage, steaming out into the fading light.

We stood long, leaning over the bulwarks and watching the lights of Bombay, at first so distinct, melt gradually into a line of tiny stars as the gulf widened that separated us from the land where we had spent so many happy days.

I wonder if we shall ever revisit it? I trust so ... and yet— —

"As a rule it is better to revisit only in imagination the places which have greatly charmed us ... for it was not merely the sights that one beheld which were the cause of joy and peace. However lovely the spot, however gracious the sky, these things external would not have availed but for contributory movements of mind and heart and blood—the essentials of the man as then he was."[6]

[6] "Henry Ryecroft"

APPENDIX I

BIG GAME LICENSE No. I,
Price Rs. 60 (sixty only).

This license will remain in force from the 15th of March 190 to the 15th November 190, and is subject to the Kashmir Stata Game Laws; it permits the Licensee to shoot the undermentioned game in the Districts and Nullahs open to sportsmen, and, subject to Rules 8 and 9 of these Laws, small game between the above dates.

Name of Animal.	No. permitted to be shot.	No. actually shot.	Size of heads.	District.
Markhor of any variety	2			
Ibex	4			
Ovis Hodgsoni (Ammon)	1			
Ovis Vignei (Sharpu)	4			
Ovis Nahura (Burhal)	6			
Thibetan Antelope	6			
Do. Gazelle	1			
Kashmir Stag	2			
Serow	1			
Brown Bears	2			
Tehr	6			
Goral	6			
Pigs, Black Bears and Leopards	No limit.			

_Name   of   Licensee_____

_Address_____ _Signature of Licensee on returning License_____

N.B.—This portion of the License to be returned to the Secretary, Game Preservation Department.

NAME OF SHIKARIES, &c., EMPLOYED

Serial No.	Name of Shikari or Coolie.	Father's Name.	Nature of employ-ment.	Place of Residence.			REMARKS.
				Village	Tehail	District	

This License does not permit the Licensee to shoot in any of the closed tracts or preserves mentioned in Rules 2 and 10, Kashmir State Game Laws, nor in the Gilgit district, nor in the Astor or Kaj-nag districts, without the special permit laid down under Rule 2.

Dated ____ (Sd.) AMAR SINGH, GENERAL, RAJA, *The* _____ *Vice-President of Council, Jammu and Kashmir State.*

I certify that a copy of Kashmir State Game Laws, 190, has been issued herewith,

Signature of Official granting License _____

NOTE—This License will be shown on demand and is not transferable. A fee of Re. 1 will be charged for a duplicate copy.

APPENDIX II

From the earliest times the Kashmiris have been objects of contempt and derision, whilst the women have been—perhaps unduly—lauded for their looks and general excellence.

The Kashmiris themselves are of opinion that "once upon a time" they were an honourable and valiant folk, brought gradually to their present condition by foreign oppression.

To a certain extent this is probably true, but, according to the *Rajatarangini Kulan*, they were noted for dishonesty and cunning long before the evil days of conquest and adversity. Bernier speaks well of the men, calling them witty and industrious. Doubtless the Kashmiri character, originally none too good, was ruined during the long years of cruelty and injustice to which he was subjected by the Tartars, Afghans, and Sikhs, who, from the day when Akbar put him into women's clothes, treated him as something lower than a brute.

Forster, writing in 1783, abuses the Kashmiri, whom he stigmatises as "endowed with unwearied patience in the pursuit of gain." He speaks of the vile treatment to which he was subjected by his then rulers the Pathans, observing that Afghans usually addressed Kashmiris by striking them with a hatchet, but, he concludes, "I even judged them worthy of their adverse fortune."

Elphinstone (1839) is of opinion that "the men are excessively addicted to pleasure, and are notorious all over the East for falsehood and cunning;" and again, "The Cashmerians are of no account as soldiers."

"Many fowls in a yard defile it, and many Kashmiri in a country ruin it," says the proverb. Lawrence goes very fully into the Kashmiri character, and dwells upon its few good points, giving him credit for great artistic feeling, quick wit, ready repartee, and freedom from crime against the person. He considers the last merit, though, to be due to cowardice and the state of espionage which exists in every village!

I was told (but perhaps by a prejudiced person) of a Kashmiri who, during the great flood of 1903, he being safely on the shore, saw his brother being swept down the boiling river, clinging to his rapidly disintegrating roof. The following painful conversation ensued:—

"Whither sailest thou, oh brother, perched upon the birch bark of thine ancestral roof?"

"Ah! brother dear. Save me quick! I drown!"

"Truly that can I; but say, what recompense wilt thou give me?"

"All I have in the world, brother—two lovely rupees."

"Tut, tut, little one; thou takest me for a fool. Two rupees, forsooth, for five perchance I will deign to save thy worthless life."

"Three, then, three, carissimo—'tis all I have—and make haste, for I feel my timbers parting, and I know not how to swim."

"Farewell, oh, dearest brother! I could not possibly think of taking so much trouble for three rupees, especially as, now I come to think of it, I can borrow a singhara pole, and, in due time, will prod for thy corpse in the Wular! Mind thou wrappest the lucre snugly in thy cummerbund, that it be not lost—farewell, little brother!"

While the gentlemen of the Happy Valley have been lashed by the tongue and pen of every traveller, the ladies, on the contrary, have been rather overrated.

In all communities where the men are invertebrate the women become the real heads of the family, doing not only most of the actual work, but also taking the dominant position in affairs generally. This I have observed strikingly in the case of the three "slackest" male races I know—the Fantis of the Gold Coast, the Kashmiri, and the crofters of the West Highlands.

Opinion is divided on the question of female loveliness in Kashmir.

Marco Polo (who probably only got his ideas of "Kesmur" from hearsay) echoed the prevalent opinion by saying, "The women although dark are very comely" (ch. xxvii.). Bernier is enthusiastic: "Les femmes surtout y sont très-belles," and hints at their popularity among the Moguls.

Moorcroft, Vigne, and others swelled the laudatory chorus until Forster, "having been prepossessed with an opinion of their charms, suffered a sensible disappointment," and even was so rude as to criticise the ladies' legs, which he considered thick!

Lawrence saw "thousands of women in the villages, and could not remember, save one or two exceptions, ever seeing a really beautiful face;" but the heaviest blow was dealt them by Jacquemont, who, as a gay Frenchman, should have been an excellent judge: "Je n'avais jamais vu auparavant d'aussi affreuses sorcières!"

APPENDIX III

I had hoped to have given, through the kindness of Colonel Ward, a full list of the birds of Kashmir. Up to the time of going to press, however, the complete list has not been made out. A very large proportion, however, has been published in the *Journal of the Bombay Nat. Hist. Society*. I would refer those desirous of a knowledge of the birds of Kashmir to the above Journal for 23rd April and 20th Sept. 1906, and 15th Feb. 1907. Also to Hume and Henderson's *Lahore to Yarkand*, and to Le Mesurier's *Game, Shore, and Water Birds of India*, to which I am indebted for the following:—

"In Kashmir, out of 116 genera of land birds, 34 have a wide range, 32 are characteristic of the Palar Arctic, 29 of the Indian, and 21 of the Himalo-Chinese sub-region. Only one species is peculiar to Kashmir, a very normal bullfinch (pyrula)."

The flora, which is most interesting, has yet (as far as I know) to be treated independently of the neighbouring regions. Royle is scientific but antiquated, and I know of no better list than that given by Lawrence in his *Valley of Kashmir*.

APPENDIX IV

It may interest any one intending a trip to Kashmir to see a note of reasonable expenses as incurred by two people during a nine-month absence from England. Therefore I append a précis of ours.

It is to be remembered that a saving might be effected in many particulars by any one knowing something of the country. We had to buy our experience. Fully £10 or £12 could be saved in wages, as at first we had a fighting tail like "Ta Phairson" of "four-and-twenty men and five-and-thirty pipers"—and pipers have to be paid! We also hired tents when we did not really require them. Against these outgoings, however, it should be borne in mind that, thanks to the kindness of friends, we paid a merely nominal rent for a "State" hut at Gulmarg. At Abbotabad, Jaipur, and Udaipur, also, we had no hotel bills to meet.

PRÉCIS OF EXPENSES—TWO PERSONS

LONDON TO KARACHI (25 Days)

	£	s.	d.	£	s.	d.
Half-Return fares, 1st class, London to Trieste, and thence by Austrian Lloyd (unaccelerated)	60	0	0			
Hotels, sleeping-car, gratuities, wine bills, &c.	16	15	0			
Baggage expenses	8	15	7			
				85	10	7

BOMBAY TO LONDON (25 Days)

	£	s.	d.	£	s.	d.
Share of fares	60	0	0			
Hotel expenses and sundries, as before	10	6	8			
Baggage expenses, dock dues, &c.	17	11	4			
				87	18	0

KARACHI TO SRINAGAR (16 Days)

	£	s.	d.	£	s.	d.
Rail and baggage expenses to Pindi	12	6	8			
Landau and two ekkas to Srinagar, inclusive of gratuities, tolls, &c.	10	10	8			
Hotels, Dàk bungalows, &c.	13	18	9			
Duty on firearms (repayable on leaving)	1	16	8			
Resais, waterproof for luggage, kettles, &c.	1	19	3			
Servant's fare to Karachi, wages, &c.	2	12	8			
				43	4	8
Carry forward				216	13	3

EXPENSES IN KASHMIR (6 Months)

	£	s.	d.	£	s.	d.
Brought forward				216	13	3
Food, wine, washing, cigars, &c.	72	7	3			
Wages, inclusive of various clothes	42	9	9			
Amusements, golf and tennis subscriptions, &c.	11	7	2			
Hire of boats, tents and equipment	17	6	5			
Transport coolies and ponies	33	14	11			
Hire of hut at Gulmarg	5	6	8			
Sundry furniture, cooking gear, yakdans, &c.	9	0	8			
				191	12	10

BARAMULA TO BOMBAY (1 Month)

	£	s.	d.	£	s.	d.
Landau and four ekkas, with gratuities and tolls.	13	14	0			
Dâk bungalows, hotels, &c.	18	5	8			
Wages, inclusive of gratuities	6	14	0			
Rail, Pindi to Bombay (*viâ* Udaipur)	16	17	0			
Baggage	5	2	8			
Hire of carriages, &c.	1	4	11			
				61	18	3
Loss by exchange on cheques.				5	19	7
Total				476	3	11

INDEX AND NOTES

ABBOTABAD, A frontier station garrisoned by a mobile force of Gurkhas and Royal Artillery, whence any descent from the Black Mountain or Chilas country can be checked. Named after Lieutenant Abbot, who reduced the neighbourhood to order in 1845-48.

Aden, Occupying a warm corner just outside the straits of Babol-Mandeb; was the first addition made to the British dominions in the reign of Queen Victoria, having been taken from the Arabs in 1839.

Agates,

Agra, Rose to importance under the Moguls, becoming their seat of government after Akbar quitted the city he had built, Fatehpur-Sighri, until Aurungzeb removed the seat of government to Delhi.

Akbar, The third, and in many ways the greatest, of the six "Great Mogul" Emperors of India. A warrior first, he consolidated his conquests with the genius of an enlightened statesman.

Alsu, A small village on the north-west shore of the Wular Lake.

Amar Singh (General Raja Sir Amar Singh, K.C.S.I.), Brother of His Highness Sir Pratab Singh, G.C.S.I., Maharaja of Jammu and Kashmir; is Vice-President of the States Council and owner of much land in Kashmir, the prosperity of which he has done much to promote.

Ambér, The ancient capital of Jaipur; was built in the eleventh century, its Rajput rulers being the powerful allies of Chitor during her struggles against the Mohammedan invasion. The Palace was built by Raja Maun, *circa* 1600, in the days of Akbar, whose cousin he was by marriage (*comp.*). Ambér was deserted in 1728 by Jey Singh for his new city of Jaipur.

Amethyst, This stone should be much worn in Scotland, particularly on New Year's Day, it having been (according to the Greek derivation of the name) an antidote to drunkenness!

Amira Kadal, The highest of the seven bridges at Srinagar; a fine modern structure, replacing that built by Amir Khan Jawan Sher, the Pathan, who also built Sher Garhi.

Anda, Egg.

Anna, the sixteenth part of a rupee, value one penny.

Apharwat, One of the Pir Panjal range, which rises above Gulmarg, height 14,500 feet.

Aru, A small village, beautifully situated about seven miles above Pahlgam.

Asti, "Go slow."

Astor, A district on the main route from Kashmir to Gilgit, the village is about ninety-two miles from Bandipur. Two passes (the Rajdiangan, or Tragbal, 11,800 feet, and the Boorzil, 13,500 feet) have to be crossed. About ten passes are issued each season to sportsmen, markhor and ibex being the game.

Atchibal, A village seven miles from Islamabad, where many springs burst out from the rocks. Atchibal was a favourite pleasure-garden of the Mogul Emperors, the remains of which still exist.

Aurungzeb, The last of the six "Great Moguls"; deposed and imprisoned his predecessor Shah Jehan in 1658, and reigned until 1707. Bigoted and intolerant, he shares with Sikander the odium of having destroyed many of the ancient Hindu temples of Kashmir.

Avantipura, The modern village is near the extensive ruins named after King Avanti Verma, which formed once the capital of Kashmir.

Bahamarishi, (_Baba-pam-Rishi=_Father Smoothbeard.) A village some three miles below Gulmarg; the ziarat is named after a rishi, or ascetic, of the sixteenth century.

Baloo, (Kashmiri, *Harpat*) "Rara avis in terras, nigroque similima cignis." *Anglicè*, a bear.

Bandipur, An important village on the north shore of the Wular Lake, the starting-point for Gilgit, &c. Oddly enough, Bandipur is not marked on the Ordnance Map.

Bandobast, A bargain or arrangement.

Bappa, An eighth-century Rajput hero, and ancestor of the present chiefs of Mewar; appears to have had strong Mormon proclivities.

Baramula, The third town in Kashmir, having some 900 houses, is built on the Jhelum at its outflow from the Kashmir Valley: it is also built on the west focus of seismic disturbance in Kashmir, and was destroyed by an earthquake in 1885, when 3000 Baramulans were killed. We were unaware of these interesting facts on the morning of April 4! The "Palms of Baramoule," which Moore sang of, are like snakes in Iceland—they do not exist.

Bara singh, The Kashmir stag.

Bawan,

Beera,

Bejbehara, The ancient Vijayasvara, a picturesque village and bridge about four miles below Islamabad.

Bernier, F., a Frenchman attached to the court of Aurungzeb as medical adviser; wrote *Voyage à Kachemire*.

Bhanyar,

Bheostie, The Indian Aquarius—the water-bearer.

Bhils,

Birch, (Kashmiri, *Burza*) The bark used in making the paper for which Kashmir was noted, also for roofing, it being strong and impervious to water.

Blue pine, *Pinus Excelsa*, (Kashmiri, *Yar*.)

Bombay,

Books on Kashmir:(1) Bernier, *Voyage à Kachemire* (Utrecht, 1724); (2) Forster's (G) *Journey from Bengal to England* (London, 1798); (3) Moorcroft, *Travels in Kashmir, &c.* edited by Wilson, 1841; (4) Jacquomont (V), *Voyage dans l'Inde* (Paris, 1841); (5) Vigne (G. T.), *Travels in Kashmir, &c.*, 1844; (6) Hugel's *Travels*, 1845; (7) Drew, *Jummoo and, Ktishmir Territories*; and (8) Lawrence's *Valley of Kashmir* 1895.

Budmash, A scoundrel.

Bund, An embankment or dyke to bank a river.

Burra, Big, or great.

Carnelian, "Flesh-stone"—for origin read Marryat's *Pacha of Many Tales*

Chakhoti,

Chandni Chowk,

Chaplies,

Chappar, Paddle with heart-shaped blade.

Chatris, The cenotaphs of the Maharanas of Mewar; they stand in a walled enclosure between Udaipur and the railway station.

Chenar, *Plaianus Orientals* or Oriental plane. This magnificent tree is supposed to have been introduced into Kashmir by the Mogul Emperors. It grows to a great size, one measured by Lawrence being sixty-three feet five inches in circumference at five feet above the ground! There is a very fair specimen in Kew Gardens, between the pond and the "herbaceous border."

Chilas,

Chit, A note or letter, and also a character or recommendation, Every man collects something, from pictures to tram tickets—the native collects "chits." Like other collectors he will beg, borrow, or steal to improve his store, and life is made a burden by the perpetual writing and reading of these mendacious documents.

Chitor,

Chittagul Nullah, The next nullah to the south-west of the Wangat. The village of Wangat is wrongly placed in it, according to the Ordnance Map.

Chondawats, A Rajput clan.

Chota, Little, *Chota Hazri* = *petit dejeúner* or early breakfast.

Chowkidar, A functionary whose principal duty seems to be to snore in the verandah at night and scare other robbers away.

Chupatty, A flabby sort of scone.

Chuprassie,

Cockburn's Agency, The nearest approach to "Whiteley's" in Kashmir.

Dâk, Post. *Dâk Bungalow* = posting station.

Dal Lake, *Dal* means lake (in a plain), while *nag* is a mountain tarn.

Dandy, A sort of enclosed chair with four projecting arms, wherein pretty ladies are carried when it doesn't suit them to walk.

Degchies, Cooking utensils—best made of aluminium, owing to the unclean ways of native scullions.

Dekho, See, look! Delhi, The capital of the Mogul Emperors, dating from 1638, when Shah Jehan commenced to build the great fort. The ancient city lies some miles to the south. Delhi was taken by General Lake in 1803.

Deodar, (Kashmiri, *Diár.) Cedrus Lebani*, var. *Deodara*. The most valuable tree in Kashmir, where it was formerly abundant. It is now chiefly found in the north-west districts, and it is carefully cherished by the "Jungly Sahib" and his myrmidons.

Dobie, The thing that ruins all your shirts and causes you to shatter the Third Commandment.

Domel, Village with Dâk Bungalow, at the confluence of the Jhelum and the Kishenganga.

Doolie,

Doras,

Dounga, "The boats of Kashmir are very long and narrow, and are rowed with paddles from the stern, which is a little elevated, to the centre; a tilt of mats is extended for the shelter of passengers or merchandize" (Forster); the mats are made of "pits" (reed mace), a swamp plant.

Drogmulla,

Dubgam, A village at junction of the Pohru with the Jhelum, about seven miles above Baramula.

EARTHQUAKE, An upsetting event of too frequent occurrence in Kashmir. Particularly severe visitations occurred in 1827 and 1885 (*see* Baramula).

Echo Lake, A small tarn on the top of Apharwat.

Ek, One. (*Ek dam*=immediately.)

Ekka,

Embroidery,

Erin Nullah,

Eshmakam, =*Eysh Makám*("the delightful halting-place") Above the village stands the shrine of Zyn-u-din, one of the four disciples of the Kashmir patron saint, Shah Nur-u-din.

FATERPUR-SIGHRI,

Ferozepore Nullah,

Floating Gardens,

GANESBAL, The boulder, red-stained and extremely sacred, which lies in the middle of the Lidar; bears some fancied likeness to Ganésh (the elephant-headed god).

Gangabal, A sacred lake, lying under the north glaciers of Haramok at the elevation of 12,000 feet. It is said to be a source of the Ganges(!) and is an object of pilgrimage.

Ghari,

Ghari Habibullah,

Ghari Wallah, The Jehu of these parts.

Ghât,

Gold mohur,

Golf,

Gram,

Grass shoes,

Gujar, Is not a Kashmiri, being a member of the semi-nomad tribes which graze buffaloes and goats upon the hills. He speaks Parímu or Hindki.

Gulmarg, (The Rose Marg.) The most frequented resort of the English in Kashmir during July and August; stands some 8500 feet above the sea, wherefore some people find the air too rarefied. Gulmarg was first mentioned by Yusaf Khan in 1580.

Gunderbal, A village placed where the Sind River debouches into the plain. The starting-point for Leh and Thibet.

Gupkar, Town of Gopaditya(?). A wine-manufacturing suburb of Srinagar, overlooking the Dal.

Gurais, A large village on the Bandipur-Gilgit route, lying on the right bank of the Kishenganga, about forty-two miles from Bandipur.

HARAMOK, The predominating mountain (16,903 feet) of the valley, from almost every part of which his square-headed bulk is visible; hence the name, which means "all faces" or "all mouths." A legend holds that a vein of emerald lies near the summit, and that within view of this gem no snake can live

Harbagwan,

Hari Parbat, ("The Green Hill") So named on account of the gardens and vineyards which clothed its sides. Became the residence of Akbar, who built the wall round foot of hill in 1597. The fort on top was the work of the Pathan, Atta Mohamad Khan.

Haripur,

Harwan,

Hasrat Bal Mosque, (The Prophet's Hair.) Various fairs and festivals are held here, the principal one being held upon the day that the Prophet rode up to Heaven on his mule Al Barak (the Thunderer). This mule, by-the-bye, is one of the five favoured beasts which the Mohammedans believe destined to immortality; the others are (1) Abraham's Ram, (2) Balaam's Ass, (3) the one upon which Christ rode on Palm Sunday, and (4) the dog which guarded the seven sleepers.

Hassanabad Mosque, Built by Nur Jehan Begum (Nourmahal), and destroyed by the Sikhs.

Hassan Abdal, (_Abdal=_fanatic).

Hoopoe, Un-natural history of.

INSECTS, Of benign insects such as butterflies there are singularly few. Both mosquitoes and flies are very troublesome during the hot weather in the valley. Visits to native huts will probably lead to an introduction to other insects. In India ants become a nuisance: I met with a foraging party of extremely large and well-nourished ones as I entered my bath place one morning. I recognised them for the descendants—decadent somewhat—of the famous fellows who played Alberich to the Gold of Hindostan and regarding which Herodotus (commonly known as the Father of History, or of Lies, I forget which) asserted that they were of the bigness of foxes and ran with incredible swiftness. He evidently got this yarn from Pliny—

"Indicae Formicae. Aurum ex cavernus egerunt terrae Ipsis autem color Fehum magnitudo Aegypti Luporum" (Lib. xi. ch. 31)—

and passed it on to Sir J. Maundevil, who swallowed it greedily. "Theise pissmyres ben grete as houndes; so that no man dar come to the hilles, for the pissmyres wolde assaylen hem and devouren hem" (ch. xxx) For the wily method of catching the ants napping, together with other *contes drolatiques*, read Maundevil's *Travels*.

Iris, (Kashmiri, *Krishm*) Succeeds the tulip and precedes the rose as typical of Kashmirian Flora, is used as fodder, and the fibre makes ropes, which are, however, not durable.

Islamabad, (Or Anant Nag, the "Place of Countless Springs.") Is the second city in Kashmir, having about 9000 inhabitants; stands at the head of the navigable Jhelum, fifty miles by water and thirty-two by land above Srinagar.

Jade,

Jagganath,

Jain, A small sect founded by Mahavera, a contemporary of Gautama. The Jains were great temple-builders.

Jehangir,

Jeimal, With Putta, one of the national heroes of the Rajputs. They fell, while mere boys, in the heroic defence of Chitor against Akbar.

Jey Singh, (Sowar Jey Singh.) Succeeded to the throne of Ambér in 1699, founded Jaipur in 1728. He wrote the following, which I had not read when I visited his observatory at Jaipur "Let us devote ourselves at the altar of the King of Kings, hallowed be his name! In the book of the register of whose power the lofty orbs of Heaven are but a few leaves, and the stars, and that heavenly courser the sun, small pieces of money in the treasury of the Most High."

Jheel, A small lake, or pond.

Jhelum, (Kashmiri, *Veth*, Hindu, *Vetasta*, the ancient *Hydaspes*.) Rises at Vernag, becomes navigable at Kanbal, and is so for 120 miles, when it forms rapids below Baramula. Average breadth at Srinagar in December 210 feet, average depth 9 feet.

Johur,

Kaj-nag,

Kali, ("The Terrible.") Wife of Shiva or Mahadeva.

Kanbal,

Karachi,

Karewas, "Where the mountains cease to be steep, fan-like projections, with flat, arid tops, and bare of trees, run out towards the valley" (Lawrence)

Kashmir=Kashuf-mir (the country of Kashuf). Was ruled by Tartar princes from about 150-100 B.C. for several centuries; conquered after a year's struggle by Mahmoud of Guznee (1014-1015 A.D.). Invaded by Baber and Humayun, and finally conquered by latter in 1543, and formally annexed by Akbar in 1588. After the fall of Delhi (Nadir Shah) in 1739, Kashmir fell into the hands of Amirs of Cabul in 1753. It was captured by the Sikhs under Ranjit Singh in 1819, and, after the defeat of the Sikhs at the hands of the British, was handed over to Gulab Singh of Jammu for twenty-five lacs of rupees "Kailasa is the best place in the three worlds, Himalaya the best part of Kailasa, and Kashmir the best place in Himalaya" (*Rajatarangini Kulan*).

Kastoora, Merula Boulboul (the grey-winged ousel). Jane bought "Freddie" one day in Srinagar, and he has been our friend and companion ever since—being at this present (August 1907) in rude health.

Khansamah, A Cook.

Khubbar, News—usually untrustworthy.

Khud, A steep slope or precipice.

Khudstick, An alpenstock made of tough wood, usually of Cotoneaster baccillaris (lun); should be well tested before purchase, as life may depend on its strength.

Killanmarg, A wide sloping marg above Gulmarg, just above the pine forest on the slopes of Apharwat.

Kilta, Creel made of the pliant withes of the Wych Hazel, *Parrotia Jacquemontiana* (Chob-i-poh).

Kishenganga, A large affluent of the Jhelum which drains the Tilail Valley, passes Gurais, and joins the Jhelum below Muzafferabad.

Kitardaji, Forest house in the Machipura.

Kitmaghar, Bearer.

Kobala,

Kohinar,

Kolahoi, or Gwash Brari, 17,800 ft. The loftiest peak in Kashmir proper. It has not yet been ascended.

Koolan,

Kralpura,

Kulan, A peak of the Pir Panjal, at the head of the Ferozepore Nullah.

Kulgam, or Kuligam.

Kunis,

Kurnavati,

Kutab Minar,

Lacquer,

Lahore, Capital of the Punjab. An ancient and interesting city, which (like Agra and Delhi) only attained its zenith of prosperity in the days of Akbar.

Lakri, A stick (at Gulmarg also a golf-club).

Lalpura, A charming village in the Lolab.

Larch,

Lidar, Liddar, or Lambodri, Drains the Kolahoi district, and forms the first substantial affluent of the Jhelum, which it joins below Islamabad.

Lidarwat, A small Grujar village fifteen miles above Pahlgam, on the left bank of the river, about 10,000 ft. above sea-level.

Logue or Log, Folk.

Lumbadhar, The headman of a village.

Machipura, "The Place of Fish"—why, I cannot imagine! The district lying along the east foothills of the Kaj-nag.

Mahadeo, (Mahadeva or Shiva) A sacred mountain and object of pilgrimage, north of Srinagar, 13,500 feet high.

Maharaja of Jammu and Kashmir, H.H. Sir Pratab Singh, G.C.S.I., succeeded his father Ranbir Singh (who was third son of Gulah Singh) in 1885. The family is of the Rajput Dogras. "His kindness to all classes has won him the affection of his people" (Lawrence).

Maharana, H.H. the Maharana Dhiraj Sir Fateh Singh, G.C.S.I., of Udaipur, is head of the Rajput princes in point of blood, being descended from the Suryabansi, or Children of the Sun.

Mahseer,

Malingam,

Manji or Hanji, A Kashmiri water-thief or boatman.

Manserah,

Mar (snake) Canal. A dirty but most picturesque waterway between the Dal and the Anchar Lakes.

Marg,(Margh?) Persian for a garden abounding in plants.

Margam,

Martand, The principal temple in Kashmir—stands on a high karewa some few miles from Islamabad.

Metal-work,

Mewar,

Mogul, The Moguls were a warlike people of Central Asia, who, under Timur (Tamerlane) their chief, sacked Delhi in 1398. At the great battle of Panipat, in 1524, Baber the Mogul (direct descendant of Timur) defeated the Sultans of Delhi. He was the first of the six "Great" Moguls (the others being Humayun, Akbar, Jehangir, Shah Jehan, and Aurungzeb), who ruled India with unparalleled magnificence for 150 years.

Mulberry, (*Morus sp.* Kashmiri *Tul*) A very precious tree in Kashmir, on account of the silk industry. It grows to a great size, attaining a girth of 25 feet.

Murghi, A fowl.

Murree, A hill station and sanatorium, 37 miles from Rawal Pindi, on a hill 7500 feet above the sea. Its importance dates from 1850. Forster speaks of it as a small village in 1786.

Musafferabad, ("The Place of Victory") Built by Masufer Khan, Rajah of Chikri.

Mussick, Water-skin.

NAG, A mountain lake or tarn.

Nagas, Human-bodied, snake-tailed gods.

Nagmarg,

Nanga Parbat, A great mountain in the Chilas country, 26,620 feet high (the fourth in point of height in the world), Mommery and two guides were destroyed in 1895, probably by an avalanche, while attempting the ascent.

Nassim Bagh, ("The Garden of Delicious Breezes") A favourite spot in the days of the Mogul Emperors. Akbar planted 1200 chenars.

Neem tree.

Neve, Dr. A. He and his brother are surgeons to the Kashmir Medical Mission, where for many years they have carried on the somewhat thankless task of benefiting the natives.

Nishat Bagh, ("The Garden of Drink")

Nopura, A village on the Pohru.

Nourmahal, ("Light of the Palace"), or, more properly, Nur Jehan Begum ("Light of the World"), was the wife of Jehaugir, celebrated in Mooree's *Lalla Rookh*. Her life story was very curious. See Forster's *Journey from Bengal to England*, London, 1798.

Nullah, A valley or ravine.

Numdah,

ONTALA,

Oodi Singh,

PADMANI, "The Lotus-lovely Lady."

Pagdandy, A short cut.

Pahlgam, "The Shepherd's Village," A Kashmiri summer resort for those who like quiet. It is 27 miles from Islamabad up the Lidar Valley, and is somewhat over 7000 feet above the sea.

Pampur, (Padma-pur, city of Vishnu, or Padmun-pur, "the place of beauty"), principally noted now for its Pampur roti or bread, a speciality of the place.

Pandrettan, or Pandrenthan, =Puranadhisthana, "the old capital." Was built in the time of Partha by his Prime Minister, Meru.

Parana Chauni,

Patan. "The City" or "Ferry," the ancient Sankarapura, Sankaravarma having built two temples there at the end of the eighth century.

Peechy, Afterwards, later, by-and-bye

Peri Mahal, "The Abode of the Fairies." Built on the hill above Gupkar by Prince Dara Shikoh, probably for astronomical purposes

Piasse, The onion.

Pice, See Rupee.

Pichola Lake,

Pir Panjab, Pir=Dogri for peak Pantzal, Kashmiri for ditto Pir also meant a saint, particularly one who lived in the pass in the days of Shah Jehan and Aurungzeb and who was interviewed by Bernier. The Pir Panjal was the route followed by the Moguls when coming to Kashmir, and, rough as it is, they sent elephants along it. The highest peak of the Pir Panjal is Tatakuti, 15,500 feet.

Pohru,

Poonch, A native state lying south-west of Kashmir, to which it is tributary. The Raja Buldeo Singh is cousin to the Maharajah of Kashmir.

Poplar. There are two varieties of Poplar in Kashmir, the Italian or Black Poplar, and the White, the latter attains a great size, one near Gurais measuring 127 feet in height and 14-1/2 feet in girth.

Porcelain,

Port Saïd,

Puttoo, Native cloth.

RAINAWARI,

Rajput, The brave and chivalrous inhabitants of Rajputana. Bernier, probably influenced by Mogul opinion, attributes much of their valour to opium, as the following curious extract shows "Ils sont grands preneurs d'opium, et je me suis quelque fois etonné de la quantité que je leur en voiois prendre; aussi ils s'y accoutûmerent dès la jeunesse; le jour d'une bataille ils ne s'oublient pas de doubler la dose; cette drogue les anime ou plutot les enyvre, et les rend insensibles an danger, de sorte quils se jettant dans le combat comma des bêtes furieuses, ne sachant ce que c'est de fuir … c'est un plaisir de les voir ainsi avec leur fumée d'opium dans la tête s'entre embrasser quand on est prêt de combattre et se dire adieu les uns aux autres, comme gens qui sont resolus de mourir." —Vol. i. p. 54.

Ramble-tamble egg, Scrambled eggs.

Ram chikor, The great snow partridge (*Tetragallus Himalayensis*).

Rampur. A small village in the Jhelum Valley, and a village on the way into the Lolab *viâ* Kunis.

Rawal Pindi,

Rassad, "Field Allowance" or extra rations given to coolies when doing any mountain work or away from supplies.

Resai,

Roorkhee chair, An extremely comfortable and portable chair made by the R.E. at Roorkhee.

Rope bridge,

Rupee=one fifteenth of a sovereign, or 1s. and 4d. 12 pice (or pies)= 4 paisa = 1 anna = 1 penny 16 annas = 1 rupee.

SAAF kuro, "Make clean."

Saktawats, A Rapjut clan.

Sari, A woman's garment, usually brilliant in colour, blood-red and dark blue being favoured.

Sekwas,

Sellar,

Serow, *Nemorhaidus bubalerius.*

Sesodia, The ruling family of Udaipur, formerly known as Gehlote.

Shadipur, "The Place of Marriage" —probably with reference to the junction of the Sind and Jhelum rivers.

Shah Jehan, The greatest builder of the Mogul Emperors. Ruled from 1627 to 1658, when he was deposed and imprisoned by Aurungzeb.

Shalimar,

Shalimar Bagh,

Shambrywa, One of the peaks of the Kaj-nag.

Shiah, A Mohammedan sect, usually much at variance with those of Sunni persuasion.

Shikara, A light sort of canoe.

Shikari, A necessary joint in the "fighting tail" of the sportive visitor to Kashmir. Usually a fraud, but, if not too proud, makes quite a good golf caddy.

Shisha Nag, "The Glassy or Leaden Lake."

Silver fir, *Abies Webbiana* (Kashmiri, *Sungal*). Grows to a great height, being known 110 feet high and 16 feet in girth.

Sind Desert,

Sind Valley,

Singhara, Meaning "horned nut," the water chestnut *(Trapa bispinosa)*. An article of diet much prized by the Kashmiri.

Sogul,

Sonamarg, "The Golden Marg." A summer station high up the Sind Valley on the route to Leh and Ladak.

Sopor, =Sonapur, or the Golden City. A somewhat unclean little town of some 600 houses on the Jhelum, about eight miles by road and twelve by water above Baramula.

Spill Canal, Cut in 1904, after the Great Flood of 1903, to carry some of the river clear of Srinagar and ease the pressure on the bund.

Spruce, *Picca, Morunda*. (Kashmiri, *Kachal*.)

Srinagar, *Surga Nagur*, City of the Sun. Has a population of 120,000. Became capital in 960 A.D., when the ancient city of Pandrettan was burnt in the reign of Abimanyu. The city was called Kashmir until recently, Martand being called Sringar by Jacquemont.

Sultanpur,

Sumbal, Said to be the site of the ancient city Jayapura.

Sunt-i-kul = "Apple-tree Canal."

TAJ MAHAL, The magnificent tomb of Mumtez Mahal, favourite wife of Shah Jehan.

Takht-i-Suleiman, A steep isolated hill rising nearly 1000 feet above Srinagar, crowned by a temple which is built on the ruins of a very ancient edifice. The Takht or Throne of Solomon is, according to the legend, the place which Solomon occupied during his mythical visit to Kashmir.

Tangmarg, "The Open Marg". Is the village about 1500 foot below Gulmarg, which is the nearest point to Gulmarg attainable by wheeled conveyance.

Tattoo, A pony.

Tehsildhar, The functionary who has jurisdiction over a tehsil.

Temples, For full description read Lawrence (*Valley of Kashmir*, chap. vi.) Their ruined state is partly due to earthquakes, but probably still more to the iconoclastic activity of Sikandar (*d.* 1416) and Aurungzeb.

Tilail,

Tonga,

Topaz, Name derived from the Greek "to conjecture" —because no one knew whence they came!

Tower of Fame,

Tower of Victory,

Tragbal,

Tragam, A large village south-west of the Lolab, whence a route leads to Musafferabad.

Tret, A station at the foot of the Murree hills on the road to Rawal Pindi.

Trieste,

Tronkol,

Turquoise,

UDAIPUR, The capital of the ancient and powerful Rajput State of Mewar, founded by Oodi Singh after the fall of Chitor. Uri,

VERNABOUG,

Vernag,

WALNUT, A valuable tree in Kashmir, where its fruit and timber are both greatly esteemed; grows to a very large size, one in the Lolab having a girth of 18 feet 10 inches.

Wangat,

Wardwan, The mountainous district on the east of Kashmir.

Water buffalo, An ungainly and "sneevish" beast beloved of Gujars and nobody else.

Weights 2 lbs. (English)=1 seer. 40 seers = 1 maund.

Wood carving,

Wular, Means "cave". The largest lake in India, being 12-1/2 x 5 miles in average extent. In floods it covers much extra space.

Wych hazel, *See* Kilta.

YAKDAN,

ZIARAT, A Mohammedan shrine. Zoji La, The pass at the head of the Sind Valley which is crossed on going to Leh, height 11,300 feet.